How to Use
THE INTERNET
SECOND EDITION

How to Use
THE INTERNET
SECOND EDITION

MARIETTA TRETTER

Illustrated by
STEPH BRADSHAW

Ziff Davis Press
Emeryville, California

Copy Editor	Margo Hill
Technical Reviewer	Mark Hall
Project Coordinator	Ami Knox
Proofreaders	Carol Burbo and Jeff Barrash
Cover Design	Regan Honda
Book Design	Dennis Gallagher/Visual Strategies, San Francisco
Screen Graphics Editor	Pipi Diamond
Technical Illustration	Steph Bradshaw
Word Processing	Howard Blechman
Page Layout	M.D. Barrera
Indexer	Carol Burbo

Ziff-Davis Press, ZD Press, and the Ziff-Davis Press logo are licensed to Macmillan Computer Publishing USA by Ziff-Davis Publishing Company, New York, New York.

Ziff-Davis Press imprint books are produced on a Macintosh computer system with the following applications: FrameMaker®, Microsoft® Word, QuarkXPress®, Adobe Illustrator®, Adobe Photoshop®, Adobe Streamline™, MacLink® *Plus*, Aldus® FreeHand™, Collage Plus™.

If you have comments or questions or would like to receive a free catalog, call or write:
Macmillan Computer Publishing USA
Ziff-Davis Press Line of Books
5903 Christie Avenue
Emeryville, CA 94608
800-688-0448

ISBN 1-56276-348-2

Manufactured in the United States of America
10 9 8 7 6 5 4 3 2 1

To Lucy and Lee

TABLE OF CONTENTS

INTRODUCTION

 You've read about this great new thing called the Internet and you're interested in trying it out, but you don't have much experience with computers and you've never used a computer network or a bulletin board. This book is for those with limited computer experience and little or no Internet experience.

The first 14 chapters contain basic tools for using the Internet with few resources. Chapters 15 through 22 introduce you to some very easy-to-use freeware software packages that will make your Internet experiences very enjoyable and productive. Going through this book sequentially will give you a comprehensive introduction to the Internet. However, you may want to occasionally skip to the later chapters for a more user-friendly approach.

Books about computer programs usually cover a specific version of a specific program. Unfortunately, it's not possible to write such a book about the Internet for the following reasons: First, getting on the Internet involves using several different programs, and you're likely to come across a number of slightly different versions of these programs. Second, the Internet is growing rapidly, so resources move around and are changed in a relatively short period of time. This is, of course, one of the exciting aspects of the Internet, but it means that some of what you see on the screen displays in this book may differ from what shows up on your computer screen. Don't be alarmed!

To minimize any confusion caused by differences between programs, the screens created for this book need to be similar to those that will be seen by the greatest number of its readers. To do this, I've made the following assumptions about who will be using this book:

1 The reader has or will get access to the Internet via an account on a computer shared by many users. (If you don't already have access to the Internet, you'll find that the Appendix lists four of the many

Internet service providers. If you are a college student, check with your campus computing center about getting free access to the Internet.)

2 The reader's Internet account uses UNIX commands (and may be referred to as a UNIX shell account by the Internet service provider).

3 The reader connects to the shared computer using a telephone line, a modem, a telecommunications program, and a PC, Macintosh, or Amiga computer.

If your setup matches these assumptions, this book will work very well for you. Even if your account differs from the profile described, this book can provide a useful foundation for understanding the Internet.

Each chapter of this book presents several related topics. Since each topic spans two facing pages, everything you need to know is in front of you at one time. Just follow the numbered steps around the pages, reading the steps and looking at the pictures. Realistic, hands-on examples are provided so you'll soon be able to use the Internet to begin collecting even more knowledge about how to use the Internet.

As you get out on the Internet and begin to use the resources discussed in this book, remember that the Internet is growing faster than anybody ever anticipated. With more and more people sharing the Internet's resources, the entire system operates more slowly. Sometimes you may have to wait seconds or even minutes to interact with the Internet, whether you're logging on, sending a message, or connecting to a service. Other times, you may not even be able to connect to a resource because too many people are already using it, and you may have to wait a few hours before trying again. Try not to let these occasional delays keep you from exploring. Learning to use the Internet will make you a pioneer on an electronic frontier that will only grow in importance.

CHAPTER 1

You and the Internet

 We live in an age of constant change. Ten years ago, the idea that you could own a personal computer was just beginning to take hold. Today, personal computers are so common that many young people will learn how to use them while still in elementary school.

Today's world is also becoming more and more interconnected. This means that we can use a car phone to dial up friends halfway around the globe. We can watch live television coverage of athletes breaking Olympic and world records on other continents. We can invest in all the world's economies, because stock markets in Tokyo, London, and New York are linked electronically to form a huge 24-hour-a-day business opportunity.

One of the most exciting manifestations of this interconnectedness is the Internet. The Internet is a global collection of people and computers, all linked together by many miles of cables and telephone lines, all able to communicate because they share a common language. The next two chapters describe the building blocks of the Internet—the machines, the language, the people—and a little of its history. But this discussion won't add up to a diagram or blueprint. One of the beauties of the Internet is that it's constantly changing and growing. It's part of a new electronic frontier for communicating and exchanging ideas and resources. What it will be one year or five years from now is what its users will make of it. This book will give you the knowledge to get on the Internet and begin exploring this extraordinary resource.

Eight Cool Things You Can Do on the Internet

There are an amazing variety of things that you can do on the Internet, and the list grows daily. Here are eight possibilities.

TIP SHEET

▶ In later chapters, we'll get on the Internet and retrieve copies of some of these valuable resources.

▶ The Appendix tells you where to find additional information on the Internet.

1 You can do legal research. The Internet lets you access copies of state laws or U.S. Supreme Court opinions.

8 You can find great information and tutorials to help you do even more things on the Internet. You can track down lists of interest groups and even access entire books on using the Internet.

7 You can get *free* public domain programs for your DOS, Windows, Macintosh, UNIX, or Amiga computer. You can even get movie clips and clip art.

2 You can look at pictures of the Dead Sea scrolls on file at the Library of Congress, or see pictures in an art gallery.

3 Feel like reading? You can get an electronic copy of classics such as *Alice in Wonderland* or *Moby Dick*.

4 You can get a weather-satellite photo of the U.S. that is, at most, an hour old.

5 The Internet lets you meet people around the world with interests or hobbies similar to your own—everything from home schooling of children to Lotus automobiles.

6 The Internet gives you access to special job listings and career information. Many universities and professional associations also make their job listings available on the Internet.

What Is a Computer Network?

The widespread use of computer networks is the one development most responsible for the emergence of the new electronic frontier. A *network* is a way of connecting computers so they can communicate with each other and share resources like printers and storage space. Networks come in all shapes and sizes. Here is a quick explanation of what they are and what they do.

Three computers connected to a shared printer

▶**1** Networks allow computer users to share expensive computer equipment. For example, it would be costly to buy a separate laser printer for every personal computer in an office. Instead, equipment like printers or very large storage disks can be shared by networking. This means each computer in a network has a cable coming out of its back that eventually leads to the equipment the computers share. In this case, the cables, computers, and the printer form a very simple network in which each computer has access to a printer that is shared by all.

A local area network (LAN) consisting of three computers sharing a printer and disk storage space

2 Certain types of networks also allow users to share programs between computers and to talk to each other using computerized messages called *electronic mail* or, more simply, *mail*. A person on one computer can send mail to one or more people on other computers within the same small office. He or she can also use the network to move files from one computer to another. This type of setup is sometimes called a *local area network* (or LAN) because it is in one physical location, such as one floor of an office building.

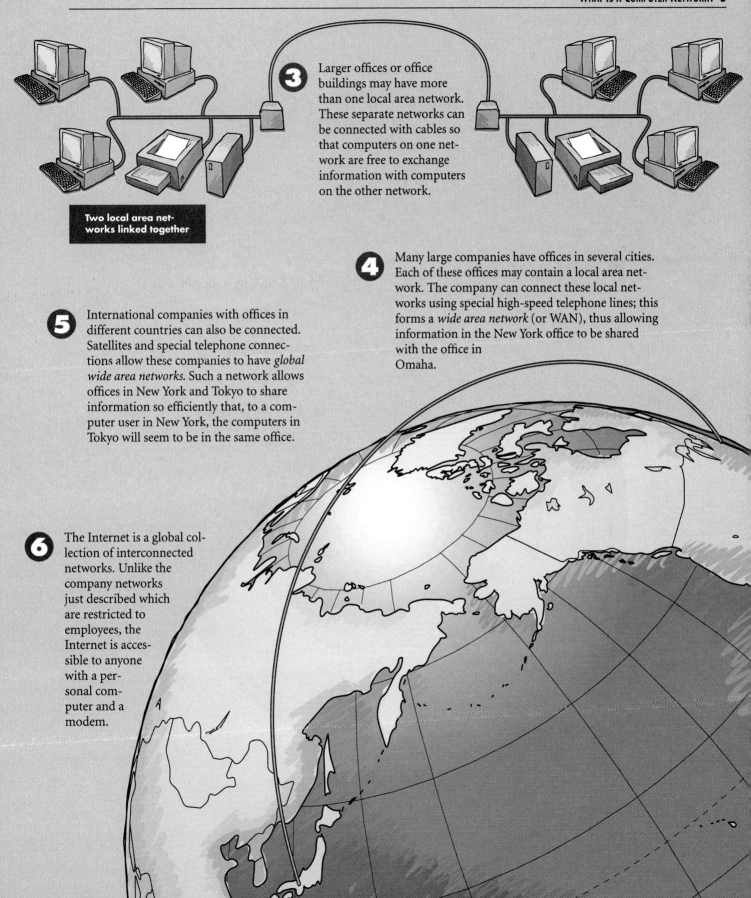

3 Larger offices or office buildings may have more than one local area network. These separate networks can be connected with cables so that computers on one network are free to exchange information with computers on the other network.

Two local area networks linked together

4 Many large companies have offices in several cities. Each of these offices may contain a local area network. The company can connect these local networks using special high-speed telephone lines; this forms a *wide area network* (or WAN), thus allowing information in the New York office to be shared with the office in Omaha.

5 International companies with offices in different countries can also be connected. Satellites and special telephone connections allow these companies to have *global wide area networks*. Such a network allows offices in New York and Tokyo to share information so efficiently that, to a computer user in New York, the computers in Tokyo will seem to be in the same office.

6 The Internet is a global collection of interconnected networks. Unlike the company networks just described which are restricted to employees, the Internet is accessible to anyone with a personal computer and a modem.

What Is the Internet?

So what is the Internet? At one level it is a vast collection of large and small interconnected computer networks extending all the way around the world. At another level it is all the people whose active participation makes the Internet a valuable information resource.

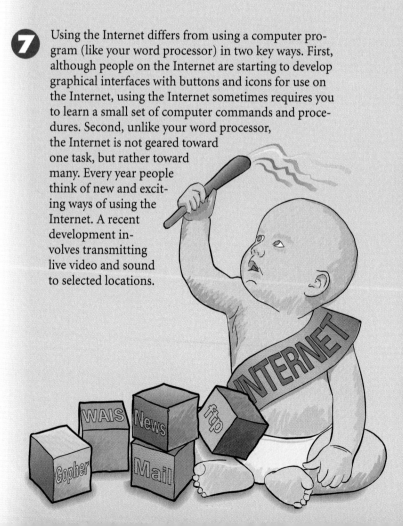

▶ **1**

The Internet is quite young. It began as a small group of military research institutions and universities in physically separate places that needed to share their computerized research data in a timely fashion. In the 1980s, the National Science Foundation created a special network connecting its five supercomputing centers. This special network (called the NSFNET) is the foundation of the Internet in the U.S.

7 Using the Internet differs from using a computer program (like your word processor) in two key ways. First, although people on the Internet are starting to develop graphical interfaces with buttons and icons for use on the Internet, using the Internet sometimes requires you to learn a small set of computer commands and procedures. Second, unlike your word processor, the Internet is not geared toward one task, but rather toward many. Every year people think of new and exciting ways of using the Internet. A recent development involves transmitting live video and sound to selected locations.

2 As computer networks have grown in popularity, universities and government departments have formed cooperative regional computer networks that connect with the NSFNET. These cooperative networks act as a link between small, local institutions and the Internet. Students and workers at these institutions use the Internet to exchange electronic mail and share all sorts of information. As the Internet continues to expand, it attracts more attention, which in turn fuels further growth.

3 While the United States develops its own regional and national computer networks, other countries do the same. The 1980s saw the beginning of connections between various national networks. Each year, more and more countries join the Internet in order to share its resources.

4 The Internet has evolved into a global collection of interconnected computer networks. Nobody's in charge of the Internet; it isn't run by a company like CompuServe or IBM. The Internet depends on the continuing cooperation of all the interconnected networks. Each local network pays for its own computers and for the connection to its nearest larger network. These connections eventually lead to our huge national data highway—the NSFNET.

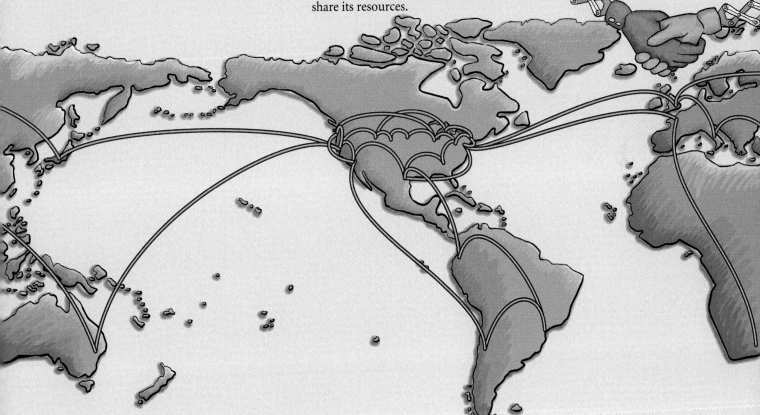

6 It should be clear by now that the Internet isn't just a collection of computers and cables. It is a global community of people who share a wide variety of resources. The Internet allows researchers to share data and publications and gives kids in faraway cities a way to collaborate on special school projects; it lets people share their experience, opinions, and information, and provides a way to create resources and share them instantly with millions of people around the world.

5 As the Internet has grown in popularity, it has become the home of a growing body of information and of the computer tools necessary for anyone on the Internet to access that information. The spirit of cooperation among the networks extends to the users. People on the Internet are very helpful and neighborly.

Exploring the Electronic Frontier

Vast, global networks of computers are one of the last frontiers of our era: the electronic frontier. The Internet is only one part of the rapidly growing system. Here's your opportunity to stake a claim in this exciting area.

▶ **1** The Internet isn't the only global computer network. There are also global commercial networks like CompuServe (CIS), MCI Mail and America Online. These networks are fully owned by a company and charge users for access. Like the Internet, these networks are used by people all around the world.

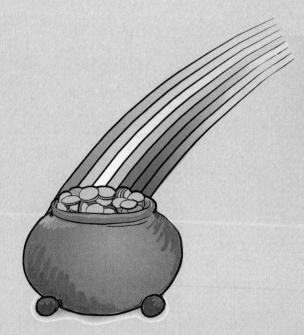

6 As a user of the Internet in the mid 90's, you are still a pioneer on this larger electronic frontier. You should be willing to experiment, to do some exploring. The payoff will be an incredible wealth of useful information, and the opportunity to meet some truly fascinating people who, like you, are colonizing this new electronic frontier.

TIP SHEET

▶ **In Chapters 3 and 16 you'll find out how to send electronic mail to your friends who may be on the Internet or any number of other places on the electronic frontier.**

▶ **Some companies let you shop and order merchandise using these electronic networks. CompuServe and Prodigy offer such services. The Internet has several locations where you can order books and compact disks.**

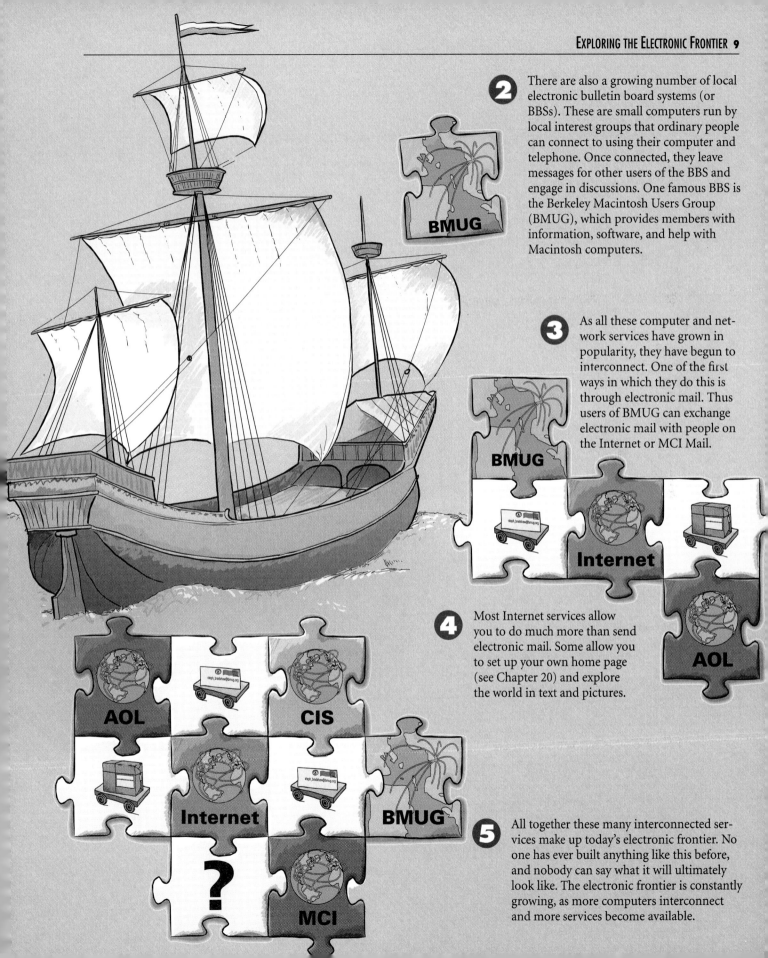

2 There are also a growing number of local electronic bulletin board systems (or BBSs). These are small computers run by local interest groups that ordinary people can connect to using their computer and telephone. Once connected, they leave messages for other users of the BBS and engage in discussions. One famous BBS is the Berkeley Macintosh Users Group (BMUG), which provides members with information, software, and help with Macintosh computers.

3 As all these computer and network services have grown in popularity, they have begun to interconnect. One of the first ways in which they do this is through electronic mail. Thus users of BMUG can exchange electronic mail with people on the Internet or MCI Mail.

4 Most Internet services allow you to do much more than send electronic mail. Some allow you to set up your own home page (see Chapter 20) and explore the world in text and pictures.

5 All together these many interconnected services make up today's electronic frontier. No one has ever built anything like this before, and nobody can say what it will ultimately look like. The electronic frontier is constantly growing, as more computers interconnect and more services become available.

CHAPTER 2

Understanding the Internet

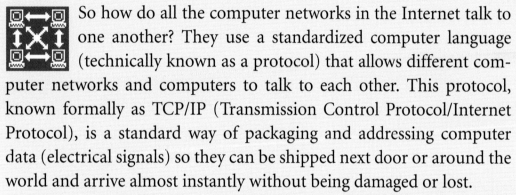 So how do all the computer networks in the Internet talk to one another? They use a standardized computer language (technically known as a protocol) that allows different computer networks and computers to talk to each other. This protocol, known formally as TCP/IP (Transmission Control Protocol/Internet Protocol), is a standard way of packaging and addressing computer data (electrical signals) so they can be shipped next door or around the world and arrive almost instantly without being damaged or lost.

Computers on the Internet have special programs that allow them to speak in TCP/IP. When you get an account on the Internet, you are renting space on a computer that speaks TCP/IP. This computer allows many people to use it at the same time. Since everyone can't sit down at this computer simultaneously, it allows you to connect using your personal computer, a telephone line, and a device called a *modem*, which translates computer signals into telephone signals and vice versa. Once your personal computer is connected, the Internet computer (called a host) waits for you to press keys on your computer keyboard and sends answers that are displayed on your computer screen.

This series of connections allows you to take full advantage of the many resources available on the Internet. In this chapter you'll learn about the various pieces of this connection. Armed with this knowledge, you'll be ready to connect with the Internet.

How Does the Internet Work?

As you've learned, the Internet is a global collection of distinct national, regional, and local computer networks capable of talking to each other. To the Internet user, these distinct networks appear as a seamless whole. Here's how this illusion of unity is maintained.

▶ **1** To move data between two specific computers on a network consisting of many computers, two things are required: the address of the destination and some means of safely and instantly moving the electronic signals that make up the data. It is very easy to lose or damage electronic data during its trip.

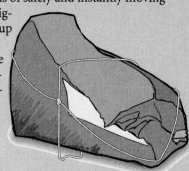

7 To a user, the Internet appears as one giant, seamless, global network that responds almost instantly to requests. Computers, gateways, routers, and protocols ensure that this illusion is maintained.

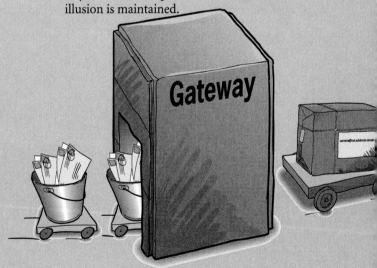

6 Special machines called *gateways* allow different types of networks on the electronic frontier to talk to the Internet using TCP/IP. Gateways translate a computer network's native language into TCP/IP and vice versa.

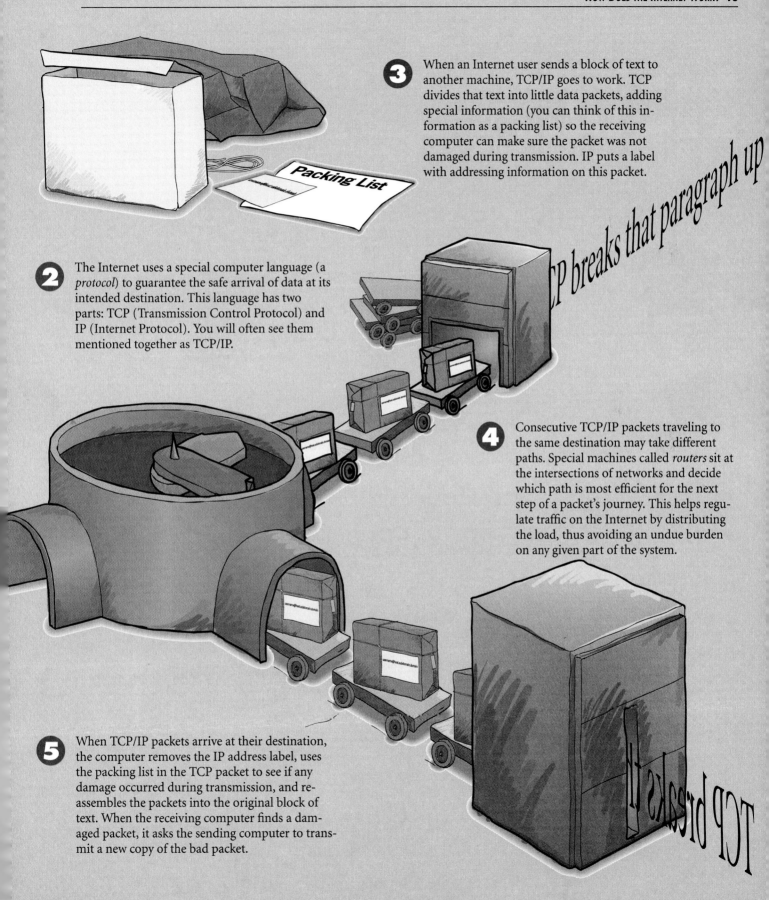

3 When an Internet user sends a block of text to another machine, TCP/IP goes to work. TCP divides that text into little data packets, adding special information (you can think of this information as a packing list) so the receiving computer can make sure the packet was not damaged during transmission. IP puts a label with addressing information on this packet.

Packing List

CP breaks that paragraph up

2 The Internet uses a special computer language (a *protocol*) to guarantee the safe arrival of data at its intended destination. This language has two parts: TCP (Transmission Control Protocol) and IP (Internet Protocol). You will often see them mentioned together as TCP/IP.

4 Consecutive TCP/IP packets traveling to the same destination may take different paths. Special machines called *routers* sit at the intersections of networks and decide which path is most efficient for the next step of a packet's journey. This helps regulate traffic on the Internet by distributing the load, thus avoiding an undue burden on any given part of the system.

5 When TCP/IP packets arrive at their destination, the computer removes the IP address label, uses the packing list in the TCP packet to see if any damage occurred during transmission, and re-assembles the packets into the original block of text. When the receiving computer finds a damaged packet, it asks the sending computer to transmit a new copy of the bad packet.

TCP breaks it

How to Decipher an Internet Address

Addresses are a central part of virtually everything you will do on the Internet. Any interaction you want to have with another person or machine will require an address. The IP (Internet Protocol) in TCP/IP is a mechanism for providing addresses for computers on the Internet. The IP wrapper on a packet is an address label that tells where an individual packet gets sent. Internet addresses take two forms—one that machines understand (expressed as numbers) and one that people can work with easily (expressed as words).

▶ **1** Addresses usually take the form shown in the illustration. The *username* generally refers to the person who holds the Internet account. It is the name you use to identify yourself when logging in to the computer on which you have your Internet account. (*Logging in* is simply the process of gaining access to your personal account on a computer shared by several users.) When your Internet account is created, you can usually choose your username. An example of a typical username is markhb.

TIP SHEET

▶ Be very careful to spell addresses correctly. The computer takes you literally. A misspelling may connect you to an unintended but valid host or may prevent you from making the connection you want. You could end up connected to a host but unable to log in—for no apparent reason.

▶ Even though the computer takes you literally, your use of upper- and lowercase in an address shouldn't affect your ability to connect. For example, markhb@amachine.nasa.gov and markhb@AMACHINE.nasa.GOV are equivalent.

▶ If you are trying to connect to another machine and you receive the message "Unknown host," the nameserver is unable to translate the word address you provided into a numeric equivalent. Check for typing errors. If you see none, the local nameserver may be broken. Wait 15 minutes and try to connect again.

5 Computers called *nameservers* contain huge collections (called databases) of Internet host addresses. They translate word addresses into their numeric equivalents and save you, the user, the trouble of keeping up with changes to hosts' addresses. Your Internet host will automatically access a nearby nameserver.

2 *Hosts* are usually individual machines at a particular location. Think of a host computer as a large apartment building. Your Internet account is like an apartment in that building. Sometimes the same machine will be known by several host names. What is the name of the host machine on which you have your Internet account? If you aren't sure, check your Internet mail address. Mine is shell.

3 Hosts and local networks get grouped together into *domains*, which are themselves grouped into one or more larger domains. You can think of a domain as an apartment complex, a town, or even a country. Some domains correspond to organizations you will recognize, such as Stanford or NASA or CompuServe. Sometimes an address will include more than one domain. An example of this is elvis@spacelink.msfc.nasa.gov. Spacelink is the host; msfc and nasa are both domains. In this address, msfc is like a building complex and nasa is like the town containing that complex.

4 The last part of an Internet address represents the largest domain. In the United States there are six: com (commercial), edu (educational), gov (government), mil (military), net (network), and org (organization). If an address does not end in one of these six domains, it probably belongs to a country other than the United States. Examples of other countries' domain names are ca for Canada, no for Norway, and au for Australia.

username@host.subdomain.domain

What Is a Computer Terminal?

To plug into the electronic frontier, your personal computer must be able to talk to other computers. One way it can do this is by pretending to be a terminal, as described here.

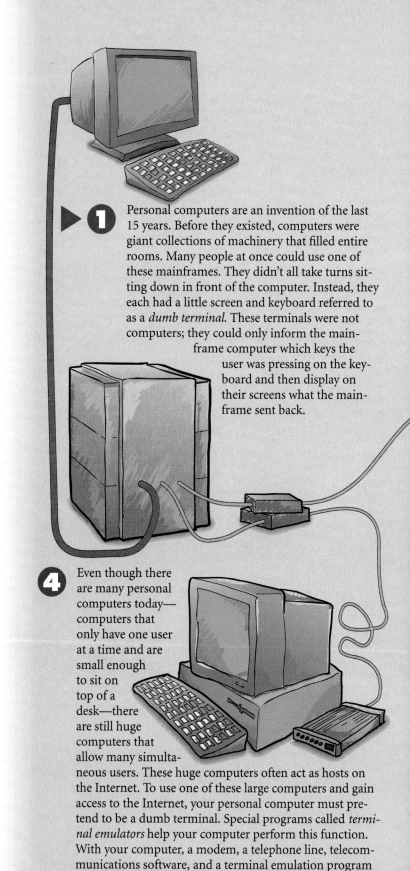

1 Personal computers are an invention of the last 15 years. Before they existed, computers were giant collections of machinery that filled entire rooms. Many people at once could use one of these mainframes. They didn't all take turns sitting down in front of the computer. Instead, they each had a little screen and keyboard referred to as a *dumb terminal*. These terminals were not computers; they could only inform the mainframe computer which keys the user was pressing on the keyboard and then display on their screens what the mainframe sent back.

4 Even though there are many personal computers today—computers that only have one user at a time and are small enough to sit on top of a desk—there are still huge computers that allow many simultaneous users. These huge computers often act as hosts on the Internet. To use one of these large computers and gain access to the Internet, your personal computer must pretend to be a dumb terminal. Special programs called *terminal emulators* help your computer perform this function. With your computer, a modem, a telephone line, telecommunications software, and a terminal emulation program you have all the equipment you need to access the Internet.

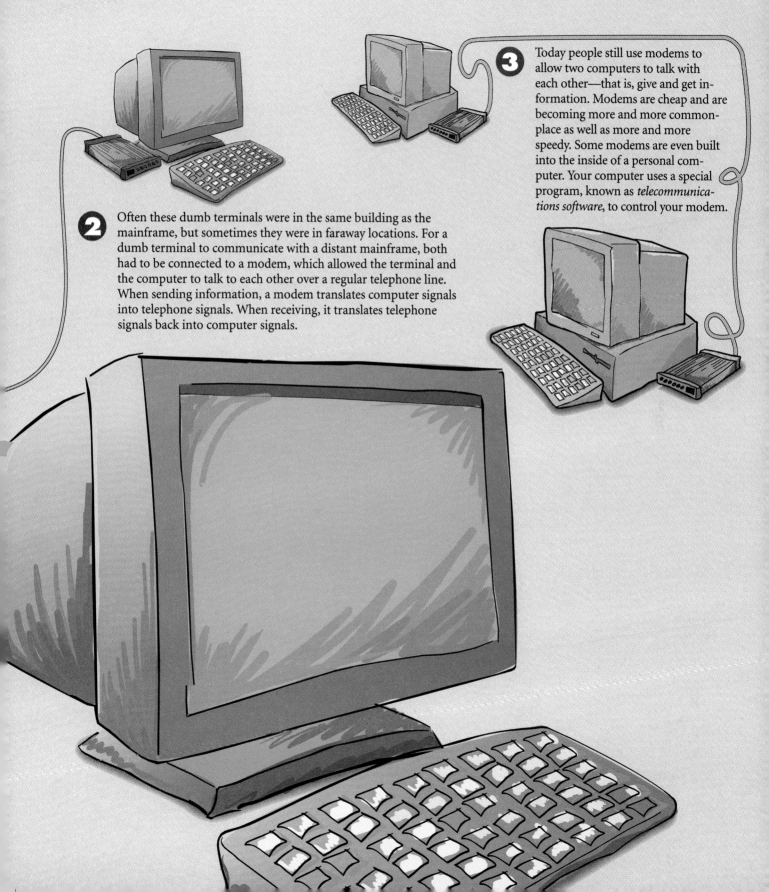

3 Today people still use modems to allow two computers to talk with each other—that is, give and get information. Modems are cheap and are becoming more and more commonplace as well as more and more speedy. Some modems are even built into the inside of a personal computer. Your computer uses a special program, known as *telecommunications software*, to control your modem.

2 Often these dumb terminals were in the same building as the mainframe, but sometimes they were in faraway locations. For a dumb terminal to communicate with a distant mainframe, both had to be connected to a modem, which allowed the terminal and the computer to talk to each other over a regular telephone line. When sending information, a modem translates computer signals into telephone signals. When receiving, it translates telephone signals back into computer signals.

What Terminal Should My Computer Emulate?

Chances are good that to access the Internet, or any other part of the electronic frontier, your computer must emulate a terminal. Telecommunications software allows you to emulate terminals of at least one of two types: line-oriented and screen-oriented. Both types will work for an Internet connection, but whenever possible you should try to use screen-oriented terminal emulation because it will give you more flexibility.

TIP SHEET

▶ Your screen might show a bunch of strange characters that look like this: "^H^H^E^E^H^C^L." If so, the host computer thinks you have a screen-oriented terminal when in fact your telecommunications program is emulating a line-oriented terminal. Those funny characters, which are usually not visible to the user, tell the screen-oriented terminal where on the screen to write various things. To remedy the problem, log in again and define the correct type of terminal at the appropriate prompt.

▶ Sometimes the bizarre characters on your screen are the result of *line noise*—random blips of electrical activity on your telephone line that cause communication with your computer to become garbled. Line noise can be caused by thunderstorms. When it happens you should log out and hang up the phone. Try again after the thunderstorm has passed.

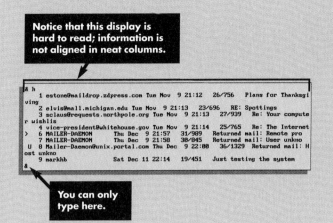

Notice that this display is hard to read; information is not aligned in neat columns.

You can only type here.

▶ **1** A *line-oriented terminal*—sometimes referred to as a *tty* or *teletype* display—inserts characters in the line at the bottom of your terminal screen. You can only alter text on this line. When the line is full or you press the ↵ (Enter or Return) key, the lines all shift up by one. (Throughout this book, ↵ will be used to indicate the Enter or Return key.) This is the simplest form of terminal emulation. It provides the least amount of flexibility in terms of what is displayed on your computer screen.

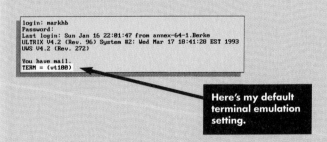

Here's my default terminal emulation setting.

4 Don't worry too much about the details of terminal emulation. When you access or log in to your Internet account, the host computer will ask you what type of terminal you have and will offer a default setting.

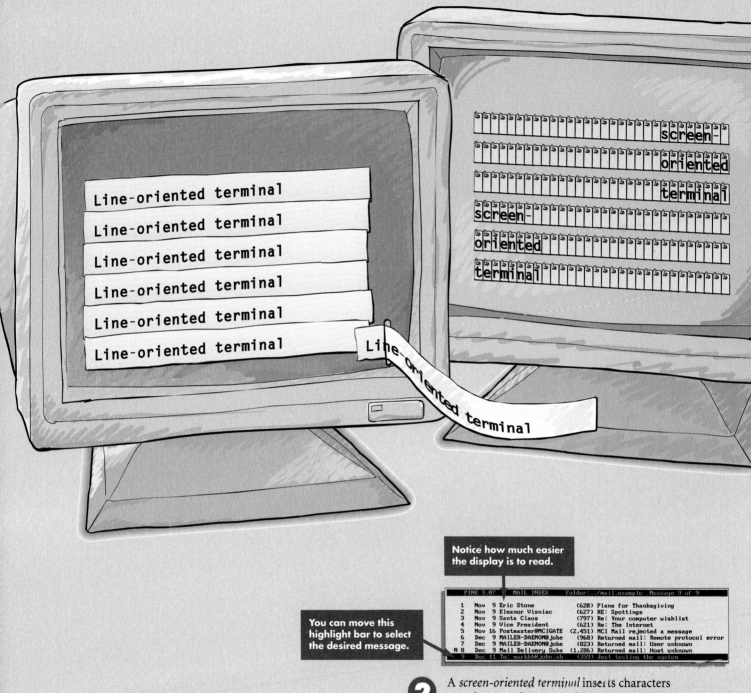

Line-oriented terminal
Line-oriented terminal
Line-oriented terminal
Line-oriented terminal
Line-oriented terminal
Line-oriented terminal

Line-oriented terminal

screen-
oriented
terminal
screen-
oriented
terminal

Notice how much easier the display is to read.

```
     PINE 3.87      MAIL INDEX      Folder:../mail.example  Message 9 of 9

   1   Nov  9 Eric Stone            (620) Plans for Thanksgiving
   2   Nov  9 Eleanor Visniac       (627) RE: Spottings
   3   Nov  9 Santa Claus           (797) Re: Your computer wishlist
   4   Nov  9 Vice President        (621) Re: The Internet
   5   Nov 16 Postmaster@MCIGATE   (2,451) MCI Mail rejected a message
   6   Dec  9 MAILER-DAEMON@jobe    (968) Returned mail: Remote protocol error
   7   Dec  9 MAILER-DAEMON@jobe    (823) Returned mail: User unknown
 N 8   Dec  9 Mail Delivery Subs  (1,286) Returned mail: Host unknown
   9   Dec 11 To: markhh@jobe.sh    (359) Just testing the system
```

You can move this highlight bar to select the desired message.

3 Screen-oriented terminals have names. Often these begin with the letters "vt," followed by a number. The most common vt terminal is the vt100. Other vt terminals include the vt220 and the vt320. The configuration options of your telecommunications software will show which vt terminals, if any, you can emulate. If your communications software will emulate a vt100 (or a number higher than that) you are all set to enjoy some great benefits such as Internet programs that are easier to use.

2 A *screen-oriented terminal* inserts characters anywhere on the terminal screen at any time, not just on the line at the bottom of the screen. This means the layout of the screen can be more graphically complex than on line-oriented terminals. A screen-oriented terminal can also vary the brightness of characters on the screen or highlight particular sections. This lets the computer do some rudimentary formatting. Screen-oriented terminals generally allow a much better presentation of information and therefore a higher degree of user friendliness.

How You Can Connect to the Internet

In order to use the Internet, your personal computer needs to speak with a computer on the Internet. There are three basic ways for this dialog—or connection—to happen. One possibility is that your computer uses a modem and terminal emulation to link with a host computer on the Internet. If your computer is not a terminal, it is actually a part of the Internet and has its own address. Two different types of direct connections are discussed below. Although you'll probably have the first type of connection, you may have more than one kind. If you are not sure which type of connection you have, ask a friend or coworker who is familiar with your system.

TIP SHEET

▶ If you do not have a computer account that provides you with Internet access, there are several ways to get one. Most colleges and universities are on the Internet. If you are a student, you can probably get an account through your school. If you are not a student, you will need to get an account through a service provider. These service providers are located around the country and will provide you with Internet access for a fee. Check in computer magazines for articles about the Internet that list current service providers.

▶ Some commercial bulletin board systems provide partial or even total access to the Internet as a service to their users. The Well in Sausalito, California and America Online in Vienna, Virginia both offer some degree of Internet access.

▶ **①** The most likely possibility is that your computer has a modem that dials out over a telephone line and connects to a host machine on the Internet. It does not matter if your computer is a PC, a Macintosh, or an Amiga. Once connected, your telecommunications software emulates a terminal, allowing you to communicate with the Internet host.

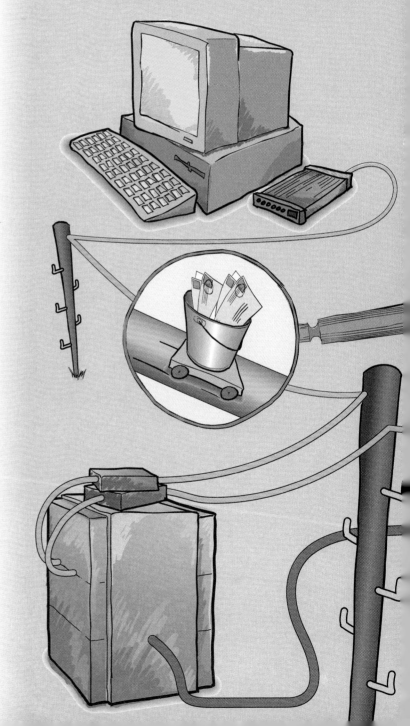

2 A second possibility is that your computer still uses the modem to dial out over a telephone line and connect to a host machine on the Internet. However, rather than pretending to be a terminal, your personal computer and the host machine will speak one of two special computer languages: SLIP (Serial Line Internet Protocol) or PPP (Point to Point Protocol). Your machine will be a physical part of the Internet and have its own host name and IP (Internet Protocol) address. The machine you connect to will forward TCP/IP packets to your computer, and your computer will have to reassemble them. This connection requires a modem that transmits data at a minimum of 9600 bits per second. However, if you want to use graphical programs such as Mosaic (see Chapters 19 and 20), you need at least a 14400 bit per second modem, and a 28800 bit per second modem is even better.

3 A third possibility is that you do not require a modem because your computer is connected by cables, such as Ethernet cables, directly to a local computer network. This network is in turn connected to the Internet. Your machine has its own host-name and IP address. As a result of this direct connection, your machine can very rapidly transmit and receive information from the Internet.

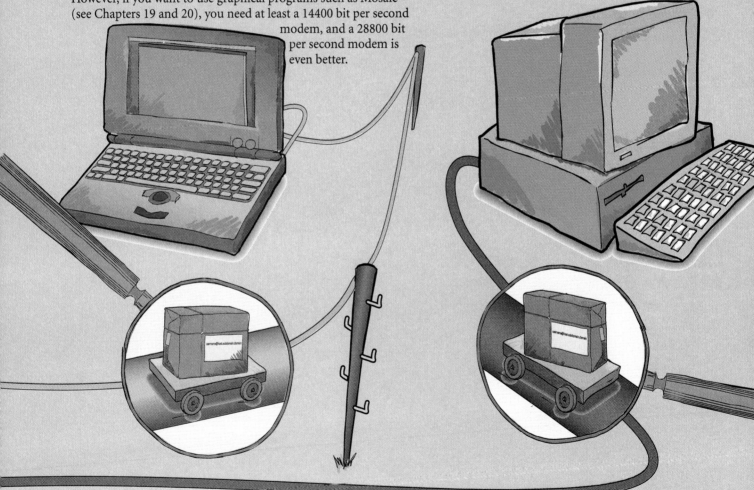

5 Regardless of the type of connection you have, in most cases you will have a computer account on a host machine shared by many users, and this account will provide you with access to the Internet. When you apply for the account, you can usually select your username and password. To use your account, you need to provide the host with that username and password. This process is referred to as logging in. Chapter 4 teaches you the basics of logging into, using, and managing your Internet computer account.

4 Actually being "on the Internet" means having access to a computer with its own IP address. You may be able to sit down in front of this computer, or you may access it using terminal emulation.

CHAPTER 3

Using Mail

One of the really great things about the Internet is that it lets you almost instantly exchange electronic messages (e-mail) with friends across the hall or around the world. Electronic mail is a popular way to communicate on the electronic frontier. If you have a friend with an account on the Internet, Att Mail, MCI Mail, CompuServe, America Online, or a whole host of other electronic networks or bulletin boards, you can exchange e-mail with him or her. If you come across an archive of humor on the Internet, or a great recipe for guacamole, or a beautiful poem, you can e-mail a copy to a friend. You can mail any electronic piece of text.

Your Internet account most likely includes an electronic mailbox. When you receive electronic mail at your Internet host computer, it is stored in your electronic mailbox. After logging in to your Internet account, one of the first things you should do is check your e-mail, just as you check your regular mail when you get home from work.

There are several e-mail programs available on Internet host computers. This chapter will show you how to use one of the most common systems: UCB Mail. Although this program is somewhat awkward to use at first, it is easy to learn, and it will be on virtually every Internet host you ever deal with.

So telephone a good friend who has electronic mail and exchange e-mail addresses with him or her. Before long you'll be able to exchange mail, and chances are you'll be another of the many people who love this cutting-edge form of communication.

How to Send Mail

Internet mail has an amazing number of uses. You can use it to talk to people and computers on the Internet. In later chapters, you'll see how to use e-mail to contact special interest groups or get information stored in Internet archives. First, you need to learn how to send mail from your Internet account.

▶ ❶ In order to send mail from your Internet account, you must first use your telecommunications software to make contact with your Internet host (unless you are working on a dumb terminal directly connected to your Internet host), as discussed in Chapter 2.

Four pieces of "bounced" mail

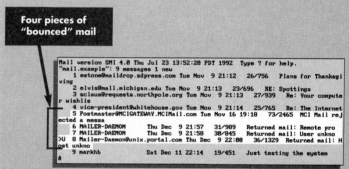

```
Mail version SMI 4.0 Thu Jul 23 13:52:20 PDT 1992  Type ? for help.
"mail.example": 9 messages 1 new
    1 estone@maildrop.zdpress.com Tue Nov  9 21:12  26/756  Plans for Thanksgi
ving
    2 elvis@mall.michigan.edu Tue Nov  9 21:13  23/696   RE: Spottings
    3 sclaus@requests.northpole.org Tue Nov  9 21:13  27/939  Re: Your compute
r wishlis
    4 vice-president@whitehouse.gov Tue Nov  9 21:14  25/765  Re: The Internet
    5 Postmaster@MCIGATEWAY.MCIMail.com Tue Nov 16 19:18  73/2465  MCI Mail rej
ected a messa
    6 MAILER-DAEMON      Thu Dec  9 21:57   31/989   Returned mail: Remote pro
    7 MAILER-DAEMON      Thu Dec  9 21:58   30/845   Returned mail: User unkno
>U  8 Mailer-Daemon@unix.portal.com Thu Dec  9 22:00  36/1329  Returned mail: H
ost unkno
    9 markhb             Sat Dec 11 22:14   19/451   Just testing the system
&
```

❼ If you have made a mistake in one or more of the addresses, only those messages with incorrect addresses will be returned to you, or *bounced back*. The returned messages show up in your mailbox with an explanation for the return. There are many reasons mail can be bounced back, but there are two you can fix: "User unknown" means that there's a typo in the username part of the address; "Host unknown" means that there's a typo in the domain name. If these words appear in the subject line of bounced mail, look closely at the username or domain name, make the needed correction, and send the message to the corrected address. In the next section you'll learn how to check the contents of your Internet mailbox.

The cc: prompt for carbon copies

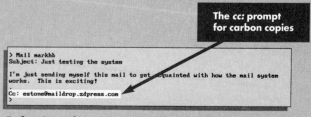

```
> Mail markhb
Subject: Just testing the system

I'm just sending myself this mail to get acquainted with how the mail system
works.  This is exciting!
Cc: estone@maildrop.zdpress.com
>
```

❻ Before it sends your message, the Mail program may prompt you with cc:. This is your opportunity to send copies of this message to others. If you don't want to send anybody a copy, just press ↵. To send copies, enter the recipients' addresses and press ↵. Separate each address with one blank space. The computer will now send your message to all the addresses you've listed.

The *login* prompt

My username

The *password* prompt

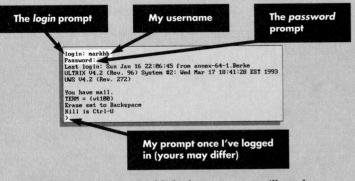

```
login: markhb
Password:
Last login: Sun Jan 16 22:06:45 from annex-64-1.Berke
ULTRIX V4.2 (Rev. 96) System #2: Wed Mar 17 18:41:28 EST 1993
UWS V4.2 (Rev. 272)

You have mail.
TERM = (vt100)
Erase set to Backspace
Kill is Ctrl-U
>
```

My prompt once I've logged in (yours may differ)

The mail command

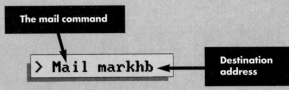

```
> Mail markhb
```

Destination address

2 Once you have established contact, you will need to log in. You do this by providing your username at the *login* prompt, pressing Enter, typing the password given to you by the people who manage your Internet host, and pressing Enter again. Once you are logged in to your account, you will see a prompt on your screen. Chapter 4 discusses the login process in greater detail.

3 Begin by sending mail to yourself just to practice. Type **mail** followed by your username—the name you use to log in—and ↵. This starts the Mail program on your Internet host. When sending mail to someone with an account on your host, you can supply just a username. When sending mail to people at other locations, type **mail** followed by their full address and ↵. As described in Chapter 2, full addresses look like this: markhb@shell.portal.com or elvis@mcimail.com. Remember that, in addresses, upper- and lowercase letters are equivalent.

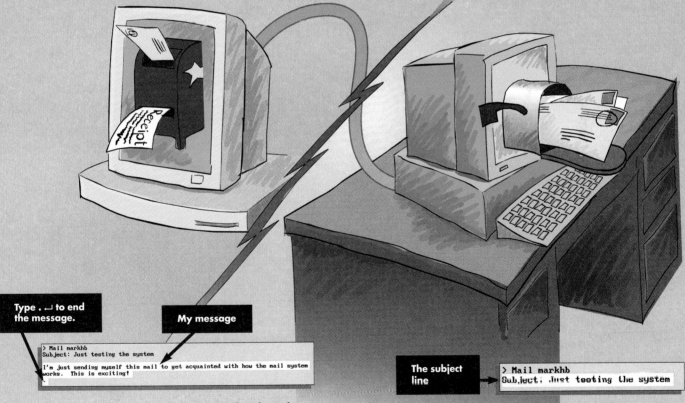

Type . ↵ to end the message.

My message

```
> Mail markhb
Subject: Just testing the system

I'm just sending myself this mail to get acquainted with how the mail system
works.  This is exciting!
.
```

The subject line

```
> Mail markhb
Subject: Just testing the system
```

5 The Mail program is now in Input mode. It's ready to accept your message and provides a blank line to type on. While in Input mode, the Mail program acts pretty much like a typewriter. You must type ↵ to end each line, but you cannot go back to previous lines to correct them. Go ahead and type a message to yourself, remembering to press ↵ at the end of each line. When you're done, go to a new line and type . ↵ at the very beginning of the line. This tells the Mail program that your message is complete and should be sent. Know that once you send a message, you cannot recall it.

4 The computer responds by displaying the subject line prompt. This is an important line on which you should briefly describe the subject of your message. When you read your electronic mail in the next section, you'll see that each message is listed by sender name and subject line. This makes it easy to decide what to read first. For practice, type **Just testing the system** ↵ on the subject line.

How to Read Your Mail

Reading mail is the flip-side of sending it. Here's what you need to know to read your mail on a UNIX host.

▶ **1** To read your mail just type **mail**. This puts the Mail program in Command mode (rather than Input mode) and lists the messages in your mailbox. If you don't get such a list, try typing **Mail** ↵. If your mailbox is empty, the Mail program will tell you so. The previous page explains how to send yourself mail so you have mail to work with in this section.

5 To exit the Mail program type x ↵ at the & prompt.

Type h to list the contents of your mailbox.

```
& h
   1 estone@maildrop.zdpress.com Tue Nov  9 21:12   26/756   Plans for Thanksgi
ving
   2 elvis@mall.michigan.edu Tue Nov  9 21:13   23/696   RE: Spottings
   3 sclaus@requests.northpole.org Tue Nov  9 21:13   27/939   Re: Your compute
r wishlis
   4 vice-president@whitehouse.gov Tue Nov  9 21:14   25/765   Re: The Internet
   5 Postmaster@MCIGATEWAY.MCIMail.com Tue Nov 16 19:18   73/2465  MCI Mail rej
ected a messa
   6 MAILER-DAEMON        Thu Dec  9 21:57   31/989   Returned mail: Remote pro
   7 MAILER-DAEMON        Thu Dec  9 21:58   30/845   Returned mail: User unkno
 U 8 Mailer-Daemon@unix.portal.com Thu Dec  9 22:00   36/1329  Returned mail: H
ost unkno
 >  9 markhb              Sat Dec 11 22:14   19/451   Just testing the system
&
```

4 Once you've read your message, you may want to see the list of messages again. To do so when you're already in Command mode, just type **h** ↵ at the & prompt. This list can include up to 20 messages.

The contents of my mailbox

The subject line

Let's read the message I sent myself, message number 9.

```
Mail version SMI 4.0 Thu Jul 23 13:52:20 PDT 1992  Type ? for help.
"mail.example": 9 messages 1 new
   1 estone@maildrop.zdpress.com Tue Nov  9 21:12   26/756    Plans for Thanksgi
ving
   2 elvis@mall.michigan.edu Tue Nov  9 21:13   23/696    RE: Spottings
   3 sclaus@requests.northpole.org Tue Nov  9 21:13   27/939   Re: Your compute
r wishlis
   4 vice-president@whitehouse.gov Tue Nov  9 21:14   25/765   Re: The Internet
   5 Postmaster@MCIGATEWAY.MCIMail.com Tue Nov 16 19:18   73/2465  MCI Mail rej
ected a messa
   6 MAILER-DAEMON        Thu Dec  9 21:57   31/989    Returned mail: Remote pro
   7 MAILER-DAEMON        Thu Dec  9 21:58   30/845    Returned mail: User unkno
>U 8 Mailer-Daemon@unix.portal.com Thu Dec  9 22:00   36/1329  Returned mail: H
ost unkno
   9 markhh               Sat Dec 11 22:14   19/451    Just testing the system
&
```

```
& 9
Message  9:
From markhh Sat Dec 11 22:14:30 1993
Received: by jobe (4.1/1.34)
        id AA29408; Sat, 11 Dec 93 22:14:27 PST
Date: Sat, 11 Dec 93 22:14:27 PST
From: markhh (Mark - Butler)
Message-Id: <9312120614.AA294080@jobe.shell.portal.com>
To: markhh
Subject: Just testing the system
Status: R

I'm just sending myself this mail to get acquainted with how the mail system
works.  This is exciting!

I'm glad I have access to a full scale text editor here.

-mark

&
```

2 Notice the display generated by the Mail program. Each message is numbered and includes the address of the sender, the date and time the message was sent, the size of the message (lines/characters), and the subject line. The ampersand (&) character at the bottom of the list is the Mail program's Command mode prompt; this is where you will type your commands.

3 To read a message, type its number—for example 9 ↵. The Mail program will now display that message on the screen. Long messages (over 24 lines) may scroll off your screen. If this happens, try typing **more** and the message number at the & prompt. For example, **more** 9 ↵ will allow you to read message 9 one screenful at a time. Simply press the spacebar to see subsequent screens of text.

How to Reply to Your Mail

If you have received mail, you can send a reply without having to look up the sender's address. The Mail program automatically extracts a person's address from the message they have sent you. This can be useful if you don't yet know somebody's address or if you don't want to go to the trouble of typing the whole thing. In fact, you might find it helpful to have friends send e-mail to you so you can reply to them and write down their addresses as they appear in the list of messages. That way, you can avoid frustration over bounced mail.

We'll reply to our own message.

▶ **1** Start your Mail program as described on the previous two pages. Now scan the list of mail messages in your mailbox and find the number of the message you want to reply to.

Type R for a group reply.

The Mail program automatically provides the entire group's addresses.

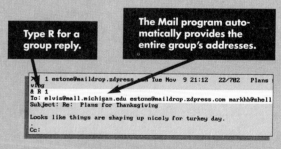

5 In some cases, you can reply to many people at once. If you've received mail that has also been sent to others, you may wish to reply to everybody without typing each address at the *cc:* prompt. To do this, type **R** (rather than r) followed by the number of the message you are replying to and press ↵. Even under these circumstances, the Mail program may offer you the cc: prompt. Just press ↵ unless you want to send copies to people that didn't receive the original message.

TIP SHEET

▶ Sometimes system administrators set up the Mail program on the host computer with the meaning of r and R reversed—r will automatically reply to everyone, and R will reply only to the sender.

▶ If you've sent mail to yourself, it may take a while to show up in your mailbox. If you don't see it, quit the Mail program and then get back in.

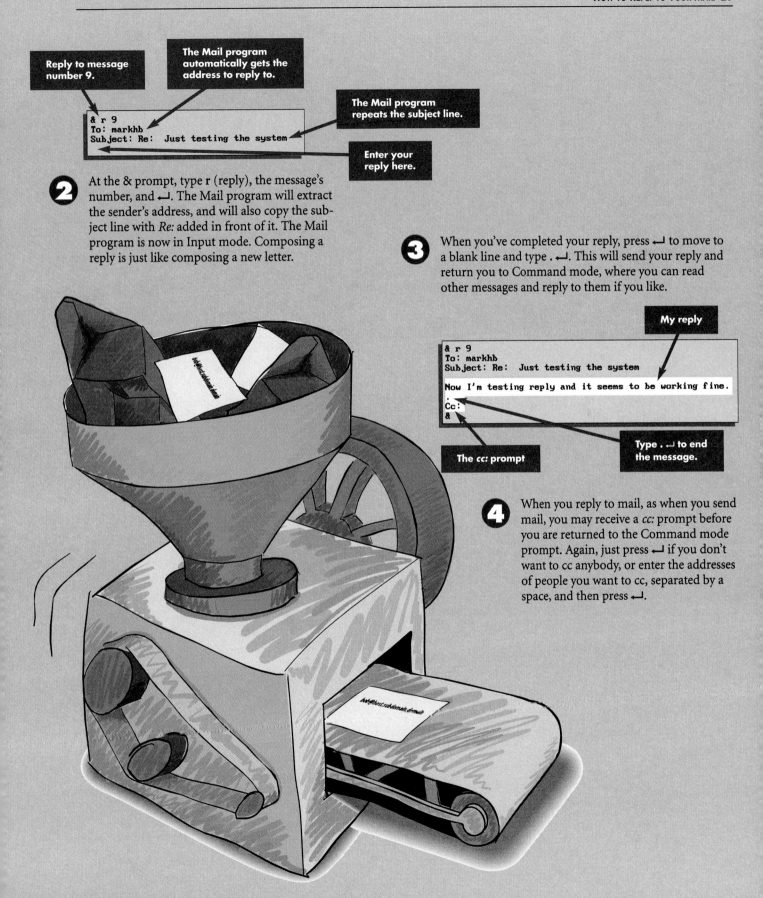

Reply to message number 9.

The Mail program automatically gets the address to reply to.

The Mail program repeats the subject line.

```
& r 9
To: markhb
Subject: Re:   Just testing the system
```

Enter your reply here.

2 At the & prompt, type **r** (reply), the message's number, and ↵. The Mail program will extract the sender's address, and will also copy the subject line with *Re:* added in front of it. The Mail program is now in Input mode. Composing a reply is just like composing a new letter.

3 When you've completed your reply, press ↵ to move to a blank line and type **. ↵**. This will send your reply and return you to Command mode, where you can read other messages and reply to them if you like.

My reply

```
& r 9
To: markhb
Subject: Re:   Just testing the system

Now I'm testing reply and it seems to be working fine.
.
Cc:
&
```

Type . ↵ to end the message.

The *cc:* prompt

4 When you reply to mail, as when you send mail, you may receive a *cc:* prompt before you are returned to the Command mode prompt. Again, just press ↵ if you don't want to cc anybody, or enter the addresses of people you want to cc, separated by a space, and then press ↵.

How to Manage Your Mailbox

Just as an apartment building has a common area for tenants' mailboxes, your Internet host has an area for everyone's mail. This means that everybody's incoming mail is stored on the same small portion of disk space on the host. As a thoughtful neighbor, you should try to minimize the amount of space you take up. You can do this by deleting messages you no longer want and saving the ones you care about in your own account's storage space. Here's how to manage you mailbox.

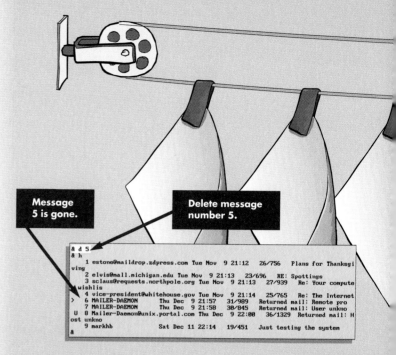

Message 5 is gone.

Delete message number 5.

▶ **1** The easiest way to manage your mailbox is to delete the items you don't want. When in Command mode, you can do this by typing **d** (delete), the message number and ↵ at the & prompt. You can probably delete most of the messages you receive immediately after reading them. If you type **h** ↵ at the & prompt after deleting messages, the deleted messages will no longer be listed.

TIP SHEET

▶ If you delete some mail messages and then list the messages in your mailbox, you'll notice that the mail program doesn't renumber the remaining messages.

▶ As your use of the Internet increases, the amount of mail you receive will also increase. If you store important messages in separate files, rather than one long file, it will be easier to find an old message you might be looking for. Chapter 4 will show you how to arrange files and the "directories" that contain them.

▶ Whether you store your old mail in one or many files, you can use the text searching tools described in Chapter 5 to help you look for particular messages in one or more text files.

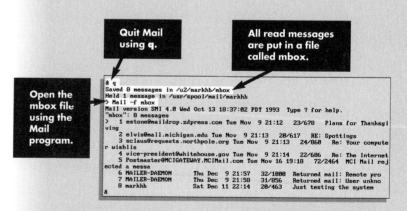

Quit Mail using q.

All read messages are put in a file called mbox.

Open the mbox file using the Mail program.

6 If you quit the Mail program by typing **q** ↵ (rather than **x** ↵) at the & prompt, all the mail that you have just read is automatically moved into a file called mbox in your home directory. This minimizes the shared disk space you use for mail, but it can become unwieldy to have all your mail stored in one file. To view the mbox file using the Mail program, type **mail -f mbox** ↵ from your home directory.

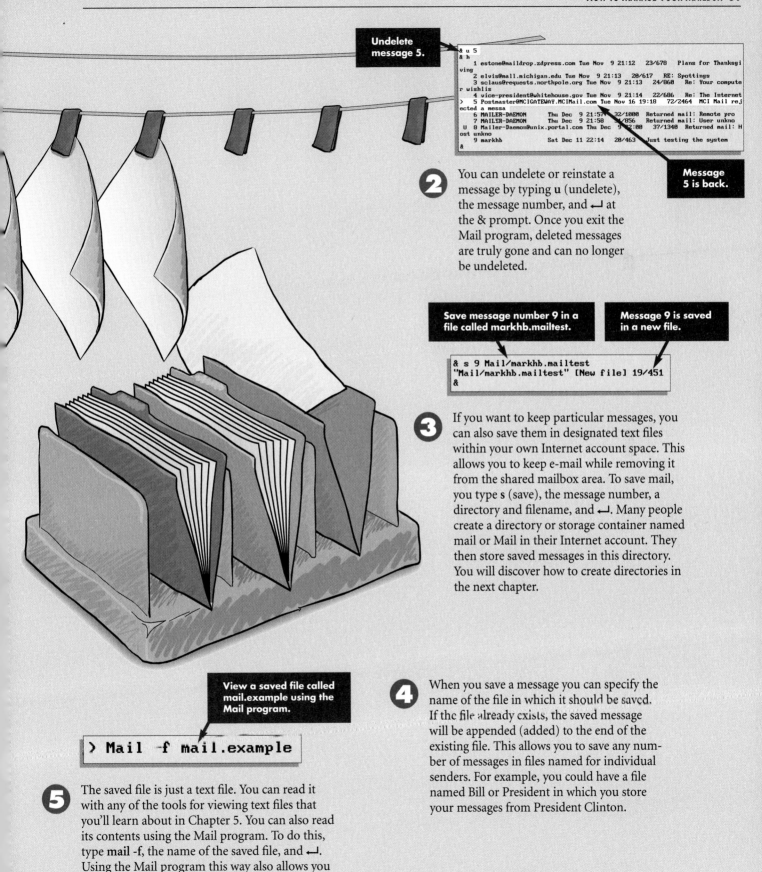

Undelete message 5.

```
& u 5
& h
    1 estone@maildrop.zdpress.com Tue Nov  9 21:12   23/678    Plans for Thanksgi
ving
    2 elvis@mall.michigan.edu Tue Nov  9 21:13   20/617   RE: Spottings
    3 sclaus@requests.northpole.org Tue Nov  9 21:13   24/860   Re: Your compute
r wishlis
    4 vice-president@whitehouse.gov Tue Nov  9 21:14   22/686   Re: The Internet
>   5 Postmaster@MCIGATEWAY.MCIMail.com Tue Nov 16 19:18   72/2464  MCI Mail rej
ected a messa
    6 MAILER-DAEMON      Thu Dec  9 21:57   32/1000  Returned mail: Remote pro
    7 MAILER-DAEMON      Thu Dec  9 21:58   4/856    Returned mail: User unkno
  U 8 Mailer-Daemon@unix.portal.com Thu Dec  9 22:00   37/1340  Returned mail: H
ost unkno
    9 markhb            Sat Dec 11 22:14   20/463   Just testing the system
&
```

Message 5 is back.

2 You can undelete or reinstate a message by typing **u** (undelete), the message number, and ⏎ at the & prompt. Once you exit the Mail program, deleted messages are truly gone and can no longer be undeleted.

Save message number 9 in a file called markhb.mailtest. **Message 9 is saved in a new file.**

```
& s 9 Mail/markhb.mailtest
"Mail/markhb.mailtest" [New file] 19/451
&
```

3 If you want to keep particular messages, you can also save them in designated text files within your own Internet account space. This allows you to keep e-mail while removing it from the shared mailbox area. To save mail, you type **s** (save), the message number, a directory and filename, and ⏎. Many people create a directory or storage container named mail or Mail in their Internet account. They then store saved messages in this directory. You will discover how to create directories in the next chapter.

View a saved file called mail.example using the Mail program.

```
> Mail -f mail.example
```

5 The saved file is just a text file. You can read it with any of the tools for viewing text files that you'll learn about in Chapter 5. You can also read its contents using the Mail program. To do this, type **mail -f**, the name of the saved file, and ⏎. Using the Mail program this way also allows you to reply to a message you've already saved.

4 When you save a message you can specify the name of the file in which it should be saved. If the file already exists, the saved message will be appended (added) to the end of the existing file. This allows you to save any number of messages in files named for individual senders. For example, you could have a file named Bill or President in which you store your messages from President Clinton.

CHAPTER 4

UNIX Commands and Your Internet Account

 Most Internet users will have an account on a host computer that uses UNIX as the main program that runs their host computer, much as DOS runs a PC or System 7 runs a Macintosh. UNIX was created before personal computers existed and is designed to let many people share the same computer simultaneously. Thus many users can have private Internet accounts on a UNIX host machine.

You can think of the shared host computer as an apartment building, where each user's account entitles him or her to an apartment and the use of a number of services. Your username is your apartment number, and your password is the key to your door. While some areas of the building (such as the mailbox area discussed in the last chapter) are shared by all the users, your apartment is like a private storage space that you are free to arrange as you see fit.

UNIX was developed before the use of Windows or pointing and clicking with a mouse. UNIX has a *command line interface* (just like DOS), which means that to interact with the computer you must type all instructions (called *commands*) at the prompt on the screen. (The prompt is UNIX's way of saying it is ready for your next instruction; your prompt may be a >, a %, or some other character or characters.) UNIX then processes the commands and displays the results on the screen. Although there are lots of commands that you can use in UNIX, you actually need to know only a few to be able to arrange your storage space and use the Internet. The more user-friendly Internet software described in Chapters 15–21 requires very little UNIX expertise. However, you may find situations where some knowledge of UNIX is desireable. This book gives you that basic knowledge.

Logging in and Getting Your Bearings in UNIX

I t is very important to have a sense of place when exploring the data inside a computer or traveling around the Internet. The storage space in a computer is organized in a hierarchical directory structure in which *directories* are containers holding either files or other directories. Directories within a directory are called *subdirectories* and can contain other subdirectories. Windows and the Macintosh represent these directories and subdirectories as folders and can show you several levels of folders at once. In UNIX you can only see one level at a time. To get somewhere in the directory structure, you must tell the computer exactly what directories and subdirectories to go through to reach your destination. This information is called a *pathname* or *path.* You must know your current location, often referred to as your current working directory, in order to supply UNIX with the path. Before learning how to determine your current working directory, log in to your UNIX account.

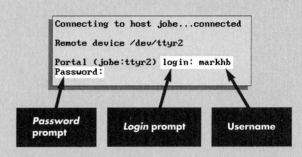

```
Connecting to host jobe...connected
Remote device /dev/ttyr2
Portal (jobe:ttyr2) login: markhb
Password:
```

Password prompt **Login prompt** **Username**

▶ **1** Think of *logging in* as the process of entering your building and getting into your apartment. Logging in is a two-step process. When you first establish contact with the host computer, it asks for your username by presenting the *login:* prompt. After you type your username, the host computer asks for your password. Notice that when you type your password the characters do not show up on the screen. This is so that other people don't see your password and thus can't break into your account. As a future reference, when you log in to an ftp site where you do not have an account, you will log in as *anonymous* and your password will be your user ID. (Ftp is explained in Chapter 10.)

5 When you are done using your account you must log out. Type **logout** ↵ at the UNIX prompt to do this. *Don't forget to log out.* If you leave your machine without logging out, another person with access to your terminal can use your account.

TIP SHEET

▶ **Your password is the key that opens the lock to your Internet account. It must not be easy to guess. Do not simply scramble the letters of your name or use complete words. Mix and match letters, numbers, and punctuation to create a password that you can easily remember but that someone will have a hard time guessing, such as zX09,me2.**

```
login: markhb
Password:
Last login: Sun Jan 16 22:06:45 from annex-64-1.Berke
ULTRIX V4.2 (Rev. 96) System #2: Wed Mar 17 18:41:28 EST 1993
UWS V4.2 (Rev. 272)

You have mail.
TERM = (vt100)
Erase set to Backspace
Kill is Ctrl-U
>
```

My UNIX prompt. Yours may look different.

2 When the machine confirms your password, it logs you in and places you in your *home directory* on the host machine. Think of this directory as the apartment you have rented. Your home directory is where you will keep your files and create your own subdirectories to help organize those files. Once you are logged in, UNIX will display its prompt, letting you know it is ready for you to type some instructions. Some systems provide users with a menu of choices after they log in. If this happens to you, select *shell* or the menu item that will let you access the command line. The rest of this book assumes you can type on the command line.

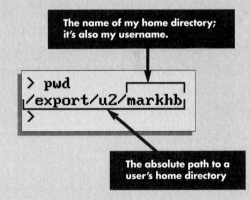

The name of my home directory; it's also my username.

```
> pwd
/export/u2/markhb
>
```

The absolute path to a user's home directory

3 To travel around in a directory structure you need to know your current working directory. UNIX has a command, pwd, that provides this information. Immediately after logging in, type **pwd** ↵. UNIX displays the path to your home directory.

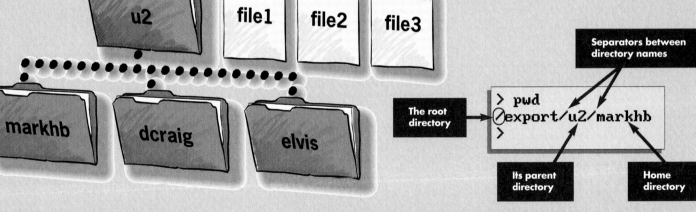

Separators between directory names

The root directory

```
> pwd
/export/u2/markhb
>
```

Its parent directory

Home directory

4 The pwd command gives your current location in the directory structure as an *absolute pathname*, a sequential list of all the directories you must travel through to get to where you currently are. The directory names in the path are separated from each other by a slash (/). The very top of the directory structure is known as the *root* and is denoted by the slash (/) at the beginning of the pathname. All absolute pathnames begin with the root. *Relative pathnames* begin with the current working directory rather than the root and specify the path to follow relative to it. You use relative pathnames to travel to nearby directories or subdirectories.

How to Create and Navigate a Directory Structure

N ow that you can log in and out and have the tools for discovering where you are in the directory structure, how do you travel around within this space? This section will show you how to create a personal subdirectory, travel there, and return home. You'll use these skills to arrange your filing system within your personal storage space, to move around within it, and, in later chapters, to move around in public spaces throughout the Internet.

▶**1** Before setting out on this journey, let's make a place to go, a subdirectory within your home directory. Immediately after logging in to your account, type **mkdir testdir** ↵. This will make a new subdirectory called testdir in your current directory. Notice that the command has two parts separated by a blank space. Mkdir (make directory) is the action being performed; testdir is the object of that action. Most UNIX commands follow this action/object syntax. See the Tip Sheet for information about naming directories and files.

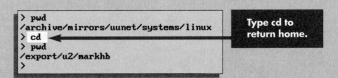

```
> pwd
/archive/mirrors/uunet/systems/linux
> cd
> pwd
/export/u2/markhb
>
```

Type cd to return home.

5 Here's one final navigational tool: Typing cd ↵ without any subsequent pathname will always take you back to your home directory. So if you are ever terribly lost, remember that cd ↵ will take you home.

TIP SHEET

▶ **Notice that UNIX pathnames use a slash (/) rather than the backslash (\) used in DOS. If you are a DOS user, this convention will be aggravating at first, but you'll adjust to it after a while.**

▶ **Most UNIX systems will allow file and directory names that are 32 characters long. Take advantage of this by giving descriptive names to files and directories.**

▶ **File and directory names are case sensitive. In other words, UNIX accepts directory, Directory, and DIRECTORY as three different names.**

▶ **File and directory names cannot contain blank spaces, semicolons, asterisks, or question marks. They can contain periods.**

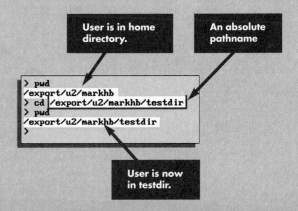

User is in home directory.

An absolute pathname

```
> pwd
/export/u2/markhb
> cd /export/u2/markhb/testdir
> pwd
/export/u2/markhb/testdir
>
```

User is now in testdir.

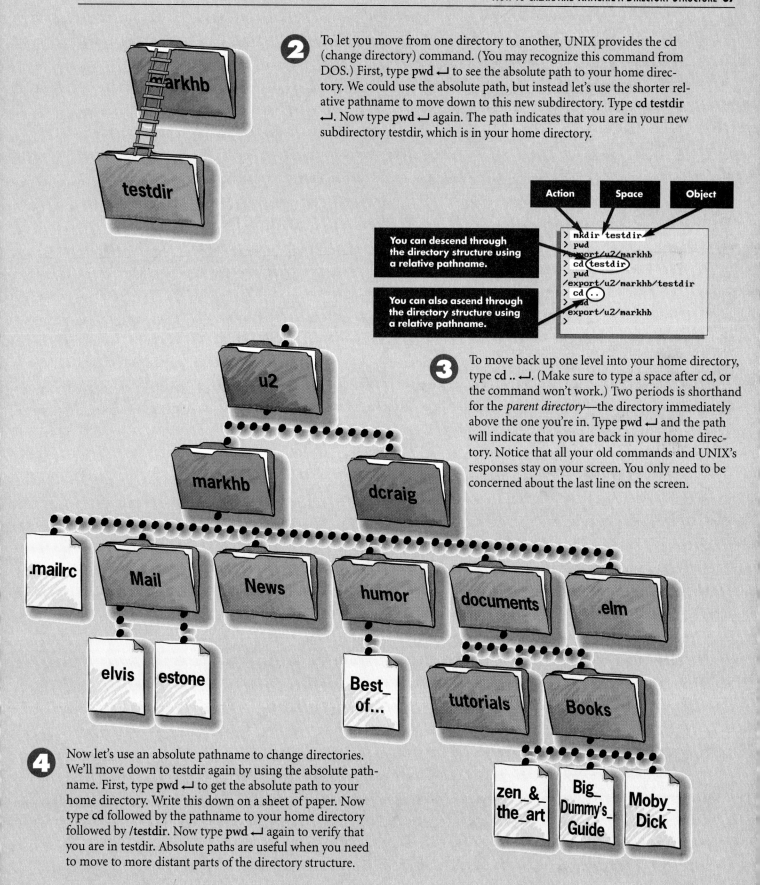

2 To let you move from one directory to another, UNIX provides the cd (change directory) command. (You may recognize this command from DOS.) First, type **pwd** ↵ to see the absolute path to your home directory. We could use the absolute path, but instead let's use the shorter relative pathname to move down to this new subdirectory. Type **cd testdir** ↵. Now type **pwd** ↵ again. The path indicates that you are in your new subdirectory testdir, which is in your home directory.

Action   **Space**   **Object**

You can descend through the directory structure using a relative pathname.

You can also ascend through the directory structure using a relative pathname.

```
> mkdir testdir
> pwd
/export/u2/markhb
> cd testdir
> pwd
/export/u2/markhb/testdir
> cd ..
> pwd
/export/u2/markhb
>
```

3 To move back up one level into your home directory, type **cd ..** ↵. (Make sure to type a space after cd, or the command won't work.) Two periods is shorthand for the *parent directory*—the directory immediately above the one you're in. Type **pwd** ↵ and the path will indicate that you are back in your home directory. Notice that all your old commands and UNIX's responses stay on your screen. You only need to be concerned about the last line on the screen.

4 Now let's use an absolute pathname to change directories. We'll move down to testdir again by using the absolute pathname. First, type **pwd** ↵ to get the absolute path to your home directory. Write this down on a sheet of paper. Now type **cd** followed by the pathname to your home directory followed by **/testdir**. Now type **pwd** ↵ again to verify that you are in testdir. Absolute paths are useful when you need to move to more distant parts of the directory structure.

How to List the Contents of a UNIX Directory

Now that you can create and travel to new directories, it's helpful to see a list of the contents of a directory so you can see what files are stored there. The UNIX command ls (list; similar to the dir command in DOS) provides this information. Like most other UNIX commands, ls allows you to add *modifiers*, often referred to as *flags*. If you add a flag to a command, UNIX will modify the output of that command, often providing additional information or changing the format of the output.

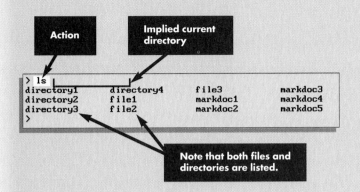

1 Using ls without any modifiers produces the simplest form of directory listing: a multicolumn list of the contents of your current working directory. The ls command is the action; since you don't specify an object, UNIX assumes you mean the current directory. This list provides only the names of things in the directory; it does not distinguish subdirectories from files. If you've just begun to use your Internet account there may not be anything in your home directory except for the subdirectory testdir that you just created. You can create files by saving some of your e-mail messages. To do so, follow the instructions in Chapter 3, under "How to Manage Your Mailbox."

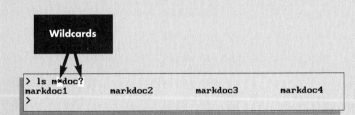

5 Like DOS, UNIX allows you to use *wildcards*—characters that stand for any set of letters in a filename. Wildcards in filenames work the same way as wildcards in card games. You can use the wildcard ? to represent any single character. You can also use the wildcard * to represent any number of characters, from zero on up. For example, if you type ls m*doc? ↵ UNIX will list all the files and directories in the current directory that begin with *m* and end with the letters *doc* followed by any single character. It doesn't matter how many letters come between the *m* and the *doc* in the file or directory name. Wildcards are very helpful when you can only remember part of a filename or when you want to do something—such as delete—more than one file at a time.

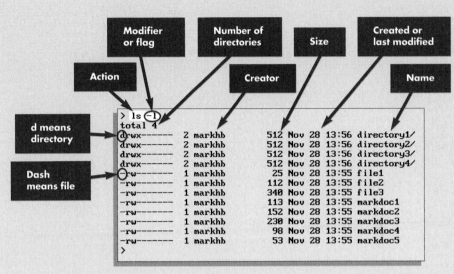

2 One of the most common flags used to modify ls is -l. When you use this flag, ls supplies lots of additional information such as the date each file or directory was created or last modified, size, and creator. This type of listing also differentiates between files (marked with -) and directories (marked with *d*). Type ls -l ↵ to get a long listing of your current working directory.

Modifier or flag

Number of directories

Size

Created or last modified

Action

Creator

Name

d means directory

Dash means file

```
> ls -l
total 4
drwx------   2 markhb        512 Nov 28 13:56 directory1/
drwx------   2 markhb        512 Nov 28 13:56 directory2/
drwx------   2 markhb        512 Nov 28 13:56 directory3/
drwx------   2 markhb        512 Nov 28 13:56 directory4/
-rw-------   1 markhb         25 Nov 28 13:55 file1
-rw-------   1 markhb        112 Nov 28 13:55 file2
-rw-------   1 markhb        340 Nov 28 13:55 file3
-rw-------   1 markhb        113 Nov 28 13:55 markdoc1
-rw-------   1 markhb        152 Nov 28 13:55 markdoc2
-rw-------   1 markhb        230 Nov 28 13:55 markdoc3
-rw-------   1 markhb         98 Nov 28 13:55 markdoc4
-rw-------   1 markhb         53 Nov 28 13:55 markdoc5
>
```

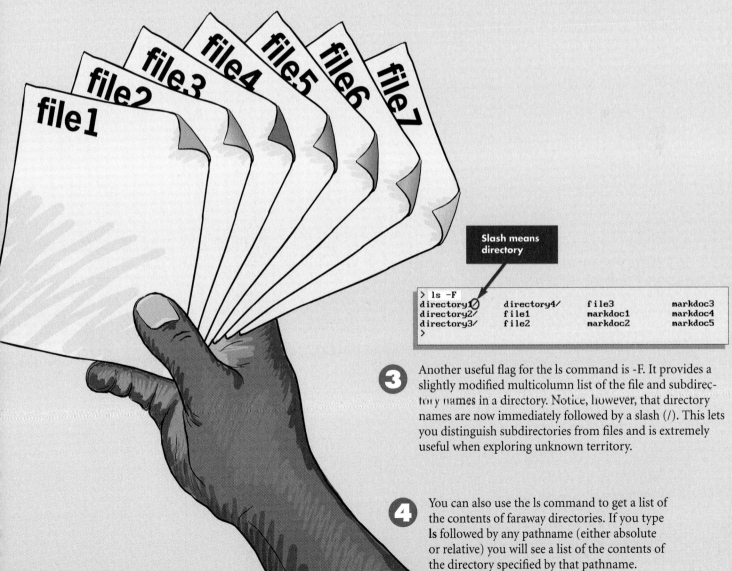

Slash means directory

```
> ls -F
directory1/   directory4/   file3      markdoc3
directory2/   file1         markdoc1   markdoc4
directory3/   file2         markdoc2   markdoc5
>
```

3 Another useful flag for the ls command is -F. It provides a slightly modified multicolumn list of the file and subdirectory names in a directory. Notice, however, that directory names are now immediately followed by a slash (/). This lets you distinguish subdirectories from files and is extremely useful when exploring unknown territory.

4 You can also use the ls command to get a list of the contents of faraway directories. If you type ls followed by any pathname (either absolute or relative) you will see a list of the contents of the directory specified by that pathname.

Rearranging and Cleaning Your UNIX Living Space

As you spend more time on the Internet, you'll collect a growing pool of information stored as files in your home directory. You wouldn't store all your papers in a single pile, and you don't need to store all your electronic files in one directory. UNIX commands allow you to copy, move, and remove unwanted files and, in some cases, remove subdirectories. When you carry out these operations, be sure you're in the appropriate directory—your home directory or a subdirectory you've created. Here are the basics of rearranging and cleaning your directories.

List directory contents.

```
> ls -F
myfile          testdir/
> cp myfile myfile.backup
> ls -F
myfile          myfile.backup    testdir/
>
```

Copy the text file.

Original

Copy

1 You use the cp (copy) command to make a copy of any file. First, create a text file by saving one of your e-mail messages. Follow the instructions in Chapter 3, in the section "How to Manage Your Mailbox," and save one of your messages in a file named myfile. Then, from your home directory, type **cp myfile myfile.backup** ↵ to make a copy of myfile named myfile.backup. Now you have two files identical in content but with different names in your current directory.

6 There is also a command for removing directories. Move to the parent directory and type **rmdir** followed by the directory's name to remove it from your directory structure. (Remember, the parent directory is the one immediately above the directory in question.) If you move to your home directory and type **rmdir testdir** ↵, you will delete the directory you created at the beginning of this chapter. You have to delete all the files in a directory before you can remove that directory.

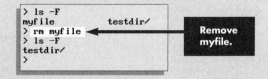

```
> ls -F
myfile          testdir/
> rm myfile
> ls -F
testdir/
>
```

Remove myfile.

5 You should avoid hanging on to outdated and unnecessary files or you'll have a harder time finding things when you want them. UNIX provides the rm (remove) command for removing unwanted files. If you type **rm myfile** ↵ you will delete the file named myfile from your directory.

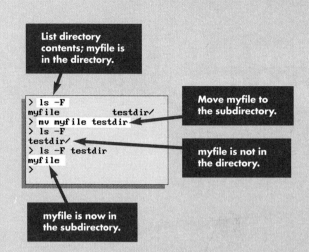

Subdirectory is empty (ls command just returns you to prompt).

```
> ls -F
myfile          myfile.backup    testdir/
> ls -F testdir
> cp myfile testdir
> ls -F testdir
myfile
>
```

Copy file to subdirectory.

Subdirectory contains a copy of myfile.

List directory contents; myfile is in the directory.

```
> ls -F
myfile          testdir/
> mv myfile testdir
> ls -F
testdir/
> ls -F testdir
myfile
>
```

Move myfile to the subdirectory.

myfile is not in the directory.

myfile is now in the subdirectory.

2 You can also copy a file into another directory. Type **cp myfile testdir** ↵ to place a copy of the file named myfile in your testdir subdirectory. If you don't have a directory named testdir, please create one first by following the instructions in the section "How to Create and Navigate a Directory Structure."

3 Sometimes you just want to move a file from one location to another without making an additional copy. UNIX provides the mv (move) command for this purpose. If you have created a subdirectory called testdir and you type **mv myfile testdir** ↵, you are telling UNIX to move the file myfile into the subdirectory testdir.

```
> ls -F
myfile          testdir/
> mv myfile myfile.backup
> ls -F
myfile.backup    testdir/
>
```

Rename the file.

File has been renamed.

4 If you don't specify a directory, UNIX assumes you want to leave the file in the current working directory but give it a new name. Thus **mv myfile myfile.backup** ↵ asks the computer to rename the file myfile as myfile.backup and leave it in the current working directory.

How to Get Help with UNIX

One of the great things about UNIX is that an electronic version of the manual is available on the computer. This means you always have access to some kind of help. Unfortunately, the *manual pages*—that is, all the text devoted to a particular topic—are not always easy to understand, so a really good book devoted to UNIX can be helpful (see the Appendix for a few suggestions). Nevertheless, the on-line help system is a good place to start if you need advice or emergency assistance.

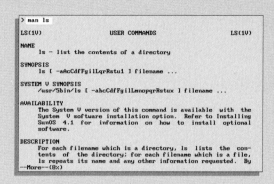

1 The UNIX command for opening manual pages is man. If you know the name of the command you need help with, type **man** followed by that command name. For example, typing **man ls** ↵ will display the manual page for the directory listing command. This help command will work in any directory.

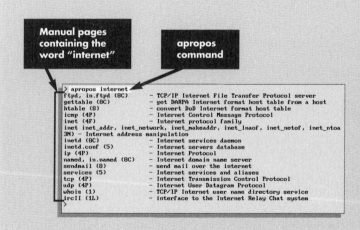

4 The man command works very well, provided you know the name of the command you want help with. But often you won't. If you type **apropos** and one or more words that describe the command you are looking for, UNIX will list the commands whose manual pages contain those words. Scan this list and type **man** followed by the name of the most promising command.

TIP SHEET

▶ When using apropos, try to provide a word that does not occur frequently. Typing apropos file **will result in a very lengthy (and not very useful) list because the word "file" probably appears in a large percentage of the manual pages.**

▶ **Your Internet host also provides manual pages for some of the programs you'll use to access the Internet later in this book, including Gopher and Archie.**

```
DESCRIPTION
     For each filename which is a directory, ls lists the con-
     tents of the directory; for each filename which is a file,
     ls repeats its name and any other information requested. By
--More--(8%)
```

You've seen one screen, which in this case is 8 percent of the total manual page. Press spacebar to see the next screenful of information.

2 Since manual pages are usually long, you will be able to view a screenful of text at a time. Generally, you will need to press the spacebar to move to the next screen. On some machines, you'll be able to move forward and backward through the manual pages. Check with your system administrators or support people to find out the capabilities of your host computer.

UNIX MANUAL

3 Manual pages have a specific format that is generally used throughout UNIX systems. At the top is the name of the command, followed by a synopsis and a description. The synopsis shows you the flags and other information you can use with the command. The description explains what a command does and how each flag modifies its output. Sometimes a manual page gives examples of how a command should be used, and sometimes it ends with a "See Also" section that lists other manual pages with pertinent information.

```
> man cd
CD(1)                      USER COMMANDS                      CD(1)

NAME
     cd - change working directory

SYNOPSIS
     cd [ directory ]

DESCRIPTION
     directory becomes the new working directory. The process
     must have execute (search) permission in directory. If cd
     is used without arguments, it returns you to your login
     directory.  In csh(1) you may specify a list of directories
     in which directory is to be sought as a subdirectory if it
     is not a subdirectory of the current directory; see the
     description of the cdpath variable in csh(1).

SEE ALSO
     csh(1), pwd(1), sh(1)

Sun Release 4.1   Last change: 9 September 1987            1
--More--(99%)
```

CHAPTER 5

Viewing and Altering Files in Your UNIX Account

 With the new Internet software tools described in Chapters 15–21, viewing and using Internet files require few UNIX skills. However, Internet archives contain many text files and you communicate with people on the Internet by sending and receiving text. Although much of this can be accomplished with your own word processor, conversion of these files for different systems can require a working knowledge of UNIX text procedures.

There are many different ways of working with text on the Internet. UNIX provides commands for displaying the contents of a text file and for searching through multiple files for a particular group of characters. Your Internet host also provides word processing programs, usually called *text editors*, that let you both view and edit text files. This chapter introduces you to the most basic UNIX commands for viewing text files, and to a text editor called "vi."

Text editors on computers controlled by UNIX are fairly old and not as convenient as the word processing programs you may be used to, especially if you work in Windows or on the Macintosh. Using these editors means having to memorize a certain number of commands. This chapter will help you get started. At some point, however, you may want to buy a reference book for a text editor like vi so you can learn some of its advanced capabilities. You can also use your knowledge of the Internet to hunt for tutorials and information about UNIX-based text editors.

How to View the Contents of a Text File

UNIX provides you with two ways of reading a text file. You can also view the contents of a text file by using a text editor. Here is a quick introduction to all three of these approaches.

▶ **1** If you don't have a text file to view, you can create one by saving a piece of e-mail in a text file. The section "How to Manage Your Mailbox" in Chapter 3 explains how to do this.

4 Your third option for viewing a text file is the text editor vi, short for visual editor. Type **vi** followed by the name of the file you want to view to see the designated file one screenful at a time. The vi text editor also lets you move backward and forward through a text file. Be cautious with vi: Since it's an editor, it lets you both display and *modify* the contents of a file. To quit vi without modifying the file, type **:q!** ↵. Make sure the q is lowercase; uppercase does not work. You'll learn about editing text with vi later in this chapter, under "How to Edit a Letter with vi."

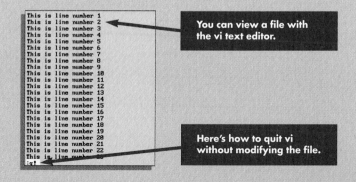

```
This is line number 1
This is line number 2
This is line number 3
This is line number 4
This is line number 5
This is line number 6
This is line number 7
This is line number 8
This is line number 9
This is line number 10
This is line number 11
This is line number 12
This is line number 13
This is line number 14
This is line number 15
This is line number 16
This is line number 17
This is line number 18
This is line number 19
This is line number 20
This is line number 21
This is line number 22
This is line number 23
:q
```

You can view a file with the vi text editor.

Here's how to quit vi without modifying the file.

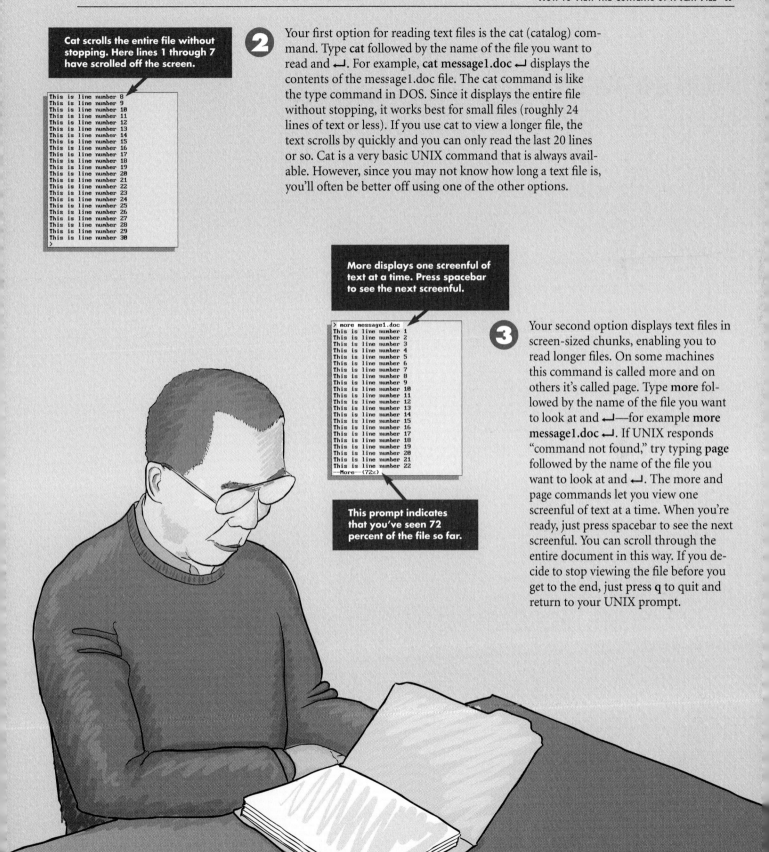

2 Your first option for reading text files is the cat (catalog) command. Type **cat** followed by the name of the file you want to read and ↵. For example, **cat message1.doc** ↵ displays the contents of the message1.doc file. The cat command is like the type command in DOS. Since it displays the entire file without stopping, it works best for small files (roughly 24 lines of text or less). If you use cat to view a longer file, the text scrolls by quickly and you can only read the last 20 lines or so. Cat is a very basic UNIX command that is always available. However, since you may not know how long a text file is, you'll often be better off using one of the other options.

Cat scrolls the entire file without stopping. Here lines 1 through 7 have scrolled off the screen.

```
This is line number 8
This is line number 9
This is line number 10
This is line number 11
This is line number 12
This is line number 13
This is line number 14
This is line number 15
This is line number 16
This is line number 17
This is line number 18
This is line number 19
This is line number 20
This is line number 21
This is line number 22
This is line number 23
This is line number 24
This is line number 25
This is line number 26
This is line number 27
This is line number 28
This is line number 29
This is line number 30
>
```

More displays one screenful of text at a time. Press spacebar to see the next screenful.

```
> more message1.doc
This is line number 1
This is line number 2
This is line number 3
This is line number 4
This is line number 5
This is line number 6
This is line number 7
This is line number 8
This is line number 9
This is line number 10
This is line number 11
This is line number 12
This is line number 13
This is line number 14
This is line number 15
This is line number 16
This is line number 17
This is line number 18
This is line number 19
This is line number 20
This is line number 21
This is line number 22
--More--(72%)
```

This prompt indicates that you've seen 72 percent of the file so far.

3 Your second option displays text files in screen-sized chunks, enabling you to read longer files. On some machines this command is called more and on others it's called page. Type **more** followed by the name of the file you want to look at and ↵—for example **more message1.doc** ↵. If UNIX responds "command not found," try typing **page** followed by the name of the file you want to look at and ↵. The more and page commands let you view one screenful of text at a time. When you're ready, just press spacebar to see the next screenful. You can scroll through the entire document in this way. If you decide to stop viewing the file before you get to the end, just press **q** to quit and return to your UNIX prompt.

How to Write a Letter with vi

One of the earliest text editors, vi was created before people gave a lot of thought to making programs easy to use. Although there are other UNIX-based text editors, vi was the standard editor and is still most likely to be the editor on your Internet host. Unlike today's word processors—which include menus, buttons, and mice—vi only lets you use commands and the keyboard. Although vi may seem foreign at first, it won't take long for you to get used to it. This and the next section provide the information you need to get started. The best way to become proficient is to practice and play. Try typing several letters to yourself using the instructions that follow. Once you are done you will feel more comfortable using vi.

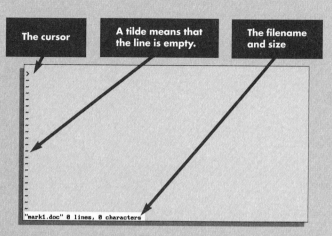

The cursor | A tilde means that the line is empty. | The filename and size

"mark1.doc" 0 lines, 0 characters

1 Type **vi** followed by a filename and ↵ to get the program started. If the file you've named already exists, vi will display its contents; if it doesn't exist, vi will create a new file with that name. In vi, empty lines have a tilde (~) at the beginning. When you open a new file, every line on your screen except the first will begin with a tilde. In the top line you'll see a little flashing dash called the *cursor*, which indicates where the next character you type will appear.

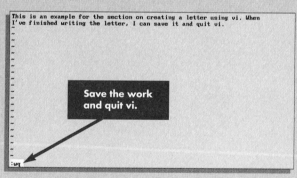

This is an example for the section on creating a letter using vi. When I've finished writing the letter, I can save it and quit vi.

Save the work and quit vi.

:wq

6 When you are ready to quit vi and want to save your file, return to Command mode by pressing Esc. Then type **:wq** ↵. This tells vi to first save the file to your current working directory and then quit the program. (Remember, you named the file when you opened it.) Don't forget that you can force vi to quit without saving changes by typing **:q!** ↵ while in Command mode.

2 The tricky thing about using vi is that it operates in two modes, Insert mode and Command mode. *Insert mode* allows you to type new text; *Command mode* lets you change existing text. Keys on the keyboard have different meanings depending on the mode you are in. If you type **x** in Insert mode, an *x* will appear on your screen. In Command mode typing **x** deletes the character the cursor is currently on. In other words, you need to remember which mode you're in and how to get from one mode to another. Unfortunately, there is no indication on the screen of your current mode.

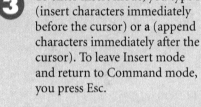

3 To enter Insert mode, you type **i** (insert characters immediately before the cursor) or **a** (append characters immediately after the cursor). To leave Insert mode and return to Command mode, you press Esc.

4 In some ways using vi is like using a typewriter. When entering text you must press ↵ at the end of each line because vi does not automatically move the cursor to the next line the way advanced word processors do.

5 To save your work without exiting vi, return to Command mode by pressing Esc and then type **:w** ↵. This saves the file in your current working directory. Note that when you type a vi command that begins with a colon (:), the entire command appears at the bottom of your screen.

How to Edit a Letter with vi

When you are working on a first draft of a document, you can just type away steadily, left to right, line after line. When editing and correcting that document, however, you need to be able to move anywhere in the document, deleting and inserting text as the need arises.

▶ **1** To edit a text file, first open it by typing **vi** and the file's name—for example, **vi my-draft.doc ↵**.

7 To paste lines in your document, you must first cut or copy them. Then move the cursor to where you want to insert that text, make sure you're in Command mode and type **p**.

6 You can cut, copy, and paste in vi. To cut (delete) a line of text, use the dd command mentioned earlier. To copy a line, move the cursor to that line and, while in Command mode, type **yy**. As with the dd command, you can specify how many lines to copy by typing the number of lines and then typing **yy**.

TIP SHEET

▶ **Initially, you may make mistakes because you think you are in Command mode when you're really in Insert mode, or vice versa. When first learning to use vi you will need to pay close attention to your current mode. Unfortunately, vi provides no on-screen indication of mode. Remember, however, if you press Esc while in Command mode, your computer will beep.**

▶ **You can delete a single word by moving the cursor to the word's first letter and typing** dw **while in Command mode.**

▶ **When you delete text, vi will not fill in the blank areas with words from another line.**

3 If your arrow keys aren't moving the cursor properly in Command mode, press **j** to move the cursor down one line and **k** to move it up one line. Press the spacebar (or **l**) to move to the right one character at a time; press backspace (or **h**) to move to the left one character at a time.

2 Remember, you must be in Command mode to delete text and in Insert mode to add text.

We live in an age of constant change. Ten ~~y~~ ago, the idea that you could own a pers~~~~ computer was just beginning to take ~~h~~ Today, personal computers are so comm~~~~ at many young people will learn how to ~~~~em while still in elementary school. Today's world is also ~~~~ing more and more ~~~~ that we can use a car phone to dial up friends halfway around the globe. We can watch live television coverage of athletes

Nine lines deleted

```
This is line number 1
This is line number 2
This is line number 12
This is line number 13
This is line number 14
This is line number 15
This is line number 16
This is line number 17
This is line number 18
This is line number 19
This is line number 20
This is line number 21
This is line number 22
This is line number 23
This is line number 24
This is line number 25
This is line number 26
This is line number 27
This is line number 28
This is line number 29
This is line number 30
~
~
9 lines deleted
```

Here vi tells you that 9 lines have been deleted.

4 While in Command mode, type **dd** to delete the entire line containing the cursor. If you want to delete more than one line, enter the number of lines to be deleted followed by **dd**. For example, typing **9dd** will delete nine consecutive lines beginning with the line containing the cursor.

Press Ctrl **and** g **to see what line the cursor is on.**

```
This is line number 1
This is line number 2
This is line number 3
This is line number 4
This is line number 5
This is line number 6
This is line number 7
This is line number 8
This is line number 9
This is line number 10
This is line number 11
This is line number 12
This is line number 13
This is line number 14
This is line number 15
This is line number 16
This is line number 17
This is line number 18
This is line number 19
This is line number 20
This is line number 21
This is line number 22
This is line number 23
"message1.doc" line 9 of 30 --30%--
```

5 If you want to move a long distance, the arrow keys are not very efficient. Fortunately, there's an easy way to move to a specific line. If you want to go directly to, say, the 100th line of a file, type **:100** ⏎ while in Command mode. Line numbers are not displayed on the screen, but if you hold down the Ctrl key and press **g** the line number the cursor is on shows up at the bottom of the screen. You can type **G** to go directly to the bottom line in your document and **:1** ⏎ to go to the top.

How to Search for Text

A s the number of text files you have in your home directory or a subdirectory increases, you will eventually want to find some text contained within a file without reading the entire file. You may forget a file's name, for example, but remember that it contains the name of your 3rd grade teacher, Mrs. Rumplemeyer. The text you are searching for is called a *character string*, or *string* for short. UNIX provides many ways of searching for strings.

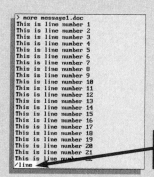

You can search for text in vi.

1 If you are already viewing a file using the more or page command, type a / followed by the string you are looking for in that document and press ↵. The cursor will move to the next occurrence of those characters in the file. As an example, typing /**line** ↵ will move the cursor to the next occurrence of the string "line." Note that if the cursor is already past the last occurrence of the designated characters, nothing will be found.

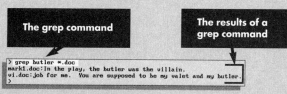

The grep command

The results of a grep command

4 If you forgot the name of a file but know it contains the string "eunuchs," you don't need to open each file and read it; instead you can use the grep command. Type **grep** followed by the string you want to search for, the files to search in, and ↵. This is a great opportunity to take advantage of wildcards, which were discussed in Chapter 4. For instance, the command **grep butler *.doc** ↵ will list each file in which the string was found and the line of text on which it occurred.

```
This is line number 1
This is line number 2
This is line number 3
This is line number 4
This is line number 5
This is line number 6
This is line number 7
This is line number 8
This is line number 9
This is line number 10
This is line number 11
This is line number 12
This is line number 13
This is line number 14
This is line number 15
This is line number 16
This is line number 17
This is line number 18
This is line number 19
This is line number 20
This is line number 21
This is line number 22
This is line number 23
/26
```

You can search for text in more.

2 While in Command mode in vi, you can also type a / followed by the search string and ↵ to move the cursor to the designated string. Typing **n** will move the cursor to the next occurrence of the string.

3 Vi and certain UNIX commands can carry out sophisticated string searches. Say you are looking for the one numbered list in a 100-page report. Suppose also that you know that each line in this list includes two tabs, a number, a period, and a space. To find the list, you can search for any line beginning with two tab characters, followed by a numeral, a period, a blank space, and some unspecified text. Again, a vi reference book can teach you the advanced aspects of vi.

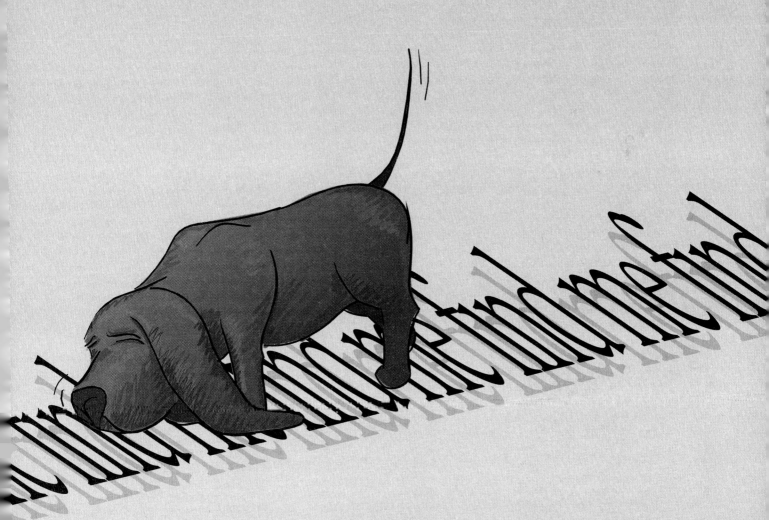

CHAPTER 6

Simplifying Mail

 Chapter 3 introduced the UCB Mail program; this chapter describes some ways of making mail easier to use. Since electronic mail is one of the most widely used services on the Internet, a lot of work has gone into making it user-friendly. For instance, you can create aliases—that is, nicknames for frequently used addresses. Rather than having to remember your friends' e-mail addresses, you can use their first names as aliases. Aliases are both easier to remember and quicker to type

Several computer programs also make mail easier by taking advantage of the screen-oriented terminal capabilities discussed in Chapter 2. These programs present mail in a more visually pleasant and manageable fashion. They provide a text editor, such as vi, for writing and editing your mail. They assist you in maintaining archives of mail you have sent out and mail you have received. Finally, they provide menus and prompts so that you don't have to memorize another batch of commands.

This chapter presents two of the alternative mail programs: Pine and Elm. Unfortunately, these programs are not on every host on the Internet. If they are accessible to your Internet account, you are encouraged to try them and use whichever one you like best. If they are not available on your machine, talk to your system administrator or support personnel about having them installed. Both are available for free over the Internet.

In Chapter 16 you will learn how to use the Windows Eudora Mail software, which is very user friendly.

How to Make Addresses Easier to Work With

Your home directory may contain a file called .mailrc. Since this file's name begins with a period, you don't usually see it in your list of files. (See Chapter 4, "How to List the Contents of a UNIX Directory," for details.) The .mailrc file lets you make mail easier to use by assigning aliases to addresses that you use frequently. (Don't worry if you don't already have a .mailrc file; you can create one easily.)

My .mailrc file before I add any aliases. Yours may look different.

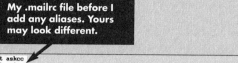

```
set askcc
set crt
~
~
~
```

▶ **1** You can change the way the Mail program works by adding certain lines of text to your .mailrc file. And since the .mailrc file is a text file, you can edit it with vi, as described in Chapter 5. Before altering any file like this you should always make a copy of the original in case something goes wrong. (Chapter 4 explains how to copy files.) So, copy the file by typing **cp .mailrc .mailrc.orig** ↵. Now, open the original .mailrc file with vi by typing **vi .mailrc** ↵. If you do not already have a .mailrc file, vi will now create one for you.

5 When you're done adding aliases to the .mailrc file, you should save the file and leave vi by getting into Command mode (press Esc) and typing **:wq** ↵. (Refer back to Chapter 5 if you want to refresh your memory on creating, editing, and saving files in vi.)

You can add group aliases.

```
set askcc
set crt
alias mary mazybri@594unix.gcb.xyz.edu
alias mark markhb@shell.portal.com
alias eleanor elvis@mall.michigan.edu
alias pals bob@lilac.xyz.edu jerry@zippy.xyz.edu elvis@mall.michigan.edu
```

4 You can also use an alias as a nickname for a group of addresses. If you enter a line like

```
alias pals bob@lilac.xyz.edu jerry@zippy.xyz.edu
   elvis@mall.michigan.edu
```

in your .mailrc file, and you send mail to pals (by typing **mail pals** ↵), your message will automatically be sent to Bob, Jerry, and Elvis.

TIP SHEET

▶ If you make a mistake in your .mailrc file and you made a backup copy following the instructions in step 1, you can restore the original (and get rid of your mistake) by typing cp .mailrc.orig .mailrc ↵.

▶ When entering an alias for a group of addresses, do *not* press ↵ at the end of each line. Just keep typing until you get to the last address. The Mail program thinks all aliases end with ↵, and will get confused if it encounters this character in the middle of an alias.

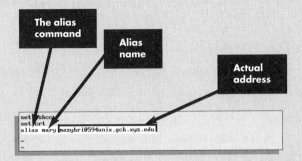

The alias command

Alias name

Actual address

```
set askcc
set crt
alias mary mazybri@594unix.gcb.xyz.edu
~
~
```

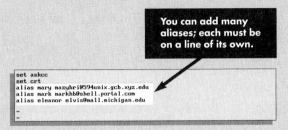

You can add many aliases; each must be on a line of its own.

```
set askcc
set crt
alias mary mazybri@594unix.gcb.xyz.edu
alias mark markhb@shell.portal.com
alias eleanor elvis@mall.michigan.edu
~
~
```

2 One of the best things about the .mailrc file is that you can use it to assign aliases to addresses. Say your friend Mary's address is mazybri@594unix.gcb.xyz.edu. Rather than having to type those 27 characters each time you send her a message, you can give the address an alias of Mary. Now when you send her mail you simply type **mail mary** ↵ and the mail is automatically sent to mazybri@594unix.gcb.xyz.edu.

3 To add an alias to your .mailrc file, go to the bottom line of the file (right after the last line of text) and type, on its own line, **alias**, the name of the alias, and then the real address. Be sure to leave one blank space between each part of the command. You can add as many of these aliases as you like, as long as you type each one on its own line and follow it with a ↵. It's that easy. Using aliases will make your mailing life a lot happier.

How to Use the Pine Mail Program

Pine is a program designed to simplify your interaction with electronic mail on the Internet. It provides the same functions as the Mail program discussed in Chapter 3, but makes life easier by always displaying your command options at the bottom of the screen and by providing *word wrap*, so you don't have to press ↵ at the end of every line. Pine requires screen-oriented terminal emulation in your telecommunications software as described in Chapter 2. Here is a brief introduction to Pine. If you like what you see, you are encouraged to try it.

TIP SHEET

▸ While looking at your mail index, you can tell Pine to delete a message by highlighting it and typing d. Pine will delete all marked messages when you quit.

▸ Pine will maintain an address book that includes the aliases you assign to addresses. For the details, you should consult your documentation.

▸ When using the Composer to create or reply to a message, hold down the Ctrl key and type g to see a document about using the Composer.

▶ **1** To start Pine, type **pine** ↵. The very first time you use Pine, it will create a directory called mail in your home directory. If UNIX tells you "Pine: Command not found," the program is not available on your Internet host.

7 To quit Pine, just type **q** while you are at the main menu or looking over the list of messages in your mailbox. Pine will ask if you really want to quit the program. Type **y** for yes.

Enter your new message text here.

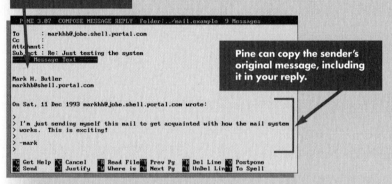

Pine can copy the sender's original message, including it in your reply.

6 Besides sending new messages, you can reply to mail you've received. This saves you from having to type in addresses. From within your list of messages, use the arrow keys to highlight the message you sent to yourself in Chapter 3 and type **r** (for reply). Pine asks if you would like to include the original message in your reply. Type **y** (for yes). This is a good way of reminding the sender what he or she said originally. Pine creates an electronic form with addressing information at the top, a message area in the middle, and the sender's original message at the bottom. You can now type your reply. When you're done, hold down the Ctrl key and type **x** to send your message. When Pine asks if you want to send the message, type **y** (for yes).

The menu for Pine's text editor, Composer

5 To send a new message in Pine, first type **c** (for compose) at Pine's main menu. Enter an address at the *To:* prompt and a subject at the *Subject:* prompt. Then type your message. You're in Pine's text editor, the Composer, which is pretty easy to use. It has word wrap, so you don't have to press ↵ at the end of each line. In addition, it doesn't have separate Command and Insert modes like vi, and all your commands are listed at the bottom of the screen. In this context, a caret (^) stands for the Ctrl key. That is, you can hold down Ctrl and press **x** to send a message, and you can hold down Ctrl and press **c** if you decide *not* to send a message.

② Pine begins by displaying its *main menu*, a list of the options from which you can choose. Among other things, you can type **?** to see the help file, **c** to create and mail a message, or **i** to see a list of the mail in your mailbox. (If your version of Pine is different, your main menu may not look exactly like this.)

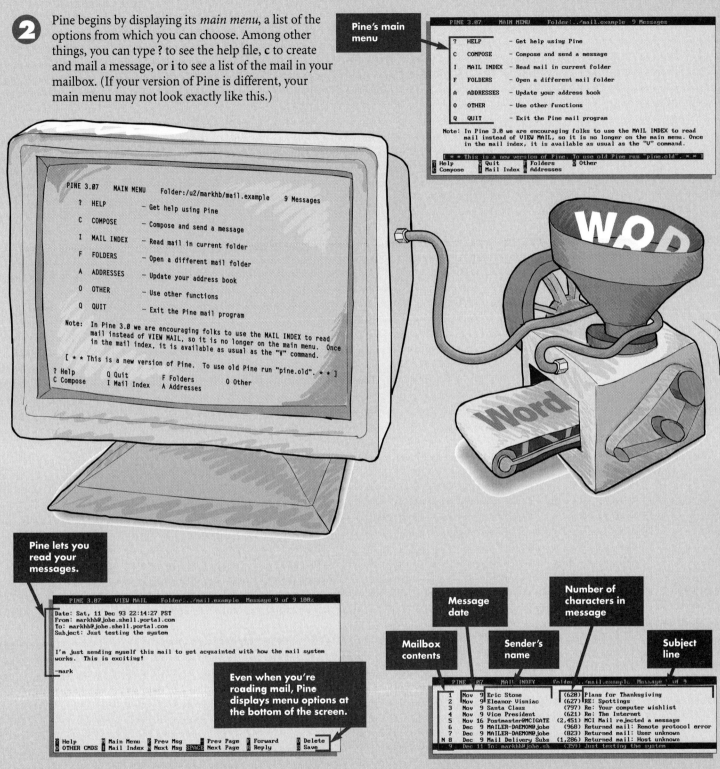

Pine's main menu

```
PINE 3.07    MAIN MENU    Folder:../mail.example  9 Messages

    ?   HELP         - Get help using Pine
    C   COMPOSE      - Compose and send a message
    I   MAIL INDEX   - Read mail in current folder
    F   FOLDERS      - Open a different mail folder
    A   ADDRESSES    - Update your address book
    O   OTHER        - Use other functions
    Q   QUIT         - Exit the Pine mail program

Note: In Pine 3.0 we are encouraging folks to use the MAIL INDEX to read
      mail instead of VIEW MAIL, so it is no longer on the main menu. Once
      in the mail index, it is available as usual as the "V" command.

[ * * This is a new version of Pine. To use old Pine run 'pine.old'. * * ]
? Help        Q Quit          F Folders      O Other
C Compose     I Mail Index    A Addresses
```

```
PINE 3.07    MAIN MENU    Folder:/u2/markhb/mail.example    9 Messages

    ?   HELP         - Get help using Pine
    C   COMPOSE      - Compose and send a message
    I   MAIL INDEX   - Read mail in current folder
    F   FOLDERS      - Open a different mail folder
    A   ADDRESSES    - Update your address book
    O   OTHER        - Use other functions
    Q   QUIT         - Exit the Pine mail program

Note: In Pine 3.0 we are encouraging folks to use the MAIL INDEX to read
      mail instead of VIEW MAIL, so it is no longer on the main menu.  Once
      in the mail index, it is available as usual as the "V" command.

[ * * This is a new version of Pine.  To use old Pine run "pine.old". * * ]
? Help        Q Quit          F Folders      O Other
C Compose     I Mail Index    A Addresses
```

Pine lets you read your messages.

```
PINE 3.07    VIEW MAIL    Folder:../mail.example  Message 9 of 9 100%

Date: Sat, 11 Dec 93 22:14:27 PST
From: markhb@jobe.shell.portal.com
To: markhb@jobe.shell.portal.com
Subject: Just testing the system

I'm just sending myself this mail to get acquainted with how the mail system
works.  This is exciting!

-mark

? Help       M Main Menu    P Prev Msg    - Prev Page    F Forward    D Delete
O OTHER CMDS I Mail Index   N Next Msg    SPACE Next Page R Reply     S Save
```

Even when you're reading mail, Pine displays menu options at the bottom of the screen.

Message date

Number of characters in message

Mailbox contents

Sender's name

Subject line

```
PINE 3.07    MAIL INDEX    Folder:../mail.example  Message 1 of 9

    1   Nov  9  Eric Stone          (620)  Plans for Thanksgiving
    2   Nov  9  Eleanor Visniac     (627)  RE: Spottings
    3   Nov  9  Santa Claus         (797)  Re: Your computer wishlist
    4   Nov  9  Vice President      (621)  Re: The Internet
    5   Nov 16  Postmaster@MCIGATE  (2,451) MCI Mail rejected a message
    6   Dec  9  MAILER-DAEMON@jobe  (960)  Returned mail: Remote protocol error
    7   Dec  9  MAILER-DAEMON@jobe  (823)  Returned mail: User unknown
  N 8   Dec  9  Mail Delivery Subs  (1,286) Returned mail: Host unknown
    9   Dec 11  To: markhb@jobe.sh  (359)  Just testing the system
```

④ Pine displays one screenful of text at a time. Press the spacebar to move to the next page or type – (the minus sign) to move to a previous page. Most importantly, notice the menu of options at the bottom of the screen. This list saves you from having to memorize commands. Type **i** to return to your list of messages.

③ If you type **i**, Pine lists the mail in your mailbox in nicely aligned columns, indicating the date of the message, the name of the sender, the number of characters in the message, and the subject line. Pine highlights the most recent message. Press ↵ to view that message, or use the arrow keys to move the highlighting to another message you want to read and then press ↵.

How to Use the Elm Mail Program

Elm is another program designed to simplify your interaction with electronic mail on the Internet. Like Pine, Elm makes e-mail easier to use by always displaying your command options at the bottom of the screen. Elm requires screen-oriented terminal emulation in your telecommunications software (see Chapter 2). Here is a quick introduction to Elm. If your system provides both Pine and Elm, you should experiment with both of them to find out which you prefer.

▶ While looking at the list of messages in your mailbox, you can highlight a message and type d to mark it for deletion. When you quit Elm, all such messages will be deleted. If you mark a message for deletion and then change your mind before quitting, you can "undelete" the message by highlighting it and typing u.

▶ Elm allows you to maintain a list of aliases. At the list of messages in your mailbox, type a to access Elm's aliasing capabilities. For the details on this convenient feature, consult your documentation.

```
> elm

Notice:
This version of ELM requires the use of a .elm directory in your home
directory to store your elmrc and alias files. Shall I create the
directory .elm for you and set it up (y/n/q)? y
```

1 To start Elm, type **elm** ↵. The very first time you use Elm, it will ask you if it can create two directories in your home directory. Type y to answer yes. If UNIX tells you "elm: Command not found", the program is not available on your Internet host.

7 To quit Elm, type **q** while looking over the list of messages in your mailbox. Elm may ask if you want to move your read messages to a folder named "received"—Elm's equivalent of the mbox file. I personally prefer not using the received folder, and therefore answer **n**. See "How to Manage Your Mailbox" in Chapter 3 for a discussion of the merits of using the mbox file.

Elm may use vi as a text editor. Notice the tildes.

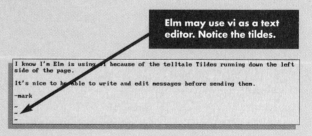

```
I know I'm Elm is using vi because of the telltale Tildes running down the left
side of the page.

It's nice to be able to write and edit messages before sending them.

-mark
~
~
~
```

6 Elm also lets you reply to messages; again this saves you the trouble of typing in addresses. Use the cursor keys to move the highlight or arrow to the message you sent to yourself in Chapter 3 and type **r** (for reply). You may be asked whether you want to include the original message in the reply. Elm displays the subject line, which you can change if you like. Type ↵ to accept it. Elm asks if you wish to send copies to anyone. Type ↵ unless you wish to send copies to someone. Elm now allows you to type in your reply. When you are done creating your reply, quit the text editor and, when prompted, either type **s** to send the message or **f** to abandon it.

Mailbox contents

Message date

Sender's name

Number of Lines in message

Subject line

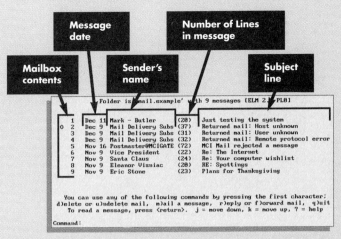

The arrow points to the current message.

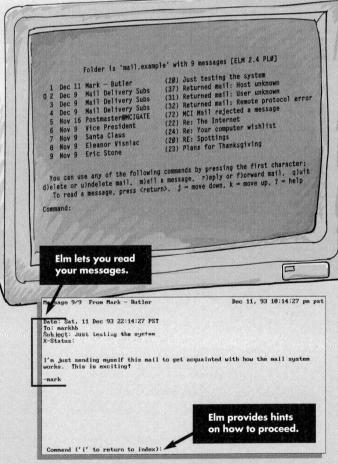

3 Depending on how your system administrator has set up Elm, it either highlights the most recent message or points to it with a little arrow on the left of the screen. Press ↵ to view that message, or use the arrow keys to move the highlight or arrow to another message you want to read and then press ↵.

2 When Elm begins, it displays a list of the messages in your mailbox, including the date of the message, the name of the sender, the number of lines in the message, and the subject line. (As with Pine, if your screen looks a little different from the ones shown here, you probably just have a slightly different version of the program.) At the bottom of the screen, Elm shows you which commands are available and which key to press to invoke a particular function.

Elm lets you read your messages.

When you quit, Elm prompts you for the next command.

```
Please choose one of the following options by parenthesized letter: s
      e)dit message, edit h)eaders, s)end it, or f)orget it.
```

5 To send a message, press **m** and, when prompted, supply an address and a subject. Then indicate whether you want to send copies to anyone. At this point you can type your message. In most cases, Elm supplies the vi editor but sometimes your system administrator will provide a different editor. You'll know Elm is using vi if you see the tilde (~) character at the beginning of each empty line. When you're done with your message, quit the text editor. Now Elm asks what you wish to do with this message. Type **s** to send it or **f** (forget it) if you decide not to send it.

Elm provides hints on how to proceed.

4 Elm displays messages one screenful at a time. Press the spacebar to move to the next page. Type **i** to return to your list of messages, **n** to view the next message, or **k** to view the previous message.

CHAPTER 7

Taking Advantage of Electronic Mailing Lists

One of the most exciting aspects of the Internet is that you can find groups of people who share your interests—whether you're inclined toward cooking, woodworking, or astronomy. Electronic mail provides a mechanism for groups of people with shared interests to establish and maintain contact. These interest groups are referred to as *mailing lists* (*lists* for short) because they are literally mailing lists of the members' e-mail addresses. Once you have subscribed to or been added to one of these lists, you receive copies of all the mail sent to the list, and you can send mail to all the subscribers.

To become a subscriber, you must contact the list's administrator and ask to be added to the list. There are two types of administrators: humans and computer programs called listservs. You can communicate with human administrators in plain English, but must speak to listservs in commands. In certain cases your request to subscribe may be refused. For example, a list for college administrators only allows administrators to join.

If you join many lists you may wind up with lots of e-mail in your mailbox. If you subscribe to several very active lists, for instance, you could receive over 100 pieces of mail every day. The amount of mail sent out depends on whether the list is moderated or unmoderated. *Moderated lists* have one or more human moderators who screen all incoming mail and only redistribute a selected portion to the list. *Unmoderated lists* just pass along all the mail.

If you're getting too much mail or just don't like a particular list, you can unsubscribe just as easily as you subscribed, by sending a request to the administrator.

Eight Cool Mailing Lists

L ists on the Internet cover a broad range of interests. Here are eight of the many possibilities. In the next section, you'll send e-mail to request a large listing of publicly accessible mailing lists on the Internet. This is an excellent way to find out what is going on in the world of electronic mailing lists.

▶ **1** If you like bagpipes, there's a mailing list for you.

8 There's even a mailing list that does nothing but notify its subscribers of new lists forming on the Internet.

7 The fitness list is for people who are interested in all kinds of physical fitness activities.

6 Catholics have a list of their own, as do many other religious groups.

TIP SHEET

▶ **The mail you receive from lists looks just like all the other mail in your mailbox, except it comes from a sender you don't recognize. The contents of the subject line often provide a good clue about which list the mail pertains to. After you've been on a list for a while you will begin to recognize the names of some of the list's regular contributors.**

▶ **Subscribe slowly to mailing lists—one or two at a time. If you subscribe to several active lists, your electronic mailbox will be inundated with messages that you may not have the time to read.**

2 The Internet also has a mailing list for people interested in woodworking.

3 Do you enjoy movies? If so, you'll want to subscribe to the cinema list.

5 There's also a list that college students can use to discuss student activism.

4 Do you have kids or are you interested in children's literature? There's a list for you too.

How to Join a Mailing List

Joining a mailing list is a simple process. You send e-mail to the list's administrator, asking to subscribe to the list. The administrator replies, and if you are accepted, gives you the address of the mailing list (which is usually different from the administrator's address). Depending on how active the members of the list are, you might receive mail immediately, or you may get nothing for several days.

Send this request for the catalog of lists to MIT.

```
> Mail mail-server@rtfm.mit.edu
Subject:

send usenet/news.answers/mail/mailing-lists/part1
```

1 You've seen eight of the possible lists you can join. Nobody has a complete catalog of all the lists on the Internet, but there is a partial one. You can ask a computer at MIT to e-mail you the first part of it. Send e-mail (see Chapter 3 for details) to mail-server@rtfm.mit.edu. Leave the subject line of the message blank. The message should say

```
send usenet/news.answers/mail/mailing-lists/part1 ↵
```

Make sure to type this message exactly as shown here; you're actually transmitting a command rather than sending a message to a person.

My request to get off the list

6 To cancel your subscription to a list, send mail to the administrator—the contact address you used to subscribe—asking that your name be removed from the list. (Try to avoid sending this request to the entire list!)

5 It's proper list etiquette to send messages to an appropriate audience so you don't clog people's mailboxes with mail that isn't relevant to them. When you receive a message of interest, you need to decide whether to reply to the list as a whole or just to the person who sent the message. If you simply want to tell someone you agree with them, you can send mail to the individual. They generally provide their name and e-mail address at the bottom of the message. If you wish to present a different point of view or add information to a group discussion, send mail to the entire list, at the same address you got when you subscribed. Remember, Chapter 3 explains how to send mail messages.

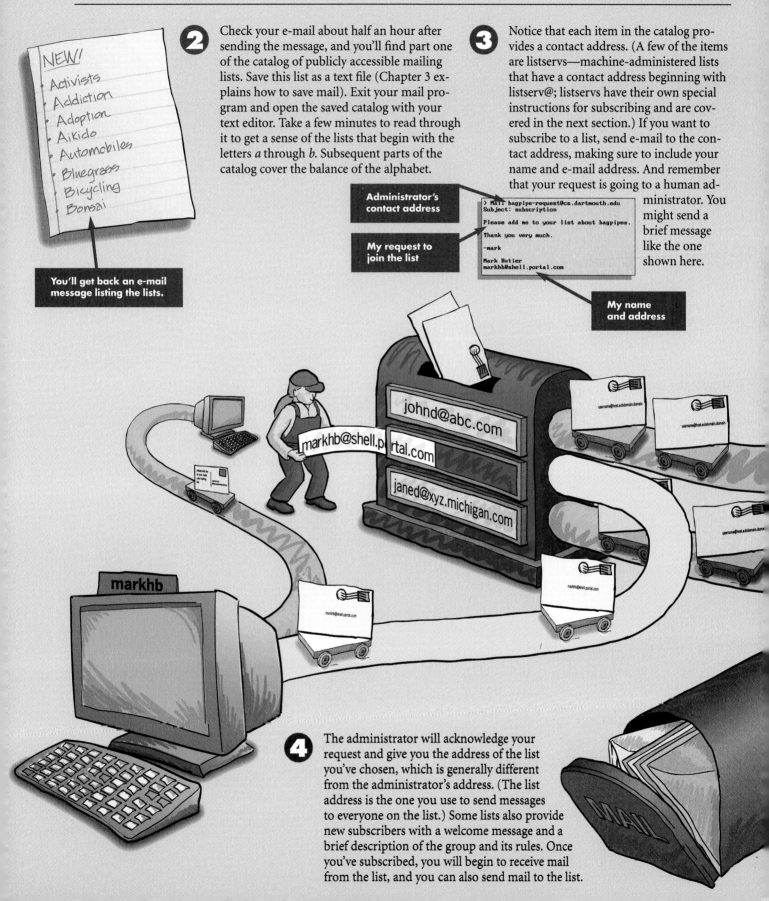

② Check your e-mail about half an hour after sending the message, and you'll find part one of the catalog of publicly accessible mailing lists. Save this list as a text file (Chapter 3 explains how to save mail). Exit your mail program and open the saved catalog with your text editor. Take a few minutes to read through it to get a sense of the lists that begin with the letters *a* through *b*. Subsequent parts of the catalog cover the balance of the alphabet.

NEW!
- Activists
- Addiction
- Adoption
- Aikido
- Automobiles
- Bluegrass
- Bicycling
- Bonsai

You'll get back an e-mail message listing the lists.

③ Notice that each item in the catalog provides a contact address. (A few of the items are listservs—machine-administered lists that have a contact address beginning with listserv@; listservs have their own special instructions for subscribing and are covered in the next section.) If you want to subscribe to a list, send e-mail to the contact address, making sure to include your name and e-mail address. And remember that your request is going to a human administrator. You might send a brief message like the one shown here.

Administrator's contact address

My request to join the list

My name and address

```
> Mail bagpipe-request@cs.dartmouth.edu
Subject: subscription

Please add me to your list about bagpipes.

Thank you very much.

-mark

Mark Butler
markhb@shell.portal.com
```

johnd@abc.com
markhb@shell.portal.com
janed@xyz.michigan.com
markhb

④ The administrator will acknowledge your request and give you the address of the list you've chosen, which is generally different from the administrator's address. (The list address is the one you use to send messages to everyone on the list.) Some lists also provide new subscribers with a welcome message and a brief description of the group and its rules. Once you've subscribed, you will begin to receive mail from the list, and you can also send mail to the list.

How to Join a Listserv Mailing List

*L*istservs are a kind of computer program that administers particular mailing lists. To subscribe to a listserv mailing list, you must contact this computerized administrator. Unlike a human, however, the listserv requires that your subscription request be in exactly the right format. The only difference between a listserv-administered list and a human-administered list is that with a listserv-administered list you must "speak" to the administrator by using precise commands. In both cases, the subscribers are people who share a common interest.

TIP SHEET

▶ **Messages to listservs should always have a blank subject line. Messages to the list itself (to all the subscribers) should always have a subject line.**

▶ **Although it is polite to say "please" and "thank you" to a human, do not include these words in the messages you send to a listserv. They may confuse the machine.**

▶ **To get help from the listserv program, send it a message that just says** help ↵**. It will reply with an abbreviated list of commands that it understands, complete with descriptions. If you send the message** info refcard ↵**, the listserv will send the complete list of commands it understands.**

1 You can recognize listservs in several ways. Many (but not all) listservs are part of the BITNET academic network, so their addresses end in .bitnet rather than .edu or .com. Often listserv lists will have names that end in -l, such as pacs-l or fit-l.

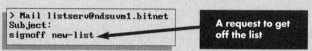

```
> Mail listserv@ndsuvm1.bitnet
Subject:
signoff new-list
```
A request to get off the list

5 To cancel your subscription to a list, send the listserv program (that is, the contact address) another mail message with no subject line and a message that reads **signoff** *listname* ↵. For example, to unsubscribe from the list of new lists, send e-mail to listserv@ndsuvm1.bitnet with a message that says **signoff new-list** ↵.

```
> Mail listserv@ndsuvm1.bitnet
Subject:
set new-list digest
```

6 Normally, each individual message for the list will be sent to your mailbox immediately. If you like, you can instead receive a *digest*—one large piece of mail incorporating all messages for the day. To do this, send e-mail to the listserv with a blank subject line and the message **set** *listname* **digest** ↵ where *listname* is the name of the list in question. If you want to receive a digest of the mail to new-list, use the message **set new-list digest** ↵.

```
> Mail listserv@ndsuvm1.bitnet
Subject:
set new-list nomail
```

7 When you leave on vacation, you should temporarily stop your mail. If you don't, your electronic mailbox in the shared mail area will overflow, leaving less space for other people's mail. To temporarily stop receiving mail from a list, send the listserv the message **set** *listname* **nomail** ↵, where *listname* is the name of the list you subscribe to. When you get back, you can begin receiving messages again by sending the message **set** *listname* **mail** ↵.

```
> Mail listserv@ndsuvm1.bitnet
Subject:
subscribe new-list Mark Butler
```

My subscription request for a listserv

The listserv's third reply

```
From: BITNET list server at NDSUVM1 (1.7f) <LISTSERV@VM1.NoDak.EDU>
Subject:    Output of your job "markhb"
To: Mark Butler <markhb@SHELL.PORTAL.COM>
Status: RO

> sub new-list Mark Butler
You have been added to list NEW-LIST.

Summary of resource utilization
_____

CPU time:        1.784 sec           Device I/O:    567
Overhead CPU:    0.178 sec           Paging I/O:      8
CPU model:       9121                DASD model:   3380
```

2 To subscribe to a listserv's list, you often have to use the same type of message. To see how it's done, let's subscribe to a listserv list that announces new mailing lists. Send an e-mail message to listserv@ndsuvm1.bitnet. Leave the subject line blank and enter the following message on one line:

subscribe new-list *YourFirstName LastName* ↵

Enter your first and last name where indicated. The name of the list you are subscribing to is new-list.

3 After 15 minutes or so you will receive three pieces of mail from the listserv program. One will confirm that your subscription to the list has been accepted (anyone can subscribe to this list). Another is a welcome, which includes a description of and rules for the new-list list. (Welcome messages generally include the list's address too.) A third piece of mail will tell you if the listserv understood your request and how much time the listserv program spent fulfilling this request. Any interaction you have with a listserv will produce at least one piece of mail that indicates how much of the computer's time you used. If the listserv doesn't understand your request, it will say so in this message.

4 After you have subscribed, you will begin to receive mail from the list. You can also begin sending messages to all the other subscribers on the list. Some lists, like new-list, are set up just for sending information to subscribers rather than fostering discussion between them. When you subscribe to a list, its welcome message will tell you whether it's for discussion or announcements. The new-list list is for announcements.

CHAPTER 8

Usenet and Newsgroups

 So far, you've learned how to communicate with others by sending electronic mail—either to individuals or to mailing lists—but there are other ways to meet people and share information on the Internet. One of the major ways is through Usenet *newsgroups*—special groups set up by people who share common interests ranging from Rush Limbaugh to Sri Lanka. There are currently thousands of Usenet newsgroups.

Usenet is another global network of computers and people that is intertwined with the Internet. Rather than operating interactively like the Internet, Usenet machines store the messages sent by users and periodically forward them to other Usenet machines. Unlike mail from mailing lists, Usenet news articles do not automatically fill up your electronic mailbox. Instead, you need a special type of program called a *news reader* to retrieve only the news you want from a local Usenet storage site and display it on your computer.

Usenet is like a living thing: New newsgroups are added, groups with too much traffic break up into smaller, more specialized groups, and some groups even decide to dissolve themselves. All of this occurs based upon some commonly accepted rules and by voting. There is no enforcement body; Usenet depends entirely on the cooperation of its computers' owners and users.

This chapter introduces Usenet and explains how to read news. You will subscribe to the special newsgroup designed for newcomers to Usenet.

At the end of this chapter and in Chapter 17 you will be introduced to accessing newsgroups with more user-friendly Windows software.

Welcome to a fascinating and exciting worldwide group!

What Is Usenet News?

U senet news represents a way other than electronic mail for people who share similar interests to communicate with one another. Usenet is a separate computer network, but most locations in the Internet provide access to a Usenet computer, making Usenet news accessible to most people on the Internet. Let's begin with a description of Usenet.

▶ **1** Usenet is a global network and community. It began in the U.S. in the early 1970s and now includes thousands of newsgroups. Usenet works on a cooperative basis by storing articles and then forwarding them from Usenet computer to Usenet computer. As with the Internet itself, there is no central authority. The administrator of a Usenet computer can decide which newsgroups will be made available to readers at a given site. Your local site may have many newsgroups or very few.

5 There are many different types of people on Usenet. Net "saints" help newcomers by answering their questions. "Wizards" have a deep knowledge and understanding of a particular area. "Flamers" respond to messages with personal insults. "Lurkers" tend to read Usenet news but never submit anything to the newsgroups. Lurking is a good way to learn about a group's interests and dynamics. Once you feel comfortable, you can stop lurking and begin posting questions to the group.

4 Most interaction on Usenet is very much like the interaction on the mailing lists described in the preceding chapter. A user submits (posts) a question on a relevant topic for the group, and other users respond with messages that either answer the question or contribute to the discussion. Each question and each response is its own Usenet article. (Note that articles can be as short as a few lines or as long as a small book.) Unlike mailing lists, nothing comes automatically to your mailbox. You must use a news reader to request the news articles you want to see when you want to see them.

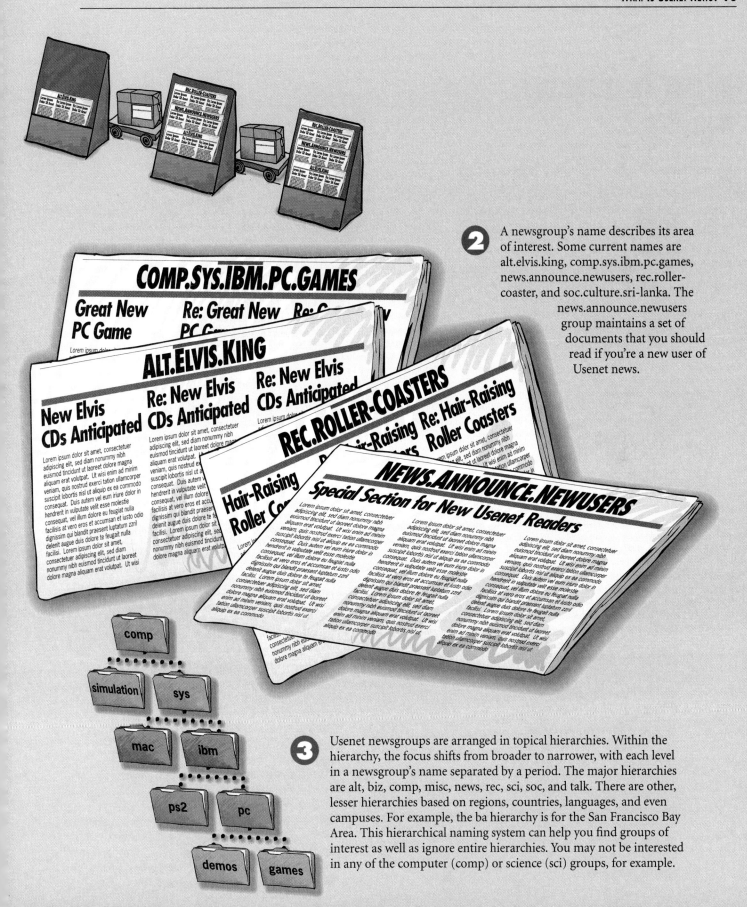

2 A newsgroup's name describes its area of interest. Some current names are alt.elvis.king, comp.sys.ibm.pc.games, news.announce.newusers, rec.roller-coaster, and soc.culture.sri-lanka. The news.announce.newusers group maintains a set of documents that you should read if you're a new user of Usenet news.

3 Usenet newsgroups are arranged in topical hierarchies. Within the hierarchy, the focus shifts from broader to narrower, with each level in a newsgroup's name separated by a period. The major hierarchies are alt, biz, comp, misc, news, rec, sci, soc, and talk. There are other, lesser hierarchies based on regions, countries, languages, and even campuses. For example, the ba hierarchy is for the San Francisco Bay Area. This hierarchical naming system can help you find groups of interest as well as ignore entire hierarchies. You may not be interested in any of the computer (comp) or science (sci) groups, for example.

What Is a News Reader?

Remember, a news reader is a program that enables you to read your news. Before you actually read news for the first time, it's useful to understand how a news reader operates. Here is a brief overview.

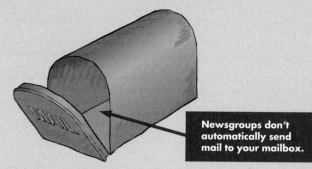

Newsgroups don't automatically send mail to your mailbox.

1 Usenet news articles do not arrive automatically in your mailbox, as do messages from mailing lists. Instead, Usenet articles are stored on a computer in your Internet domain that's called a *news server* because it serves up news to all the local people who request it. So that there's room for new messages, Usenet messages have expiration dates, set by the author, ranging from a week to a month from the date they were originally posted. The Usenet news server will delete a message after its expiration date.

6 There are several different news readers, but they all use the three-level approach to reading news. Some take advantage of screen-oriented terminal emulation to give a nicer, more organized display of articles. Some news readers let you view articles in the order of subject threads instead of the order in which articles are posted to the newsgroup. In this chapter you'll learn how to use rn— the most basic and widely distributed news reader.

TIP SHEET

► Some newsgroups maintain archives of their expired messages. Instructions for accessing these archives are provided in special documents of frequently asked questions (or FAQs) prepared by members of the newsgroup.

► Other popular news readers are trn, tin, and nn. Your Internet host may have one or more of these in addition to rn. After you become familiar with rn, you should try out these fancier news readers and see which one you like best. You'll want to choose one and stay with it rather than switching back and forth between several.

5 News readers operate at three different levels: the newsgroup level, the subject/article level, and the page level. When you start your news reader it begins at the newsgroup level and asks if you want to read the articles in one of the groups you've subscribed to. When you select the newsgroup you want to read, you move to the subject/article level, where the news reader displays the subject lines of currently posted articles. When you select an article to read, you move down to the page level, where you see the actual text (pages) of an article. When using a news reader, you need to remember which level you're on because you must use different commands at the different levels.

ALT.BACCHUS

Re: Rare Sonoma Cabernets

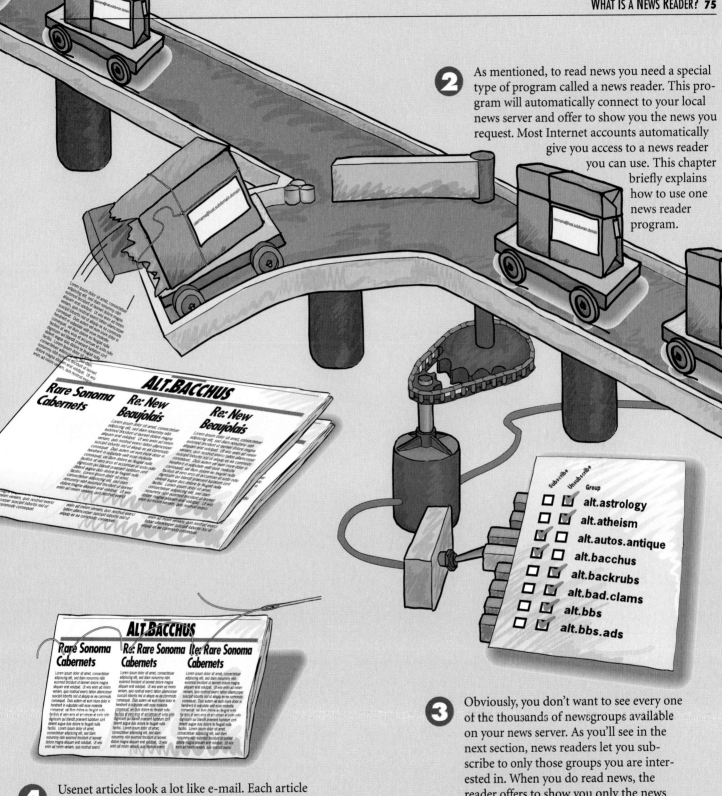

2 As mentioned, to read news you need a special type of program called a news reader. This program will automatically connect to your local news server and offer to show you the news you request. Most Internet accounts automatically give you access to a news reader you can use. This chapter briefly explains how to use one news reader program.

3 Obviously, you don't want to see every one of the thousands of newsgroups available on your news server. As you'll see in the next section, news readers let you subscribe to only those groups you are interested in. When you do read news, the reader offers to show you only the news for the groups you are subscribed to. You can unsubscribe and resubscribe to any group on the local news server whenever you like, as you'll learn in the next section.

4 Usenet articles look a lot like e-mail. Each article has a section at the beginning that indicates the sender, the date, and the subject of the article. If an article is a follow-up to a previous article, it will share the same subject line beginning with *Re:*. All articles sharing a subject within a group make up a *subject thread*. Newsgroups often have many subject threads running at the same time.

How to Get Only the News You Want

Given the thousands of newsgroups available to most people on the Internet, it is critical that you be able to distinguish those you want to read from those you have no interest in. You do this by subscribing to specific newsgroups, much as you subscribe to mailing lists of interest. Now that you have a basic understanding of how news readers operate, you can start the one called rn and use it to subscribe to a newsgroup.

Rn sets up your .newsrc file the very first time you use it.

```
> rn
Trying to set up a .newsrc file -- running newsetup...

Creating /u2/markhb/.newsrc to be used by news programs.
Done.

If you have never used the news system before, you may find the articles
in news.announce.newusers to be helpful.  There is also a manual entry for rn.

To get rid of newsgroups you aren't interested in, use the 'u' command.
Type h for help at any time while running rn.
```

1 Type **rn** ↵ to start the program. (If you get an error message when you enter the rn command, then this option may not be available on your system.) The very first time you run rn it creates a special file called .newsrc that indicates which groups are available and whether you are subscribed to them. Rn assumes you are subscribed to all the newsgroups on the local news server. Since it's unlikely you'll want to subscribe to all these newsgroups, it's best to unsubscribe to all the newsgroups and then resubscribe to only those you are interested in.

5 For now, just quit rn by typing q. When you use q to exit, rn updates your .newsrc file by marking the groups you are subscribed to. In this case, it will mark your .newsrc to indicate that you are subscribed to news.announce.newusers.

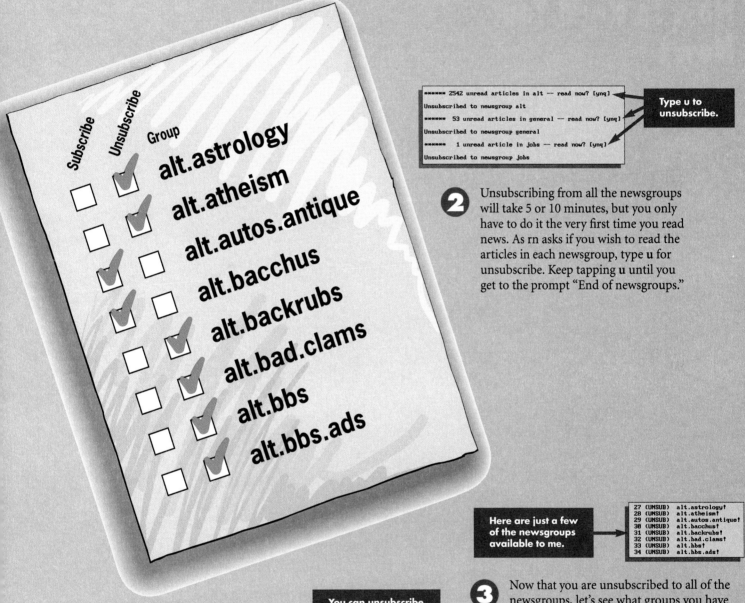

```
****** 2542 unread articles in alt -- read now? [ynq]
Unsubscribed to newsgroup alt
****** 53 unread articles in general -- read now? [ynq]
Unsubscribed to newsgroup general
******    1 unread article in jobs -- read now? [ynq]
Unsubscribed to newsgroup jobs
```

Type u to unsubscribe.

2 Unsubscribing from all the newsgroups will take 5 or 10 minutes, but you only have to do it the very first time you read news. As rn asks if you wish to read the articles in each newsgroup, type **u** for unsubscribe. Keep tapping **u** until you get to the prompt "End of newsgroups."

Here are just a few of the newsgroups available to me.

```
27 (UNSUB)  alt.astrology!
28 (UNSUB)  alt.atheism!
29 (UNSUB)  alt.autos.antique!
30 (UNSUB)  alt.bacchus!
31 (UNSUB)  alt.backrubs!
32 (UNSUB)  alt.bad.clams!
33 (UNSUB)  alt.bbs!
34 (UNSUB)  alt.bbs.ads!
```

You can unsubscribe and resubscribe as often as you like.

```
****** End of newsgroups -- what next? [qnp] g news.announce.newusers
Newsgroup news.announce.newusers is unsubscribed -- resubscribe? [yn]

****** 42 unread articles in news.announce.newusers -- read now? [ynq]
```

3 Now that you are unsubscribed to all of the newsgroups, let's see what groups you have available on your local news server. Type **L** to list the available newsgroups and your subscription status for each one. (Of course, at this point you won't be subscribed to any of them.) If you see a group that looks interesting, write down its name on a piece of paper so you can subscribe to it later. There could be literally thousands of newsgroups in this list. You may want to read it at another time since it could take a while to get through. When you are done looking at the list type **q**. You don't need to be at the end of the list to do this.

4 Try subscribing to the special newsgroup for newcomers to Usenet. Type

    g news.announce.newusers ↵

which tells the news reader to find a newsgroup named news.announce.newusers. Rn says you are unsubscribed and asks if you wish to resubscribe. Indicate yes by typing **y**. Rn asks if you would like to read the articles now; type **n** for no because you'll come back and read those articles in the next section.

How to Read Your News

Now that you have subscribed to news.announce.newusers, you're ready to find out how to read news articles. Keep in mind that your news reader operates at three different levels: the newsgroup level (which lists the available newsgroups), the subject/article level (which lists the available articles by subject), and the page level (which displays the actual text of the article). When you read news, you'll move up and down among these levels as you switch from article to article and newsgroup to newsgroup.

TIP SHEET

▶ Sometimes you don't get around to reading news for several days, and there are too many articles to go through. If you type c at the article level, rn asks if you want to mark all the articles in that group as read. Type y to mark them all as read. This process is referred to as "catching up."

▶ If you are viewing an article and would like to see the next article in the subject thread rather than the next article in the numerical list, hold down the Ctrl key and type n.

▶ If you are reading an article and you decide not to see any other articles on that subject, type k to have all the articles with that subject line or thread marked as read.

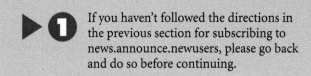

1 If you haven't followed the directions in the previous section for subscribing to news.announce.newusers, please go back and do so before continuing.

8 Quit rn by typing **q**. You may have to type **q** several times to move back up through the article and newsgroup levels. Don't worry if you press q too many times. The extra q's will just show on your command line after you have quit reading news.

Type m while reading an article to mark it as unread.

```
    This is the monthly introductory article for the moderated newsgroups
alt.answers, de.answers, comp.answers, misc.answers, news.answers,
rec.answers, sci.answers, soc.answers, and talk.answers (hereafter

Article 762 marked as still unread.
(Mail) End of article 762 (of 763) -- what next? [npq]
```

7 When you finish reading an article and go to the next one, rn marks the one you were just viewing as read. Once an article is marked as read, your news reader will not display it again (note, however, that the remaining articles are *not* renumbered). You can mark articles as unread by typing **m** while viewing them. This allows you to come back to these articles later.

6 At the page level, rn displays the first screenful of the article. To see the next screenful, tap the space-bar. You can read the entire article in this way, or you can type **n** to move to the next article. Don't look at more than one or two articles right now. Wait until the next section, where you'll learn how to save the remaining articles in your own directory.

```
> rn
Unread news in news.announce.newusers                    42 articles

Checking for new newsgroups...

Newsgroup alt.fan.addams.wednesday not in .newsrc -- subscribe? [ynYN]
(Ignoring alt.fan.addams.wednesday)
(Ignoring alt.tv.beavis-and-butthead)
(Ignoring cov.seminar.stats)
(Ignoring alt.support.tinnitus)
```

Type N to automatically cancel your subscription to all newly created newsgroups.

2 Type **rn** ↵ to start rn. If you haven't read news in a day or so, you may be asked if you want to subscribe to groups created since you last read news. Type **y** for yes or **n** for no for each group. If you want rn to mark all the new groups as unsubscribed, type **N**.

```
******  42 unread articles in news.announce.newusers -- read now? [ynq]
```

3 When rn is done checking for new and defunct (or *bogus*) newsgroups, it displays a list of the newsgroups you are subscribed to and asks you if you want to read the articles in the first one. Type **y** for yes.

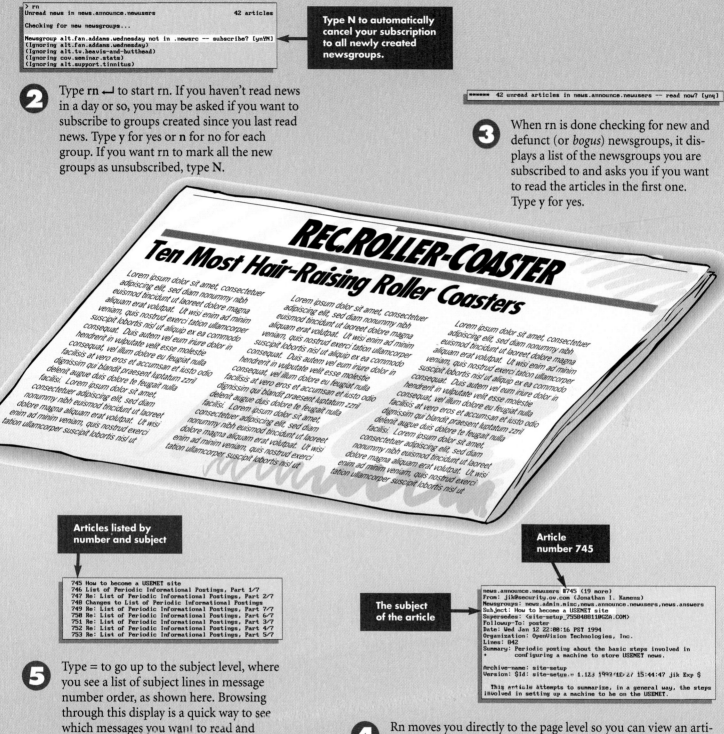

Articles listed by number and subject

```
745 How to become a USENET site
746 List of Periodic Informational Postings, Part 1/7
747 Re: List of Periodic Informational Postings, Part 2/7
748 Changes to List of Periodic Informational Postings
749 Re: List of Periodic Informational Postings, Part 7/7
750 Re: List of Periodic Informational Postings, Part 6/7
751 Re: List of Periodic Informational Postings, Part 3/7
752 Re: List of Periodic Informational Postings, Part 4/7
753 Re: List of Periodic Informational Postings, Part 5/7
```

Article number 745

The subject of the article

```
news.announce.newusers #745 (19 more)
From: jik@security.ov.com (Jonathan I. Kamens)
Newsgroups: news.admin.misc,news.announce.newusers,news.answers
Subject: How to become a USENET site
Supersedes: <site-setup_755848811@GZA.COM>
Followup-To: poster
Date: Wed Jan 12 22:00:16 PST 1994
Organization: OpenVision Technologies, Inc.
Lines: 842
Summary: Periodic posting about the basic steps involved in
+        configuring a machine to store USENET news.

Archive-name: site-setup
Version: $Id: site-setup.v 1.123 1993/12/27 15:44:47 jik Exp $

   This article attempts to summarize, in a general way, the steps
involved in setting up a machine to be on the USENET.
```

5 Type **=** to go up to the subject level, where you see a list of subject lines in message number order, as shown here. Browsing through this display is a quick way to see which messages you want to read and which you want to skip. It is not unusual for very active newsgroups to post 50 to 100 messages a day. This list of subject lines is a convenient way to cope with a large number of messages. You can scroll through this list of subjects by tapping the spacebar. To read a specific message, just type its number followed by ↵.

4 Rn moves you directly to the page level so you can view an article. (Some news readers instead move you to the subject/article level at this point.) Notice that articles have numbers. The more recent the article, the higher the number. When viewing articles, the news reader moves from the oldest available unread article to the most recent. Your newsreader ignores articles once you have read them. We'll cover read and unread articles later in this section. Write down the number of the first article you read in news.announce.newusers.

How to Save the News You Want

Many of the articles in newsgroups are things you want to read only once. However, there will also be articles you want to save for future reference. Periodically, people post lists of articles and books or other resources. Sometimes groups assemble and post lists of frequently asked questions (FAQs) and their answers. News readers allow you to save copies of these articles in your own directory. You can read this copy at your leisure, share it with friends, or even print a paper copy.

1 Type rn ↵ to start rn and begin reading the news.announce.newusers group. When rn starts, it will ask you if you want to read the available articles in groups you subscribed to. Type y for yes when rn asks if you want to read news.announce.newusers.

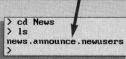

My News directory has a file called news.announce.newusers.

6 When you are done saving files, type q until you have quit rn. Move to the News directory by typing cd News ↵. Now you can use either vi or the more command to view the news.announce.newusers articles you saved.

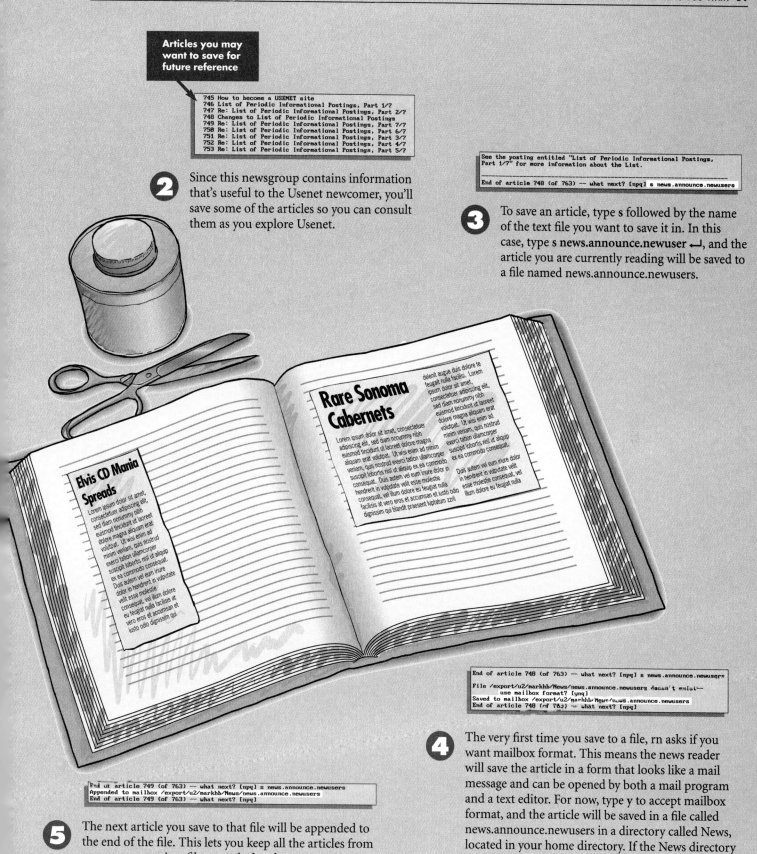

Articles you may want to save for future reference

```
745 How to become a USENET site
746 List of Periodic Informational Postings, Part 1/7
747 Re: List of Periodic Informational Postings, Part 2/7
748 Changes to List of Periodic Informational Postings
749 Re: List of Periodic Informational Postings, Part 7/7
750 Re: List of Periodic Informational Postings, Part 6/7
751 Re: List of Periodic Informational Postings, Part 3/7
752 Re: List of Periodic Informational Postings, Part 4/7
753 Re: List of Periodic Informational Postings, Part 5/7
```

2 Since this newsgroup contains information that's useful to the Usenet newcomer, you'll save some of the articles so you can consult them as you explore Usenet.

```
See the posting entitled "List of Periodic Informational Postings,
Part 1/7" for more information about the List.

End of article 748 (of 763) -- what next? [npq] s news.announce.newusers
```

3 To save an article, type **s** followed by the name of the text file you want to save it in. In this case, type **s news.announce.newuser** ↵, and the article you are currently reading will be saved to a file named news.announce.newusers.

Rare Sonoma Cabernets

Elvis CD Mania Spreads

```
End of article 748 (of 763) -- what next? [npq] s news.announce.newusers

File /export/u2/markhb/News/news.announce.newusers doesn't exist--
     use mailbox format? [ynq]
Saved to mailbox /export/u2/markhb/News/news.announce.newusers
End of article 748 (of 763) -- what next? [npq]
```

4 The very first time you save to a file, rn asks if you want mailbox format. This means the news reader will save the article in a form that looks like a mail message and can be opened by both a mail program and a text editor. For now, type y to accept mailbox format, and the article will be saved in a file called news.announce.newusers in a directory called News, located in your home directory. If the News directory doesn't exist, rn will create it for you.

```
End of article 749 (of 763) -- what next? [npq] s news.announce.newusers
Appended to mailbox /export/u2/markhb/News/news.announce.newusers
End of article 749 (of 763) -- what next? [npq]
```

5 The next article you save to that file will be appended to the end of the file. This lets you keep all the articles from one newsgroup in a file named after the newsgroup.

New Software Makes Getting News Enjoyable

The new software available (most of it is free) allows much more user-friendly access to news groups by offering a graphical Windows interface. Also the latest trend in Web browsers, such as Mosaic and Netscape, is to incorporate a news reader. In Chapter 17 there is a detailed illustration of one of these news readers.

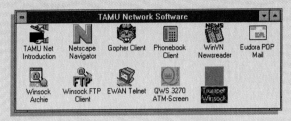

▶ **1** WinVN and Trumpet Winsock are two news readers that are available in the public domain. To use them you just double-click the left mouse button on the appropriate window icon.

TIP SHEET

▶ **WinVN is available free from several public domain sites. One of these sites is an ftp site: ftp.ksc.nasa.gov and can be found in the UNIX directory /pub/win3/winvn.**

▶ **In order to download free software, you will need to follow the instructions in Chapters 10, 11, and 15.**

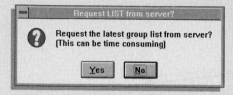

2 The first time you double-click your mouse on the WinVN icon, you will be asked to supply some network information. You simply move the cursor to each box, type in the appropriate information, and click OK when done.

3 Once you set up your personal network information, you will then be asked if you want the extensive group list.

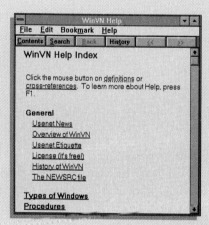

4 The really nice aspect of this window interface is that you can ask for help at any time. This makes it easy to use the program without having to remember a lot of commands.

CHAPTER 9

Interacting with People on Usenet

Newsgroups are really about interacting with people who share your interests. The previous chapter showed you half of the interaction: how to read messages posted to newsgroups of interest. This chapter will show you the other half: how to post your own questions as well as your answers to the questions of others.

When you interact with people on line, a whole new set of rules and manners—sometimes called "netiquette"—is required. In a face-to-face conversation you can see a person's hand and facial gestures and can hear the intonation of his or her voice. This helps you judge if someone is teasing, being sarcastic, or even lying. With on-line interaction, in contrast, you cannot see the person you are interacting with; you can only make judgments based on written words. The rules of netiquette help to compensate for the limitations of this on-line environment.

Usenet serves primarily as a forum for questions and answers. In order to cut down on repetitive questions, many Usenet newsgroups periodically offer subscribers a document made up of frequently asked questions (or FAQs) and their answers. You should read these documents to make sure your questions haven't already been answered. If you have a new question, people on Usenet can be extremely cooperative in helping you find the answer. When others ask questions, you may also be able to assist them. People interacting with each other help make Usenet the amazing information resource that it is.

How to Behave On Line

Like any other community, Usenet has its own set of rules or manners governing behavior, many based on common courtesy. Unfortunately, not everybody follows them. Here are some brief pointers on how to be on your best behavior on Usenet. Some of these pointers pertain to mailing lists as well.

```
**NOTE: this is intended to be satirical.  If you do not recognize
  it as such, consult a doctor or professional comedian.  The
  recommendations in this article should recognized for what
  they are -- admonitions about what NOT to do.


               "Dear Emily Postnews"

    Emily Postnews, foremost authority on proper net behaviour,
    gives her advice on how to act on the net.

==============================================================
Dear Miss Postnews: How long should my signature be? -- verbose@noisy

A: Dear Verbose: Please try and make your signature as long as you
can.  It's much more important than your article, of course, so try
to have more lines of signature than actual text.
```

▶ 1 Chapter 8 described how to subscribe to a newsgroup and read news. The newsgroup you subscribed to has documents that explain a great deal about Usenet manners. The satirical document *Emily Postnews Answers Your Question on Netiquette* is both educational and funny. If it is not there when you read news.announce.newusers for the first time, you may have to wait several weeks until it gets reposted to the newsgroup. You may also be able to find a copy in the newsgroup news.answers.

TIP SHEET

▶ Some articles contain material that might be considered offensive because it is raunchy or derogatory. A program called Rot13—short for rotate 13—provides the sender with a means of scrambling the contents of a message by changing *a* to *m*, *b* to *n*, *c* to *o*, and so on, so the message appears as random letters on your screen. To see what it really says, you must unscramble it. In rn you can do this by typing X when you're at the page level. Other news readers also provide a way of unscrambling Rot13 articles.

▶ Many people add a signature to the bottom of their messages. The signature, which takes up three or four lines at most, provides your real name, your e-mail address, and perhaps a telephone number. Some people include a funny quote or some other piece of humor in their signature.

▶ Even though this section introduces many new manners for coping with the on-line environment, you will do fine if you are simply considerate of others and their time by avoiding frivolous questions and excessively long messages.

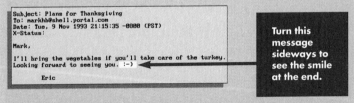

Turn this message sideways to see the smile at the end.

6 When you are speaking face to face you can use facial gestures or your tone of voice to show that you are being sarcastic, or you can wink to indicate that you are just kidding. To add this dimension to on-line speech, you can use a number of character sequences that, when viewed sideways, look something like a facial expression. For example, the wink is conveyed with ;-) and sadness is conveyed with :-(. Some of these *emoticons* or *smileys*, as they are called, are fairly complex.

2 It is a good idea to restrict yourself to reading news for a while before participating (remember, this is called "lurking"). This gives you an opportunity to observe the dynamics of a particular group. Certain things that would be acceptable in one group might not be acceptable in another. For example, some groups may collectively choose not to discuss certain aspects of their topic. Different groups will have different opinions of what is offensive or improper. For instance, jokes that are funny to some may be offensive to others. It is better to find out a group's norms through lurking than by offending someone.

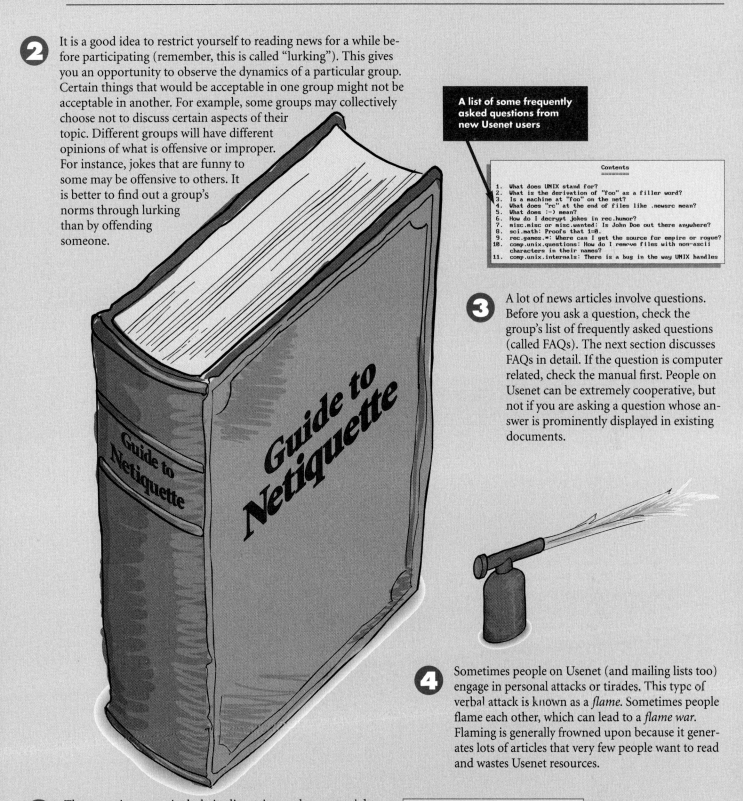

A list of some frequently asked questions from new Usenet users

```
                        Contents
                        ========

   1.   What does UNIX stand for?
   2.   What is the derivation of "foo" as a filler word?
   3.   Is a machine at "foo" on the net?
   4.   What does "rc" at the end of files like .newsrc mean?
   5.   What does :-) mean?
   6.   How do I decrypt jokes in rec.humor?
   7.   misc.misc or misc.wanted: Is John Doe out there anywhere?
   8.   sci.math: Proofs that 1=0.
   9.   rec.games.*: Where can I get the source for empire or rogue?
  10.   comp.unix.questions: How do I remove files with non-ascii
        characters in their names?
  11.   comp.unix.internals: There is a bug in the way UNIX handles
```

3 A lot of news articles involve questions. Before you ask a question, check the group's list of frequently asked questions (called FAQs). The next section discusses FAQs in detail. If the question is computer related, check the manual first. People on Usenet can be extremely cooperative, but not if you are asking a question whose answer is prominently displayed in existing documents.

4 Sometimes people on Usenet (and mailing lists too) engage in personal attacks or tirades. This type of verbal attack is known as a *flame*. Sometimes people flame each other, which can lead to a *flame war*. Flaming is generally frowned upon because it generates lots of articles that very few people want to read and wastes Usenet resources.

5 There are times, particularly in discussions, when you might want to be emphatic. You can do this by *highlighting* a word with asterisks to make it stand out. If you feel very strongly you may want to SHOUT something by capitalizing all its letters. You can also be emphatic and shout in your regular e-mail correspondence.

```
Subject: RE: Spottings
To: markhb@shell.portal.com
Date: Tue, 9 Nov 1993 21:16:19 -0800 (PST)
X-Status:

I look forward to our bird spotting next Saturday.
I just hope we *don't* have another grey day.
I'M TIRED OF THE RAIN!

     --Eleanor
```

What Is a FAQ?

One of the great resources offered by Usenet is the FAQ—the list of frequently asked questions and their responses for a particular newsgroup. There are FAQs on an incredible number of topics ranging from the new Power PC to Rhodesian Ridgeback dogs. A FAQ is an excellent starting place to learn about a topic.

Some frequently asked questions

```
                          Contents
                          ========

1.  What does UNIX stand for?
2.  What is the derivation of "foo" as a filler word?
3.  Is a machine at "foo" on the net?
4.  What does "rc" at the end of files like .newsrc mean?
5.  What does :-) mean?
6.  How do I decrypt jokes in rec.humor?
7.  misc.misc or misc.wanted: Is John Doe out there anywhere?
8.  sci.math: Proofs that 1=0.
9.  rec.games.*: Where can I get the source for empire or rogue?
```

▶ **1** All FAQs are text files or Usenet articles that generally follow a common question and answer format. Some FAQs are just a long list of questions followed by their respective answer. Other FAQs have a numbered list of all the questions up front. This makes it easier for you to search for a particular question and its answer since, for example, you may quickly find out that you want number 15. Many questions are very practical such as "how can I do xyz?" Some FAQs answer questions about where you can read more about a specific topic, and some go so far as to provide annotated bibliographies.

TIP SHEET

▶ Sometimes people have written tutorials for a topic. If a tutorial exists, the FAQ will probably tell you where it is and how to get it.

▶ Take a good look at the FAQ for news.announce.newusers. It provides a great deal of useful information about all of the topics covered in this book. You saved a copy in a file when you learned to read and save news in the previous chapter.

▶ You should also look at the FAQ in alt.internet.services. This FAQ, which is going to be published as a small book, discusses many of the things you can do with the Internet.

5 There are several methods of recovering files from the archive at rtfm.mit.edu. One of the best ways is to use a program called ftp, which stands for "file transfer protocol." The next chapter describes ftp in detail.

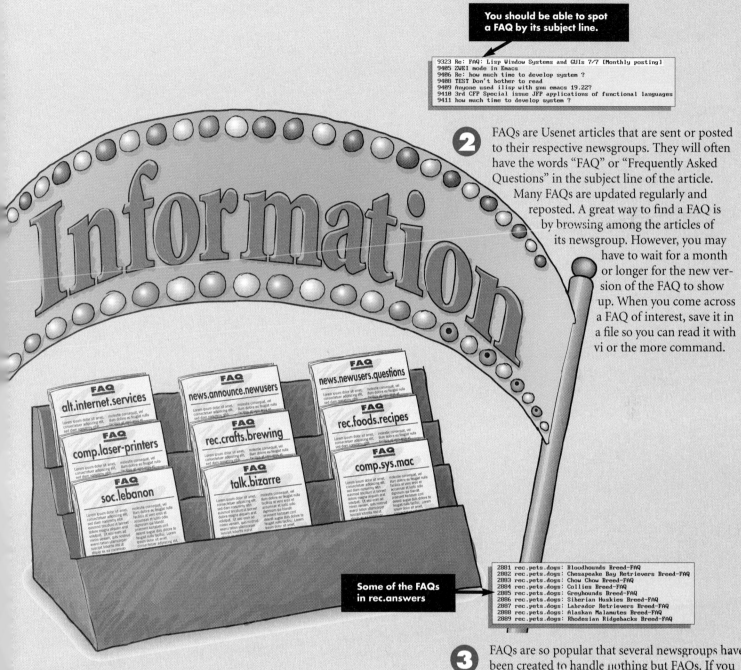

You should be able to spot a FAQ by its subject line.

```
9323 Re: FAQ: Lisp Window Systems and GUIs ?/? [Monthly posting]
9405 ZWEI mode in Emacs
9406 Re: how much time to develop system ?
9408 TEST Don't bother to read
9409 Anyone used ilisp with gnu emacs 19.22?
9410 3rd CFP Special issue JFP applications of functional languages
9411 how much time to develop system ?
```

2 FAQs are Usenet articles that are sent or posted to their respective newsgroups. They will often have the words "FAQ" or "Frequently Asked Questions" in the subject line of the article. Many FAQs are updated regularly and reposted. A great way to find a FAQ is by browsing among the articles of its newsgroup. However, you may have to wait for a month or longer for the new version of the FAQ to show up. When you come across a FAQ of interest, save it in a file so you can read it with vi or the more command.

Some of the FAQs in rec.answers

```
2881 rec.pets.dogs: Bloodhounds Breed-FAQ
2882 rec.pets.dogs: Chesapeake Bay Retrievers Breed-FAQ
2883 rec.pets.dogs: Chow Chow Breed-FAQ
2884 rec.pets.dogs: Collies Breed-FAQ
2885 rec.pets.dogs: Greyhounds Breed-FAQ
2886 rec.pets.dogs: Siberian Huskies Breed-FAQ
2887 rec.pets.dogs: Labrador Retrievers Breed-FAQ
2888 rec.pets.dogs: Alaskan Malamutes Breed-FAQ
2889 rec.pets.dogs: Rhodesian Ridgebacks Breed-FAQ
```

4 Most Usenet articles have expiration dates, and FAQs are no exception. Therefore the FAQ you need may be gone from both its newsgroup and its corresponding answers group, and you may not want to wait for it to be reposted. Fortunately, many newsgroups archive a copy of their FAQ. The address of the major FAQs archive is rtfm.mit.edu (you can also use the address pit-manager.mit.edu). The directory pub/usenet includes a separate subdirectory for each of many Usenet groups. For example, there's a subdirectory named news.announce.newusers for that group. There is also a directory for news.answers.

3 FAQs are so popular that several newsgroups have been created to handle nothing but FAQs. If you search through your .newsrc file you will find several groups whose name ends in *answers,* such as news.answers or comp.answers; these groups are devoted entirely to FAQs. When a FAQ is sent to its newsgroup, it is often posted to its corresponding answers group as well. When the FAQ for comp.lang.lisp is posted to the newsgroup, for example, it is also sent to comp.answers. Checking the articles on the relevant .answers group (that is, news.answers for Usenet, comp.answers for computers, rec.answers for hobbies and recreation, and so on) can be a rapid way of finding a FAQ.

How to Send a Message to a Newsgroup

Although you can learn a lot by simply lurking in various Usenet newsgroups, sooner or later you'll want to submit your own article or posting. Here's a quick rundown on how to do so.

▶ **1** Before you post anything, please read the articles about posting to Usenet in news.announce.newusers. You should have saved copies of them earlier in Chapter 8. If you didn't, use rn to read the articles in news.announce.newusers and save them.

Your message in misc.test

```
47159 Re: Hmm.......
47168 please ignore
47161 MAKE MONEY FA$T (was Re: Cus chamber for pirates! (Re: Raeking games))
47162 Re: Das chamber for pirates! (Re: Cracking games)
47163 Re: Cas chamber for pirates! (Re: Cracking games)
End of article 47159 (of 47163) — what next? [npq]
```

8 After about a half hour or so, start rn again and read the new articles in misc.test. One of them should be yours. If your article is not there, again mark all the articles as read (type c), quit rn (type q) and wait another half hour before reading the newsgroup again.

7 Now type c to mark all of the articles in misc.test as read, and then quit rn by typing q. Marking all the other articles as read will make it easier to find your new posting.

6 Rn starts your text editor (in my case it's vi) and provides you with a header you must fill in. Again, the header your system provides may be slightly different. For the purposes of this test, you need only fill in the Sender line with your name. Normally, you would also want to fill in the Expires line with a date that would cause the message to expire after a week to 10 days. Below the header you can type your message:

```
please ignore this message. ↵
```

Exit the text editor (type **:wq** if it's vi) and rn will ask what you wish to do. Type **send** ↵ to send off your test article.

2 There are basically two reasons for posting to a Usenet newsgroup. Either you want to begin a new subject thread or you want to follow up on an existing thread. Your news reader will allow you to do both.

3 Just to practice, let's post to a test group called misc.test. This group is designed for testing the propagation of a message through the Usenet network and is not generally read by anybody.

4 Begin by starting rn, the news reader program. (See Chapter 8 for more on rn.) At the newsgroup level, type **g misc.test** ↵. Rn asks if you want to resubscribe; type **y** for yes. Rn then tells you how many unread articles there are in misc.test and asks if you want to read them now; answer **y**. While viewing an article, type f for followup. Make sure you type a lowercase *f*.

ALT.BACCHUS

Rare Sonoma Cabernets

Lorem ipsum dolor sit amet, consectetuer adipiscing elit, sed diam nonummy nibh euismod tincidunt ut laoreet dolore magna aliquam erat volutpat. Ut wisi enim ad minim veniam, quis nostrud exerci tation ullamcorper suscipit lobortis nisl ut aliquip ex ea commodo consequat. Duis autem vel eum iriure dolor in hendrerit in vulputate velit esse molestie consequat, vel illum dolore eu feugiat nulla facilisis at vero eros et accumsan et iusto odio dignissim qui blandit praesent luptatum zzril delenit augue duis dolore te feugait nulla facilisi. Lorem ipsum dolor sit amet, consectetuer adipiscing elit, sed diam nonummy nibh euismod tincidunt ut laoreet dolore magna aliquam erat volutpat. Ut wisi

Re: New Beaujolais

My Article

Lorem ipsum dolor sit amet, consectetuer adipiscing elit, sed diam nonummy nibh euismod tincidunt ut laoreet dolore magna aliquam erat volutpat. Ut wisi enim ad minim veniam, quis nostrud exerci tation ullamcorper suscipit lobortis nisl ut aliquip ex ea commodo consequat. Duis autem vel eum iriure dolor in hendrerit in vulputate velit esse molestie consequat, vel illum dolore eu feugiat nulla facilisis at vero eros et accumsan et iusto odio dignissim qui blandit praesent luptatum zzril delenit augue duis dolore te feugait nulla facilisi. Lorem ipsum dolor sit amet, consectetuer adipiscing elit, sed diam nonummy nibh euismod tincidunt ut laoreet dolore magna aliquam erat volutpat.

—markhb@shell.portal.com

Re: New Beaujolais

Lorem ipsum dolor sit amet, consectetuer adipiscing elit, sed diam nonummy nibh euismod tincidunt ut laoreet dolore magna aliquam erat volutpat. Ut wisi enim ad minim veniam, quis nostrud exerci tation ullamcorper suscipit lobortis nisl ut aliquip ex ea commodo consequat. Duis autem vel eum iriure dolor in hendrerit in vulputate velit esse molestie consequat, vel illum dolore eu feugiat nulla facilisis at vero eros et accumsan et iusto odio dignissim qui blandit praesent luptatum zzril delenit augue duis dolore te feugait nulla facilisi. Lorem ipsum dolor sit amet, consectetuer adipiscing elit, sed diam nonummy nibh euismod tincidunt ut laoreet dolore magna aliquam erat volutpat. Ut wisi

```
Are you starting an unrelated topic? [ynq] y

Subject: please ignore
Distribution: usa

(leaving chreak mode; cwd=/export/u2/markhb)
Invoking command: QUOTECHARS=>' Pnews -h /u2/markhb/.rnhead

I see you've never used this version of Pnews before.  I will give you extra
help this first time through, but then you must remember what you learned.
If you don't understand any question, type h and a CR (carriage return) for
help.

If you've never posted an article to the net before, it is HIGHLY recommended
that you read the netiquette document found in news.announce.newusers so
that you'll know to avoid the commonest blunders.  To do that, interrupt
Pnews, get to the top-level prompt of [t]rn, and use the command
"g news.announce.newusers" to go to that group.

This program posts news to many machines throughout the country.
Are you absolutely sure that you want to do this? [ny] y
```

For a normal message, you would type the expiration date here in *dd/mm/yy* format.

```
Newsgroups: misc.test
Subject: please ignore
Summary:
Expires:
Sender: Mark Butler
Followup-To:
Distribution: usa
Organization: Portal Communications Company -- 408/973-9111 (voice) 408/973-8091
  (data)
Keywords:
Cc:

please ignore this message.

~
~
~
```

Vi's tildes; you may wind up in a different text editor.

5 Rn now begins creating an article to post. Here's the way my Internet host's rn prompts for information about an article. Your Internet host's rn might offer you slightly different prompts. Rn knows that this is your first time, so it will provide extra prompts. Rn asks if you are starting an unrelated topic; answer **y** for yes. Next, rn asks for the subject of your posting. Type **please ignore** ↵. (Remember, this is just a test.) Rn then asks about distribution. In this case type **usa** ↵ to limit the distribution of your message to the United States. Depending on the newsgroup, you may want to limit the distribution to a regional area such as New England or you may want to type **world** for world-wide distribution. Rn then asks you if you are absolutely certain you want to do this; answer **y** ↵ for yes.

CHAPTER 10

Transferring Files with Ftp

 One major reason to access the Internet is that it gives you access to all kinds of information. Files and data are scattered all around the Internet in large and small archives. These files may contain text, pictures, sounds, or computer programs. Sometimes you look at this information while it remains on a distant computer, but at other times you'll want to have your very own copy. Copying files from these archives to your personal Internet account will be one of your main activities on the Internet.

Computers on the Internet have a standard tool for transferring copies of files—a program called *ftp*, which stands for *file transfer protocol*. You can use ftp to copy any file from one Internet host to another; all you need is an account name on a host and the account's password. Your ftp program will make a special connection with the remote host, which will allow you to navigate its directories and select files for transfer. Unfortunately, there is no way to look at the contents of a file while you are connected via ftp: You must transfer the copy and look at it once it is in your own account.

When you do not have an account on a remote Internet host, ftp recognizes a special account name called anonymous. Anybody on the Internet can access a public archive through the use of anonymous ftp, and, once connected, can transfer a copy of any file in the archive. This chapter will provide you with all the skills necessary to copy files from any archive on the Internet using anonymous ftp.

New software for Windows can make ftp transfers painless (see Chapter 15). However, it is often useful to know the basic fundamentals involved in ftp.

How to Connect to an Ftp Site

Ftp allows you to transfer a copy of a file between two computers on the Internet if you have an account on both machines or if you use the anonymous account on the machine holding the archive of files. Here's how you make the initial connection.

1 Ftp allows you to copy (transfer) files from one machine to another, in much the same way as you copy files in your own account's subdirectories. With ftp you can copy files from your account to a distant or remote computer, and you can copy files on the remote machine to your account.

Type bye ↵ **to exit.**

Your anonymous ftp connection is accepted.

The *ftp* prompt

```
230 Guest login ok, access restrictions apply.
Remote system type is UNIX.
Using binary mode to transfer files.
ftp>
```

8 The machine now tells you if it accepts your connection. Occasionally, your request for a connection will be rejected because the archive already has as many anonymous connections as it will accept. Some archives display a special message when you do connect. You should take a moment to read this welcoming message. In the next section you'll learn how to move around in the archive and grab files. For now, break this connection and quit the ftp program by typing **bye** ↵ at the *ftp* prompt. This prompt is where you type commands for ftp, just as you type commands for UNIX at your UNIX prompt.

7 The remote machine now asks for a password. When you are logging in anonymously, enter your full Internet address as your password. (I enter **m-tretter@-tamu.edu**.) This allows the administrators of the archive to know who is browsing in their archive.

m-tretter@tamu.edu

MARIETTA TRETTER

2 To establish an ftp connection, as with so many other activities on the Internet, you must know the Internet address of the remote computer you wish to connect to.

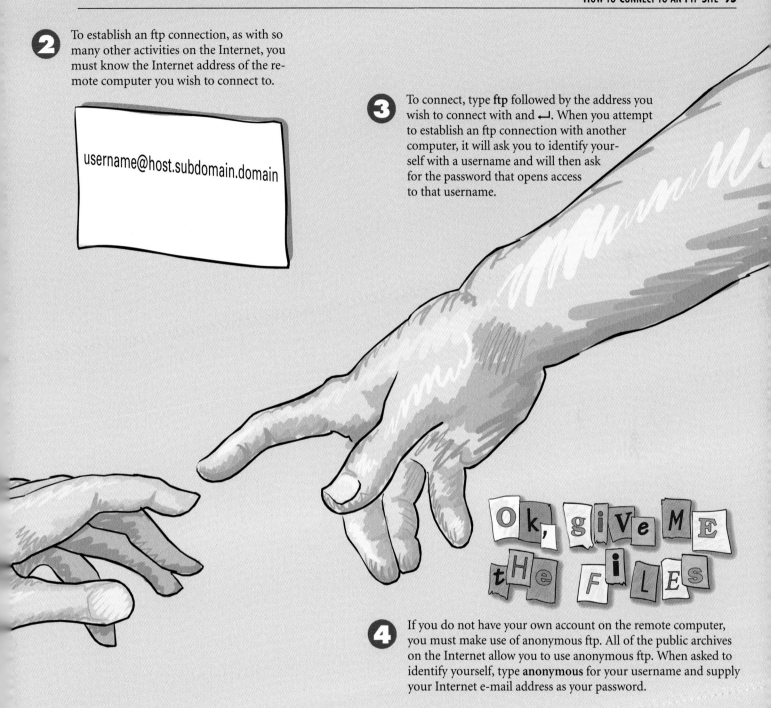

username@host.subdomain.domain

3 To connect, type **ftp** followed by the address you wish to connect with and ↵. When you attempt to establish an ftp connection with another computer, it will ask you to identify yourself with a username and will then ask for the password that opens access to that username.

Ok, give Me the Files

4 If you do not have your own account on the remote computer, you must make use of anonymous ftp. All of the public archives on the Internet allow you to use anonymous ftp. When asked to identify yourself, type **anonymous** for your username and supply your Internet e-mail address as your password.

```
> ftp rtfm.mit.edu
Connected to BLOOM-PICAYUNE.MIT.EDU.
220 rtfm ftpd (wu-2.1c(17) with built-in ls);
Name (rtfm.mit.edu:markhb): anonymous
```

```
> ftp rtfm.mit.edu
Connected to BLOOM-PICAYUNE.MIT.EDU.
220 rtfm ftpd (wu-2.1c(17) with built-in ls);
Name (rtfm.mit.edu:markhb):
```

6 When the connection is established, the remote computer will ask you for identification. If you had an account on that machine you would type your username. To employ the anonymous ftp service, type **anonymous** ↵ when prompted for a name.

5 Chapter 9 discussed the archive of Usenet newgroups' frequently asked questions lists (FAQs). Let's use ftp to see what FAQs are there. First we'll establish the connection and see what the anonymous login process looks like. Type **ftp rtfm.mit.edu** ↵. This will start the ftp program on your machine, causing it to contact the machine you specified (in this case rtfm) and negotiate for an ftp connection.

How to Navigate within an Ftp Site

Most public archives on the Internet are on computers that use UNIX. Their files will be located in directories and subdirectories. You can use your ftp connection to move through this directory structure, checking which files are in any given location. Note that ftp commands are remarkably similar to the commands for navigating in a UNIX directory structure (discussed in Chapter 4). You may also want to review the more advanced UNIX concepts and commands presented in Chapter 5 before continuing with this section.

TIP SHEET

▶ Even if the remote machine you are connected to is not using UNIX, ftp uses the commands described here. The ftp program will perform the necessary translations.

▶ When you used the pwd command earlier, you may have noticed that you were in a subdirectory of a directory called pub. The pub directory is standard to sites offering anonymous ftp services. Usually, all files in subdirectories of pub will be accessible to you. This is useful when you have the address of an ftp site but don't know the path to the file you want. To track down the file, make the ftp connection, use the cd command to switch to the pub directory, and begin looking there.

▶ ❶ Let's use a real-life example to try navigating in a remote archive. Reconnect to rtfm by typing **ftp rtfm.mit.edu** and logging on as anonymous.

❼ Now that you've seen how to scan directories and lists of files, you should exit this ftp connection. Type **bye** ↵ to close the connection and end the ftp program.

❻ Unfortunately, there is no way to look at the contents of a file while you are connected using ftp. To see what's in the file you have to transfer it to your host and then open it with the appropriate program. You'll do this in the next section.

2 To see what documents are available for new Usenet users, go to the directory with the FAQs. Use the cd (change directory) command to move around the directory structure. Type

cd pub/usenet/news.announce.newusers ↵

(In ftp, the cd command should always be followed by a pathname. You can use both relative and absolute pathnames as discussed in Chapter 4. You can also type **cd ..** to move up into the parent directory.)

Your current directory on the remote machine

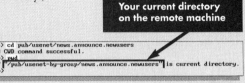

```
ftp> cd pub/usenet/news.announce.newusers
250 CWD command successful.
ftp> pwd
257 "/pub/usenet-by-group/news.announce.newusers" is current directory.
ftp>
```

3 Another ftp command that works like its UNIX equivalent is pwd. Whenever you use this command, the remote computer displays the full path of your current directory—that is, your remote location. Type **pwd** ↵ to make sure you changed to the correct directory in the last step. Your current directory on the remote machine should be /pub/usenet-by-group/news.announce.newusers.

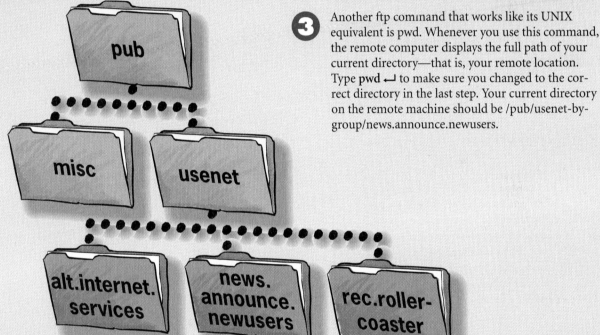

File size	Date and time last modified	Filename

```
-rw-rw-r--   8 root    3      41370 Dec 1  03:02 Publicly_Accessible_Maili
ng_Lists,_Part_6_6
-rw-rw-r--   4 root    3      17858 Oct 22 02:49 Rules_for_posting_to_Usen
et
-rw-rw-r--  10 root    3      23518 Oct 22 01:05 USENET_Software:_History_
and_Sources
-rw-rw-r--   6 root    3      22996 Nov 22 07:27 Usenet_Newsgroup_Creation
_Companion
-rw-rw-r--   6 root    3      16334 Oct 22 02:49 What_is_Usenet?
-rw-rw-r--   2 root    3       1414 Oct 11 06:54 uk.bcs.announce_-_charter
-_monthly_reminder
```

d here means directory (this examples shows only directories).

```
drwxrwxr-x   2 root    3        512 Dec 20 01:04 rec.running
drwxrwxr-x   2 root    3       1024 Dec 27 00:37 rec.scouting
drwxrwxr-x   2 root    3        512 Dec 15 05:57 rec.scuba
drwxrwxr-x   2 root    3       2048 Dec 27 09:19 rec.skate
drwxrwxr-x   2 root    3        512 Dec 15 04:14 rec.skydiving
drwxrwxr-x   2 root    3        512 Dec 27 00:37 rec.sport.dive
drwxrwxr-x   2 root    3        512 Dec 25 00:37 rec.sport.dive
drwxrwxr-x   2 root    3        512 Dec 17 05:79 rec.sport.fencing
```

5 Chapter 4 discussed how to tell the difference between subdirectories and files in a directory listing by using the ls -f command. If you are using the dir command, there's also an easy way to identify subdirectories: Each line begins with a string of letters. If an item is a directory, the line begins with the letter d; otherwise the line begins with a dash.

4 Now that you've confirmed your location, there are two ways to see the contents of a directory. You can type **dir** ↵ or use the UNIX-like ls command. Some ftp archive administrators make it so the ls command alone automatically provides the equivalent of ls -l. If not, you'll have to type **ls -l** ↵ to get the long version of the directory listing, which includes filename, file size, and the date the file was last modified.

How to Grab a File from an Ftp Site

Now that you know how to make an ftp connection and navigate in a remote archive's directory structure, you can use ftp to get a really useful file that lists a whole range of services currently available over the Internet. The list is compiled and maintained by Scott Yanoff. You should pick up this list periodically to see what new Internet services are available.

TIP SHEET

▶ **If you accidentally transfer a binary file with the transfer mode set to ascii, the file you receive will be corrupted and useless. However the reverse—transferring text files with the transfer mode set to binary— will work. If you don't know the type of file you are dealing with, set the transfer mode to binary. Your files will always transfer correctly.**

▶ **Sometimes you'll want to get multiple files from a directory. Rather than typing** get **plus the filename for each file, you can use the mget (multiple get) command with a wildcard. If you type** mget C* ↵**, the remote machine will get each file in the directory whose name begins with a *C* and ask if you want a copy of it. For each file you must answer** y ↵ **for yes or** n ↵ **for no. This technique can be a real time-saver.**

▶ **In electronic documents, references to specific Internet files will tell you where to find the file. For example, you might see a reference indicating that Scott Yanoff's updated list of Internet services can be found at rtfm.mit.edu in the directory pub/usenet/alt.internet.services. As you browse, jot down these references so you know exactly where to find files of interest.**

1 First, make an anonymous ftp connection to rtfm.mit.edu by typing **ftp rtfm.mit.edu** ↵. Enter **anonymous** as the username and your Internet e-mail address as the password.

8 Here are two quick points about viruses and the Internet. Viruses live in program files (as opposed to data or text files). If you are using the Internet to obtain files containing text, pictures, or sounds, you don't need to worry about picking up viruses. You can only infect your home computer if you transfer programs to it. If you are only using your computer as a terminal emulator and are keeping retrieved files on the host, your home computer cannot be infected by a virus from your Internet connection. If you download and run programs, you should install antivirus software and have it scan the downloaded programs *before* you run them. You can buy antivirus programs for Amigas, Macintoshes, and PCs.

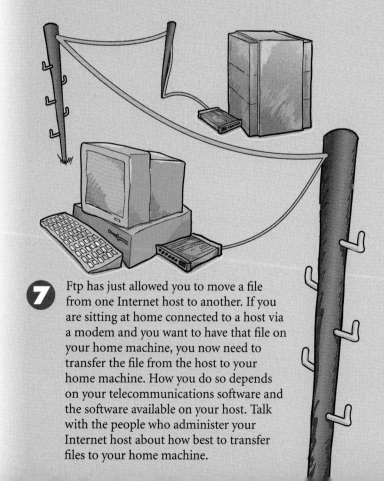

7 Ftp has just allowed you to move a file from one Internet host to another. If you are sitting at home connected to a host via a modem and you want to have that file on your home machine, you now need to transfer the file from the host to your home machine. How you do so depends on your telecommunications software and the software available on your host. Talk with the people who administer your Internet host about how best to transfer files to your home machine.

```
> ftp rtfm.mit.edu
Connected to BLOOM-PICAYUNE.MIT.EDU.
220 rtfm ftpd (wu-2.1c(17) with built-in ls); bugs to
Name (rtfm.mit.edu:markhb): anonymous
331 Guest login ok, send your complete e-mail address
Password:
230 Guest login ok, access restrictions apply.
Remote system type is UNIX.
Using binary mode to transfer files.
ftp> cd pub/usenet/alt.internet.services
250 CWD command successful.
ftp>
```

2 To travel down the directory structure to the file you want, type

`cd pub/usenet/alt.internet.services` ↵

3 When transferring files, you need to know what kind of file you are dealing with. Ftp thinks there are two kinds of files in the world: *text files* (also called *ascii files*); and all other types of files, which are collectively called *binary files*. A text file is any file that contains only plain text. Despite what you might think, word processing files, like those created by Microsoft Word, are not text files because they include formatting information along with the text. Files containing sounds or pictures are also not text files. Ftp also considers compressed files to be binary files even if they are plain text files when uncompressed. You must make ftp use the appropriate transfer mode for a file. To set the transfer mode for a binary file, type **bin** ↵; for text mode, type **ascii** ↵. The mode will remain set for the rest of this ftp session or until you change it. Type **ascii** ↵ since you'll be transferring text.

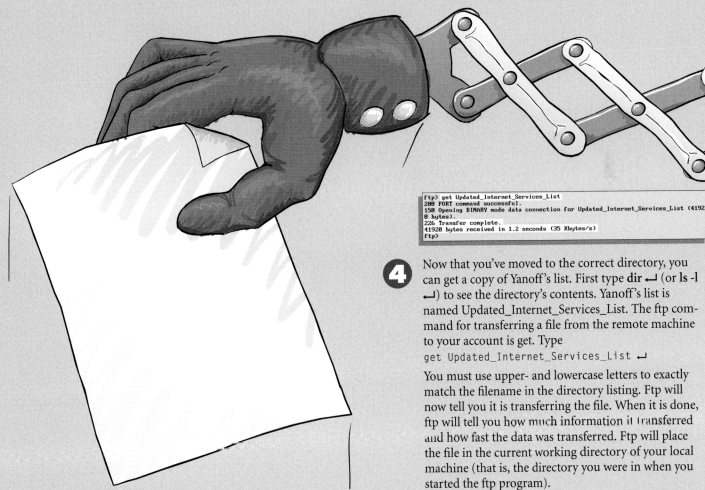

```
ftp> get Updated_Internet_Services_List
200 PORT command successful.
150 Opening BINARY mode data connection for Updated_Internet_Services_List (4192
0 bytes).
226 Transfer complete.
41920 bytes received in 1.2 seconds (35 Kbytes/s)
ftp>
```

4 Now that you've moved to the correct directory, you can get a copy of Yanoff's list. First type **dir** ↵ (or **ls -l** ↵) to see the directory's contents. Yanoff's list is named Updated_Internet_Services_List. The ftp command for transferring a file from the remote machine to your account is get. Type

`get Updated_Internet_Services_List` ↵

You must use upper- and lowercase letters to exactly match the filename in the directory listing. Ftp will now tell you it is transferring the file. When it is done, ftp will tell you how much information it transferred and how fast the data was transferred. Ftp will place the file in the current working directory of your local machine (that is, the directory you were in when you started the ftp program).

6 You can now view Yanoff's list (the file named Updated_Internet_Services_List) using page, more, or vi, as discussed in Chapter 5. Once you have finished going through this book, Yanoff's list will prove invaluable. It provides a topical listing of all sorts of resources on the Internet.

5 Once the file transfer is complete, you can transfer other files or you can quit ftp. Quit now so you can take a look at the file you just grabbed. Type **bye** ↵ to close the connection and exit the ftp program.

CHAPTER 11

Advanced Ftp

 On your PC or Macintosh you may have used a program like Stuffit, PKZip, or Compactor. This software can reduce the size of a file dramatically—sometimes as much as 90 percent. In some cases this software can even shrink entire directory structures so they can be restored intact when they are needed. There are two reasons why many archived files on the Internet are compressed: Smaller files take up less storage space, and smaller files take less time to transmit from site to site.

UNIX provides a standard program called Compress for compressing files, another called Uncompress for uncompressing files, and another called Tar for bundling multiple files and directories into one package. You will probably first encounter a tarred and compressed file at some ftp archive; you'll need to untar and uncompress your copy of such a file to use it. After you've collected a large number of your own files, you may also want to make use of Compress to store some of these files in smaller bundles. This chapter will teach you how to compress, uncompress, and untar files that you transfer from anonymous ftp archives.

How to Compress and Uncompress a File with UNIX

The shorter the file, the less time it takes ftp to transfer it, and the less disk space it takes up. As mentioned, there are special programs that shrink files without injuring their contents. These types of programs are available on all computers—PCs, Macintoshes, and UNIX hosts. Here you'll use the UNIX Compress program to compress files and the Uncompress program to restore files to their full size.

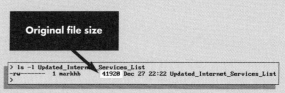

Original file size

1 Try compressing Yanoff's list, which you retrieved in the previous chapter. (You can also compress any large text file.) First see how large the file is. Type

`ls -l Updated_Internet_Services_List ↵`

and jot down the size of the file.

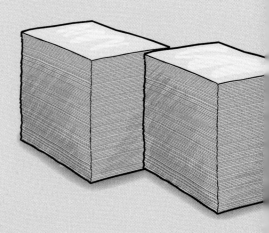

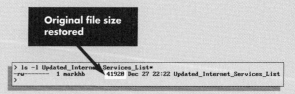

Original file size restored

5 Now type

`ls -l Updated_Internet_Services_List* ↵`

Your file will return to its original size, and the compressed file will vanish. It's easy to compress and uncompress files, and this strategy can be very useful for managing your own limited space on a UNIX host. If you keep a collection of FAQs or e-mail correspondence with a friend and don't look at the files very often, compress them. You can always uncompress them for viewing.

```
> compress Updated_Internet_Services_List
```

2 Type
`compress Updated_Internet_Services_List` ↵

The Compress program will now go to work. You can always identify UNIX compressed files because the Compress program appends a .Z to the filename. The Tip Sheet tells you how to recognize files compressed on PCs and Macintoshes.

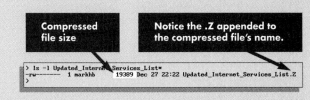

Compressed file size

Notice the .Z appended to the compressed file's name.

```
> ls -l Updated_Internet_Services_List*
-rw-------  1 markhb        19389 Dec 27 22:22 Updated_Internet_Services_List.Z
>
```

3 Now type
`ls -l Updated_Internet_Services_List*` ↵

Compare the current file size to the size you jotted down earlier. Notice that the compressed file is a lot smaller than the original text file. Most importantly, the original uncompressed file is no longer there. It has been replaced by its compressed counterpart. By contrast, compression programs on the PC and Macintosh often leave the uncompressed original unchanged and create a compressed copy.

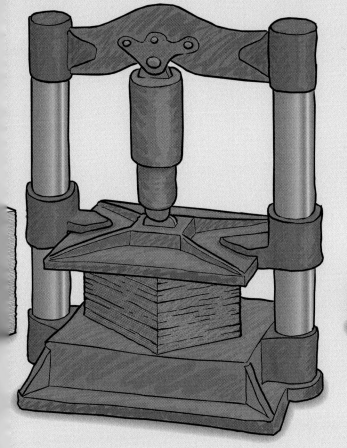

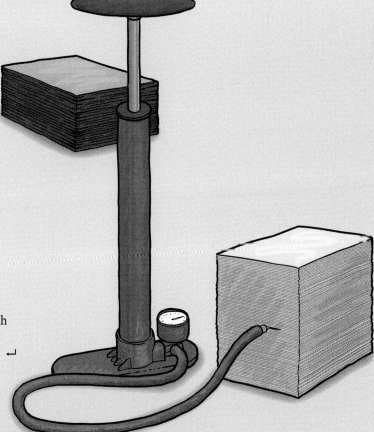

```
> uncompress Updated_Internet_Services_List.Z
```

4 To read the file again you need to uncompress it with the uncompress command. Type
`uncompress Updated_Internet_Services_List.Z` ↵

What Is a Tar File, and How Can I Untar It?

Sometimes files belong together as a group. Maybe each file is a part of a larger file like the list of mailing lists that was broken into multiple parts in Chapter 7. UNIX provides a way of bundling files together into a single file. In an archive, this saves you the trouble of having to figure out which files you need to transfer, since they are all grouped into one larger file. The UNIX program for bundling files is Tar. (This program may or may not be available to you, depending on your system setup.) You can also use Tar to "unbundle" tarred files so you can work with them individually again.

1 Tar can take a group of files and wrap them up into one bundle. Tar does not compress files; it simply groups them as one file. You can then use Compress to make a tar file much more compact. You will often find compressed tar files in ftp archives on the Internet.

The directory extracted from the tar file

The tar file

Untarring the file has recreated these directories and files within the directory testdir.

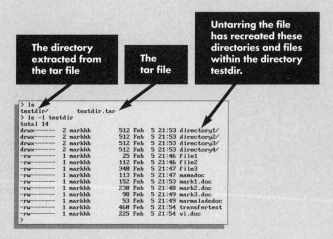

```
> ls
testdir/        testdir.tar
> ls -l testdir
total 14
drwx------  2 markhb       512 Feb  5 21:53 directory1/
drwx------  2 markhb       512 Feb  5 21:53 directory2/
drwx------  2 markhb       512 Feb  5 21:53 directory3/
drwx------  2 markhb       512 Feb  5 21:53 directory4/
-rw-------  1 markhb        25 Feb  5 21:46 file1
-rw-------  1 markhb       112 Feb  5 21:46 file2
-rw-------  1 markhb       340 Feb  5 21:47 file3
-rw-------  1 markhb       113 Feb  5 21:47 mamadoc
-rw-------  1 markhb       152 Feb  5 21:53 mark1.doc
-rw-------  1 markhb       230 Feb  5 21:48 mark2.doc
-rw-------  1 markhb        98 Feb  5 21:49 mark3.doc
-rw-------  1 markhb        53 Feb  5 21:49 marmaladedoc
-rw-------  1 markhb       460 Feb  5 21:54 transfertest
-rw-------  1 markhb       225 Feb  5 21:54 vi.doc
>
```

5 Tar files are also useful because they can incorporate directories and subdirectories along with the files they contain. When you untar the file, these directories and subdirectories will be recreated, if they do not already exist, and then extracted files will be placed in appropriate subdirectories. This could be very useful if you were receiving a copy of a report that included text and pictures in separate directories. The tar file can rebuild this directory structure and place files in their appropriate directory, which is much simpler than forcing the user to recreate the directory structure and place the files themselves.

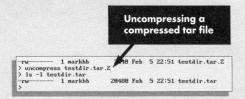

Uncompressing a compressed tar file

```
-rw--------  1 markhb        ???0 Feb  5 22:51 testdir.tar.Z
> uncompress testdir.tar.Z
> ls -l testdir.tar
-rw--------  1 markhb       20480 Feb  5 22:51 testdir.tar
>
```

2 Tarred files traditionally have the letters *tar* somewhere in the filename. Very often you will see a file with a name such as great_software.tar.Z. This file has been tarred and then compressed. The last section explained how to uncompress a file by typing **uncompress** followed by the file's name and ↵. If you did this to the preceding file, its name would become great_software.tar.

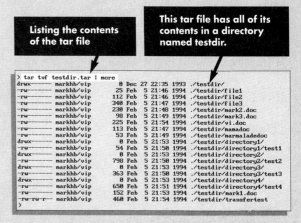

Listing the contents of the tar file

This tar file has all of its contents in a directory named testdir.

```
> tar tvf testdir.tar | more
drwx-------  markhb/vip        0 Dec 27 22:35 1993 ./testdir/
-rw--------  markhb/vip       25 Feb  5 21:46 1994 ./testdir/file1
-rw--------  markhb/vip      112 Feb  5 21:46 1994 ./testdir/file2
-rw--------  markhb/vip      340 Feb  5 21:47 1994 ./testdir/file3
-rw--------  markhb/vip      230 Feb  5 21:48 1994 ./testdir/mark2.doc
-rw--------  markhb/vip       90 Feb  5 21:49 1994 ./testdir/mark3.doc
-rw--------  markhb/vip      225 Feb  5 21:54 1994 ./testdir/vi.doc
-rw--------  markhb/vip      113 Feb  5 21:47 1994 ./testdir/mamadoc
-rw--------  markhb/vip       53 Feb  5 21:49 1994 ./testdir/marmaladedoc
drwx-------  markhb/vip        0 Feb  5 21:53 1994 ./testdir/directory1/
-rw--------  markhb/vip       54 Feb  5 21:50 1994 ./testdir/directory1/test1
drwx-------  markhb/vip        0 Feb  5 21:53 1994 ./testdir/directory2/
-rw--------  markhb/vip      798 Feb  5 21:50 1994 ./testdir/directory2/test2
drwx-------  markhb/vip        0 Feb  5 21:53 1994 ./testdir/directory3/
-rw--------  markhb/vip      363 Feb  5 21:50 1994 ./testdir/directory3/test3
drwx-------  markhb/vip        0 Feb  5 21:53 1994 ./testdir/directory4/
-rw--------  markhb/vip      650 Feb  5 21:51 1994 ./testdir/directory4/test4
-rw--------  markhb/vip      152 Feb  5 21:53 1994 ./testdir/mark1.doc
-rw-rw-r--  markhb/vip      460 Feb  5 21:54 1994 ./testdir/transfertest
>
```

3 Before you take apart a tar file you should check its contents. It may include files that have the same name as some files already in your directory, in which case the files in the tar file would replace your files. If so, you should untar the file in its own directory. Type

tar tvf *filename.tar* | more ↵

This will display the contents of the tarred file a screenful at a time. This file does not need to be taken apart in its own directory.

Extracting the contents of the tar file

```
> tar xvf testdir.tar
./testdir/
./testdir/file1
./testdir/file2
./testdir/file3
./testdir/mark2.doc
./testdir/mark3.doc
./testdir/vi.doc
./testdir/mamadoc
./testdir/marmaladedoc
./testdir/directory1/
./testdir/directory1/test1
./testdir/directory2/
./testdir/directory2/test2
./testdir/directory3/
./testdir/directory3/test3
./testdir/directory4/
./testdir/directory4/test4
./testdir/mark1.doc
./testdir/transfertest
>
```

These files were bundled together with the Tar program.

4 To have the tar file untarred—that is, pulled apart into its component parts—type

tar xvf *filename.tar* ↵

where *filename.tar* is the name of the tarred file you want to untar. As the program extracts each file from the tar file, it will display its name on your screen.

CHAPTER 12

Connecting to Remote Machines with Telnet

Telnet is a program that allows your Internet host computer to become a terminal of another host computer on the Internet. With ftp you opened a connection solely to transfer files. Telnet allows you to log in as a user on a remote machine and run the Internet computer programs that machine provides.

Telnet provides direct access to various Internet services. Sometimes these services are available on your host, but Telnet is especially useful when they're not. For example, when citizens of the electronic frontier write interfaces to help other users, Telnet lets you access their hosts and use their new interfaces. In Chapters 13 and 14 you'll use Telnet to access several programs that help users browse or find specific things on the Internet. Similarly, when someone creates a useful service, Telnet allows you to access this valuable information resource. In this chapter, we'll telnet to a service that provides current weather forecasts for cities in the United States.

Telnet is extremely simple to use. Just type **telnet** followed by the address you want to connect with. Once connected, you are a terminal on the remote machine and can interact with the programs it makes available. Telnet sits quietly in the background while you interact with the remote machine.

What Types of Services Can I Telnet To?

There is a large and constantly changing set of services you can telnet to. In Chapter 10, you grabbed a copy of Scott Yanoff's list of Internet services. After you've looked over this page, take a moment to read through his list using more, page, or vi and see all the services to which you can telnet. Here is a brief run-down of some of the types of available services.

▶ **1** There are many databases available to you on the Internet. In the next section you'll explore a weather database in Michigan.

8 And then there are the many Internet services yet to be created. Nobody has ever built anything like the Internet before. Every year brings new and better means of accessing the treasures of the Internet. Once you've mastered Telnet basics, you'll be able to telnet to future exciting services.

7 *Freenets* are community-based networks that allow free access to people who live within that community. The most famous of these—because it was the first of its kind—is the Cleveland Freenet. With your Internet account you can telnet to one of these "electronic villages."

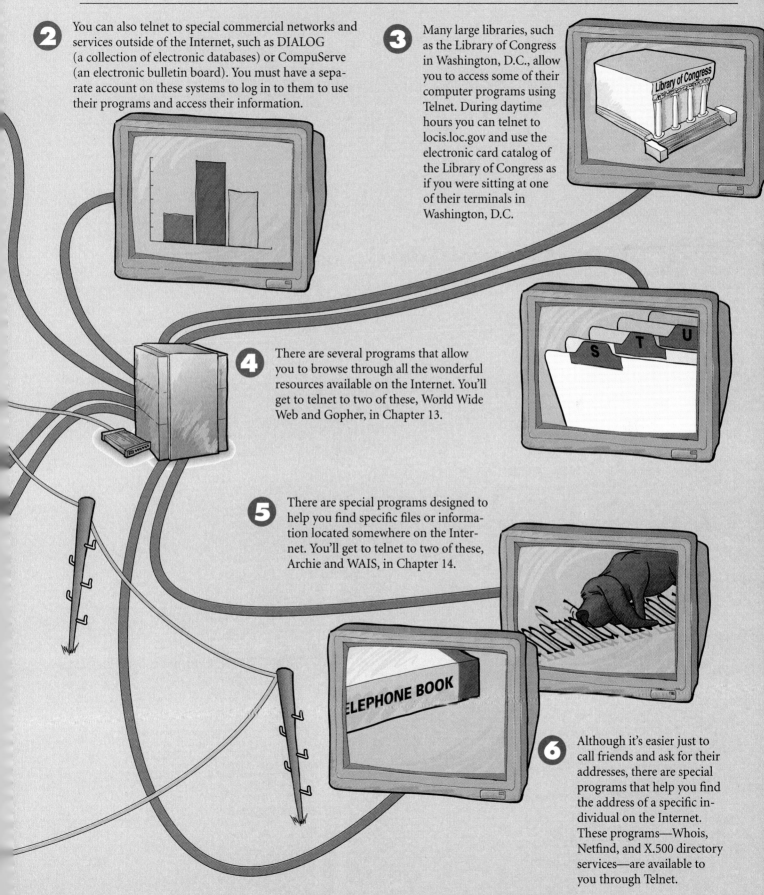

2 You can also telnet to special commercial networks and services outside of the Internet, such as DIALOG (a collection of electronic databases) or CompuServe (an electronic bulletin board). You must have a separate account on these systems to log in to them to use their programs and access their information.

3 Many large libraries, such as the Library of Congress in Washington, D.C., allow you to access some of their computer programs using Telnet. During daytime hours you can telnet to locis.loc.gov and use the electronic card catalog of the Library of Congress as if you were sitting at one of their terminals in Washington, D.C.

4 There are several programs that allow you to browse through all the wonderful resources available on the Internet. You'll get to telnet to two of these, World Wide Web and Gopher, in Chapter 13.

5 There are special programs designed to help you find specific files or information located somewhere on the Internet. You'll get to telnet to two of these, Archie and WAIS, in Chapter 14.

6 Although it's easier just to call friends and ask for their addresses, there are special programs that help you find the address of a specific individual on the Internet. These programs—Whois, Netfind, and X.500 directory services—are available to you through Telnet.

How to Telnet to Locations or Services on the Internet

Telnet is useful because of all the Internet services it allows you to interact with. Here's an interesting example involving a Michigan machine that contains a program that answers questions about current weather information. It provides you with forecasts for the cities you specify.

TIP SHEET

▶ If the remote machine stops responding to your keystrokes, you can hold down the Ctrl key and press] to return to the *Telnet* prompt on your machine; then type close ↵ at the *Telnet* prompt to close the connection to the remote machine and exit the Telnet program.

▶ If the remote machine is not responding while you're trying to connect, your Telnet program continues trying to make a connection for a minute or two. If a connection cannot be established, Telnet will be *timed out*—that is, the Telnet program will stop attempting to create the connection and will shut itself off. Timeouts occur because the remote machine is not functioning or because your Telnet program cannot translate the Internet address into the numerical IP address understood by computers. Sometimes the connection is refused at the remote end; sometimes the connection is established and then closed by the remote machine. When these things happen, your only option is to wait and try again later.

▶ As more and more people use the Internet, you are likely to have your telnet connections refused because too many others are already using the service you want.

Before you telnet you must have a destination in mind and must know its Internet address. We are going to connect to *downwind.sprl.umich.edu 3000*. The number (3000) following the address designates a *port*—the location of a specific program on the remote machine. If you telnet to the host without specifying a port, it thinks you are a regular user and will expect a valid username and password before allowing access. When you connect to a specific port, in contrast, the host doesn't ask for a username but limits you to one specialized function. In this case, rather than asking us if we want to log in, the host will automatically start the Weather program for us. This mechanism allows you to use a service without having an account on the host computer. Think of it as Telnet's equivalent of anonymous ftp.

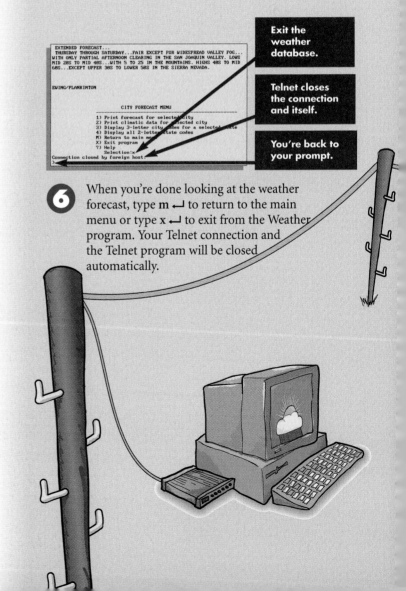

When you're done looking at the weather forecast, type **m** ↵ to return to the main menu or type **x** ↵ to exit from the Weather program. Your Telnet connection and the Telnet program will be closed automatically.

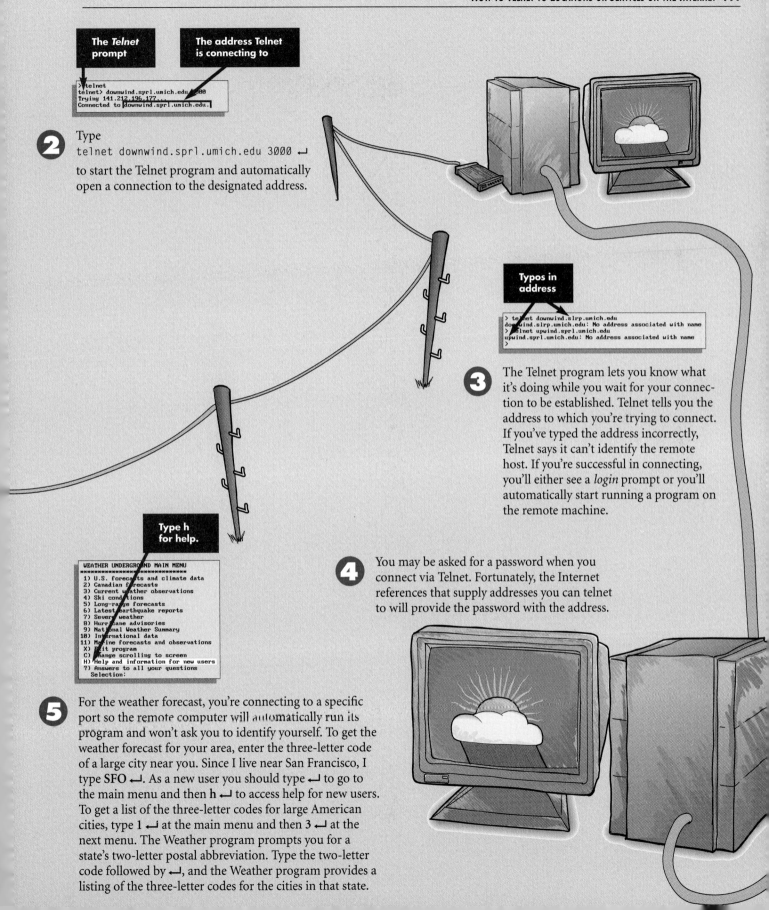

The *Telnet* prompt

The address Telnet is connecting to

```
>telnet
telnet> downwind.sprl.umich.edu 3000
Trying 141.212.196.177...
Connected to downwind.sprl.umich.edu.
```

2 Type

`telnet downwind.sprl.umich.edu 3000 ↵`

to start the Telnet program and automatically open a connection to the designated address.

Typos in address

```
> telnet downwind.slrp.umich.edu
downwind.slrp.umich.edu: No address associated with name
> telnet upwind.sprl.umich.edu
upwind.sprl.umich.edu: No address associated with name
>
```

3 The Telnet program lets you know what it's doing while you wait for your connection to be established. Telnet tells you the address to which you're trying to connect. If you've typed the address incorrectly, Telnet says it can't identify the remote host. If you're successful in connecting, you'll either see a *login* prompt or you'll automatically start running a program on the remote machine.

Type h for help.

```
WEATHER UNDERGROUND MAIN MENU
*******************************
 1) U.S. forecasts and climate data
 2) Canadian forecasts
 3) Current weather observations
 4) Ski conditions
 5) Long-range forecasts
 6) Latest earthquake reports
 7) Severe weather
 8) Hurricane advisories
 9) National Weather Summary
10) International data
11) Marine forecasts and observations
 X) Exit program
 C) Change scrolling to screen
 H) Help and information for new users
 ?) Answers to all your questions
   Selection:
```

4 You may be asked for a password when you connect via Telnet. Fortunately, the Internet references that supply addresses you can telnet to will provide the password with the address.

5 For the weather forecast, you're connecting to a specific port so the remote computer will automatically run its program and won't ask you to identify yourself. To get the weather forecast for your area, enter the three-letter code of a large city near you. Since I live near San Francisco, I type **SFO** ↵. As a new user you should type ↵ to go to the main menu and then **h** ↵ to access help for new users. To get a list of the three-letter codes for large American cities, type **1** ↵ at the main menu and then **3** ↵ at the next menu. The Weather program prompts you for a state's two-letter postal abbreviation. Type the two-letter code followed by ↵, and the Weather program provides a listing of the three-letter codes for the cities in that state.

CHAPTER 13

Browsing the Internet

In earlier parts of this book you learned about Telnet and ftp. Both of these programs require you to know the address of a specific computer to connect with; neither is conducive to just getting a general sense of what's out there on the Internet. There are an increasing number of *browsers* for the Internet that provide many of the best aspects of ftp and Telnet, as well as the ability to view text and do searches. These programs are also refreshingly easy to use, especially when compared to some of the less "friendly" UNIX-based programs you've already encountered. The addresses of locations are built into these browsers by their administrators. You don't need to remember UNIX commands or syntax. All you need to do is start them up and select from the choices they present. Using these browsers, you can go window-shopping for information on the Internet.

The first of these browsers—Gopher—presents the Internet as a series of menus containing items that point to another menu, a file, a directory within a remote host, a Telnet service, the articles of a Usenet newsgroup, or to a variety of other things. The second browser takes advantage of the World Wide Web. Rather than menus, the World Wide Web places pointers to other resources within its text. When you select one of the pointers, you automatically "jump" to the resource pointed at—even if the resource is on another computer in a different part of the country.

Gopher and the World Wide Web are designed for browsing. Their ease of use makes them two of the most popular programs on the Internet. The next chapter discusses two ways to find specific files on a specific topic. Chapters 18–22 will introduce you to some of the newer browsers.

"Surfing" the Internet

The Internet is growing so fast that it's very difficult to keep up with all the new information, archives, and other resources that are available. Periodically, you need to "surf" the Internet—venturing out just to see what you'll find. When surfing you have no particular destination in mind and no idea of what you'll discover, but you're bound to come across some amazing things.

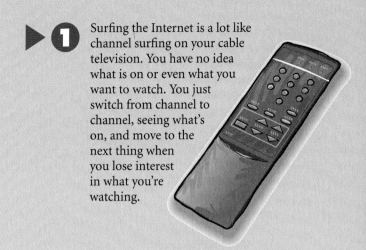

1 Surfing the Internet is a lot like channel surfing on your cable television. You have no idea what is on or even what you want to watch. You just switch from channel to channel, seeing what's on, and move to the next thing when you lose interest in what you're watching.

5 The best way to keep up with developments on the Internet and with new information sources is to go out surfing and see what you find. Gopher and World Wide Web make this a simple and enjoyable pastime. Be warned, though: It's easy to lose track of time as you explore the Internet!

TIP SHEET

▶ A growing number of documents try to list the resources available on the Internet. *The Internet Directory* by Eric Braun (Fawcett Colombine, 1994) is a recent book that provides a comprehensive listing that you can browse through in paper (rather then electronic) form. You'll find some other resources listed in the Appendix at the back of this book.

▶ Remember, the Internet is very young. Gopher and the World Wide Web are only a few years old. The latest and greatest browser, Netscape, is a multimedia program based on the World Wide Web; it allows you to hear sounds and see pictures and movies in addition to text. As the amount of information on the Internet grows, programmers will devise even better ways to browse.

▶ All this popularity has its downside. At times your browser will operate slowly, and sometimes it may not be allowed to access resources because of their overuse.

4 Internet users have grown frustrated with the lack of organization of the information on the Internet. In response, some individuals and groups have taken it upon themselves to create special subject-specific listings and archives, which are available through both Gopher and World Wide Web. These listings are like libraries that specialize in material on one subject. The people who maintain these special listings make a point of providing access to all the Internet information available on their topic and of monitoring the Internet for new, relevant information.

2 Internet services such as ftp are great for transferring a known file, but do little to let you just go out and explore. When you employ ftp you need to know the remote machine's address and the path to the file you want, and you must transfer a copy of the entire file to read it. When using Gopher or the World Wide Web, by contrast, you simply select items displayed on your computer screen. These items are really addresses that you cannot see. A connection is established to this invisible address, and the file you request is automatically retrieved and displayed on your screen.

Start Here

Start Here

Start Here

3 Both Gopher and World Wide Web give you listings of Internet resources each time you begin using them. Gopher provides main menus, and World Wide Web provides home pages of text. Furthermore, different universities and organizations provide specialized menus and home pages listing different sets of resources; these make good starting points for surfing the Internet. We'll encounter examples of all of these in this chapter as we use both Gopher and World Wide Web.

What Is Gopher?

Gopher is a program that is designed to allow you to browse the resources of the Internet. Gopher displays a set of resources on the Internet as *menus*—or lists of items from which you can choose. You travel around the Internet by selecting items from these menus—you don't need to know their addresses, and you don't need to know any commands. You just point to an item of interest and press ↵ to see its contents on the screen.

TIP SHEET

▸ **Sometimes the public Gopher clients are very busy. You may not be able to access them, or if you do get connected it may take a long time for the remote machine to respond to your commands. If possible, try to use a Gopher client on your Internet host rather than telneting to one of the public clients. Local clients cut down on network traffic and provide users with faster performance. Even with local clients, you may experience delays because the Internet is gaining so many new users and these services are so popular.**

▸ **To see if you have a Gopher client available on your Internet host, simply type** gopher ↵. **If UNIX tells you "command not found," speak with your system administrator about having a Gopher client installed. If Gopher starts up and you get a menu, you do have a local Gopher client. Try using this client; your work with Gopher will be faster and smoother.**

1 Gopher is based on the concept of clients and servers. This may sound complicated, but it's not. *Clients* are programs that request information for a user, and *servers* are programs that provide, or serve up, the information to clients. There are Gopher servers scattered all over the Internet that sit and wait for requests from Gopher client programs. You can use the Gopher client program on your Internet host, or, if one is not available, you can telnet to one of the many public Gopher clients available to anyone on the Internet. The menus on Gopher servers are created by the people who maintain the computer running the server. Menu items can point to materials on that Gopher server or to materials on other Gopher servers.

8 If you type **u** repeatedly, you will ultimately return to the main menu, where you started. This can be useful if you get lost while traveling through the menu hierarchy. When you're ready to quit Gopher just type **q**. When Gopher asks if you really want to quit, type y for yes.

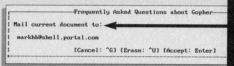

You can have interesting documents mailed to you or others.

7 If the document you are reading doesn't interest you, type **u** to move back up to the menu you just came from. If the document seems useful, you can have the Gopher client send you a copy via e-mail while you are reading it. Type **m** and, when asked for an e-mail address, enter your full Internet mail address and then press ↵. A copy will eventually show up in your electronic mailbox. After you've mailed the document, type **u** to return to the previous menu.

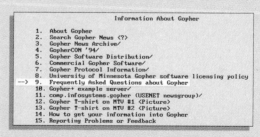

6 You will see a menu with many choices of information about Gopher. We'll look at the FAQ about Gopher. Locate the item *Frequently Asked Questions about Gopher*, noticing that a line number precedes it. Type the line number to select the item and then press ↵. You are now looking at a copy of the Gopher FAQ. You can press the spacebar to scroll through the document one screenful at a time.

2 All of the Gopher servers, their information resources, and all the Internet resources they can reach are collectively referred to as "Gopherspace." You'll hear people talk about "tunneling through Gopherspace" and "traveling around Gopherspace." The Internet has grown phenomenally in size, and Gopherspace has perhaps grown even faster.

```
> telnet consultant.micro.umn.edu
Trying 134.84.132.4...
Connected to hafnhaf.micro.umn.edu.

AIX telnet (hafnhaf)


N O T I C E : this system is very heavily used
For better performance, you should install and
run a gopher client on your own system.

Gopher clients are available for anonymous ftp from
boombox.micro.umn.edu

To run gopher on this system login as "gopher"


IBM AIX Version 3 for RISC System/6000
(C) Copyrights by IBM and by others 1982, 1991.
login: gopher
```

3 The best way to understand Gopher is to use it. Let's begin by using one of the public Gopher clients at the University of Minnesota, where Gopher was first built. Type

`telnet consultant.micro.umn.edu ↵`

At the *login* prompt, type **gopher** ↵ to run the public Gopher client. You must be using a vt100 terminal, as discussed in Chapter 2, to run Gopher. Since Gopher is one of the most popular services on the Internet, making the connection can sometimes take a while.

Move this arrow to the desired menu item.

```
            Internet Gopher Information Client 2.0 pl11

                Root gopher server: hafnhaf.micro.umn.edu

-->  1.  Information About Gopher/
     2.  Computer Information/
     3.  Internet file server (ftp) sites/
     4.  Fun & Games/
     5.  Libraries/
     6.  Mailing Lists/
     7.  News/
     8.  Other Gopher and Information Servers/
     9.  Phone Books/
    10.  Search Gopher Titles at the University of Minnesota <?>
    11.  Search lots of places at the U of M <?>
    12.  UofM Campus Information/




Press ? for Help, q to Quit                          Page: 1/1
```

5 You can select menu items either by using arrow keys and ↵ or by typing the number to the main item's left and pressing ↵. Now use your arrow keys to move the arrow to the item *Information About Gopher* and press ↵.

4 You are now at the main menu (the home site) of the Gopher at the University of Minnesota. Each item on a Gopher menu is really an address of the location of that item. Menu items that end with a slash (/) denote directories which may contain other directories or documents. Menu items ending with a <?> point to special indexes (which are beyond the scope of this book). Menu items with no special characters at the end are documents you can view.

Browsing Gopherspace

Gopherspace has expanded very rapidly in the last two years. New Gopher servers are coming on line all the time. In this section you'll travel to a menu that lets you access Gopher servers all over the world. This menu is an excellent starting point for browsing the resources on the Internet. Once you've completed this section, you'll be able to go out and explore Gopherspace on your own.

```
To run gopher on this system login as "gopher"


IBM AIX Version 3 for RISC System/6000
(C) Copyrights by IBM and by others 1982, 1991.
login: gopher
Last unsuccessful login: Fri Feb 11 18:36:22 199
Last login: Sat Feb 12 00:04:16 1994 on pts/18
TERM = (vt100) vt100
Erase is Ctrl-H
Kill is Ctrl-U
Interrupt is Ctrl-C
I think you're on a vt100 terminal
```

Gopher confirms that you are using the correct terminal.

1 Once again, connect to the public Gopher at the University of Minnesota. Type `telnet consultant.micro.umn.edu ↵`
At the *login* prompt, type **gopher ↵** to run the public Gopher client. Remember, you must be using a vt100 terminal to run Gopher.

7 When you are done looking around, type **q** to quit Gopher and **y** to confirm that you want to quit.

There are many interesting resources here besides free books.

```
      Net Info (Big Dummy's Guide to the Internet, FAQs, etc.)
 --> 1. Big Dummy's Guide to the Internet (by Adam Gaffin)/
     2. Zen and the Art of the Internet (by Brendan Kehoe)/
     3. OUTPOSTS FAQ - a list of online civil liberties organizations
     4. Search all White House Press Releases <?>
     5. Internet Resources by Subject/
     6. Guides to the Internet (NCSU)/
     7. Electronic Addresses (Email) Directories/
     8. Clearinghouse for Subject-Oriented Internet Resource Guides (UMich../
```

6 Select the *Net Info* item and press ↵. On the next menu the top item is a free book about the Internet—*Big Dummy's Guide to the Internet (by Adam Gaffin)*. This book is a good source of information on the Internet. You can read it using Gopher or you can mail yourself a copy to read at your leisure by selecting the text version labeled ASCII, typing **m**, and then typing your Internet e-mail address when it's requested. (Be sure you are reading the document you want mailed when you type **m**; the m command will only send you the document you are viewing. If you are not reading a document, typing **m** will return you to your main menu.) *Big Dummy's Guide to the Internet* provides an excellent discussion of the Internet, its resources, and its history. The ASCII text version is readable on any computer, while other versions like PostScript require a special viewer or printer.

TIP SHEET

▶ **If you have a Gopher client on your Internet host, you can use it to connect directly to a specific Gopher server by typing** gopher **followed by the address of the server. To connect directly to the University of Minnesota Gopher server we've been using, type**
gopher consultant.micro.umn.edu ↵
This direct connection will allow faster response rates and may save you the trouble of having to remember all the menus required to get to a location.

▶ **To find out the address a specific menu item points to, move the arrow to it and then type** =. **Gopher will display some information about the item you have selected, including its address on the Internet. You can go directly to this item—rather than moving through a series of menus—by typing** gopher **followed by the address exactly as Gopher just displayed it.**

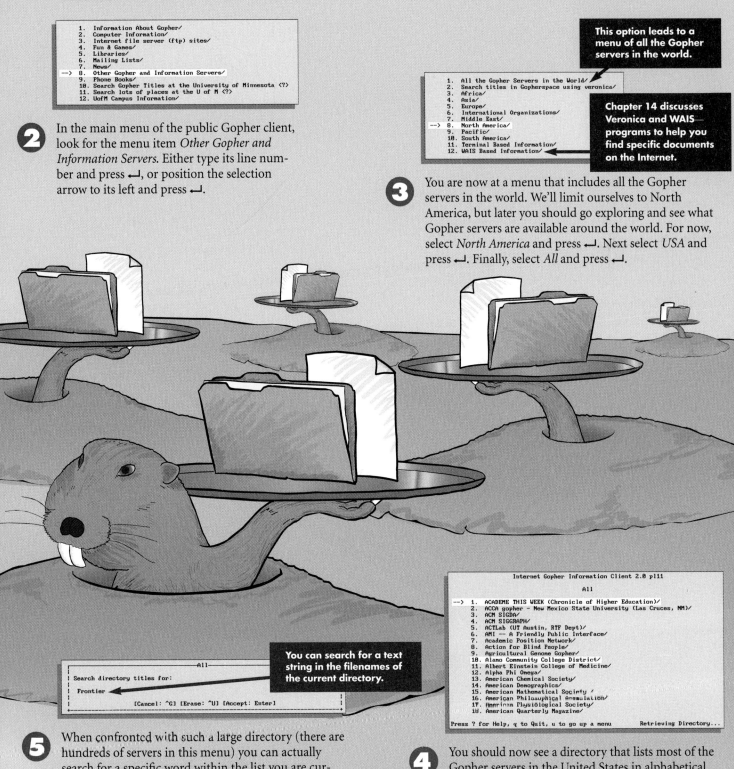

```
    1.  Information About Gopher/
    2.  Computer Information/
    3.  Internet file server (ftp) sites/
    4.  Fun & Games/
    5.  Libraries/
    6.  Mailing Lists/
    7.  News/
--> 8.  Other Gopher and Information Servers/
    9.  Phone Books/
    10. Search Gopher Titles at the University of Minnesota <?>
    11. Search lots of places at the U of M <?>
    12. UofM Campus Information/
```

This option leads to a menu of all the Gopher servers in the world.

```
    1.  All the Gopher Servers in the World/
    2.  Search titles in Gopherspace using veronica/
    3.  Africa/
    4.  Asia/
    5.  Europe/
    6.  International Organizations/
    7.  Middle East/
--> 8.  North America/
    9.  Pacific/
    10. South America/
    11. Terminal Based Information/
    12. WAIS Based Information/
```

Chapter 14 discusses Veronica and WAIS—programs to help you find specific documents on the Internet.

2 In the main menu of the public Gopher client, look for the menu item *Other Gopher and Information Servers*. Either type its line number and press ↵, or position the selection arrow to its left and press ↵.

3 You are now at a menu that includes all the Gopher servers in the world. We'll limit ourselves to North America, but later you should go exploring and see what Gopher servers are available around the world. For now, select *North America* and press ↵. Next select *USA* and press ↵. Finally, select *All* and press ↵.

```
                Internet Gopher Information Client 2.0 p111

                                    All

-->  1.  ACADEME THIS WEEK (Chronicle of Higher Education)/
     2.  ACCA gopher - New Mexico State University (Las Cruces, NM)/
     3.  ACM SIGDA/
     4.  ACM SIGGRAPH/
     5.  ACTLab (UT Austin, RTF Dept)/
     6.  AMI -- A Friendly Public Interface/
     7.  Academic Position Network/
     8.  Action for Blind People/
     9.  Agricultural Genome Gopher/
     10. Alamo Community College District/
     11. Albert Einstein College of Medicine/
     12. Alpha Phi Omega/
     13. American Chemical Society/
     14. American Demographics/
     15. American Mathematical Society /
     16. American Philosophical Association/
     17. American Physiological Society/
     18. American Quarterly Magazine/

Press ? for Help, q to Quit, u to go up a menu        Retrieving Directory...
```

You can search for a text string in the filenames of the current directory.

```
                         -----All-----
    |                                                    |
    | Search directory titles for:                       |
    |                                                    |
    | Frontier                                           |
    |          [Cancel: ^G] [Erase: ^U] [Accept: Enter]  |
    |                                                    |
```

5 When confronted with such a large directory (there are hundreds of servers in this menu) you can actually search for a specific word within the list you are currently viewing. Type /, and the Gopher client displays a box in which you can type a word or words to search for. Gopher doesn't care whether you type in upper- or lowercase—it matches both. Try typing **Frontier** ↵ in this box; the arrow will move to the item *Electronic Frontier Foundation*. Press ↵ to connect with and view the contents of this Gopher server.

4 You should now see a directory that lists most of the Gopher servers in the United States in alphabetical order. Take a few minutes to move through it. You can use the spacebar to move down one screenful at a time. Many of the Gopher servers are identified by their location (for example, Alamo Community College District), but a growing number are identified by their subject matter (for example The Chronicle of Higher Education).

What Is the World Wide Web?

Menus are not the only way to browse the Internet. The World Wide Web offers a competing approach. The World Wide Web doesn't require you to learn a lot of commands. You simply read the text provided and select the items you wish to jump to for viewing. You can follow many different "trails" of information in this way, much as you might skip from one word to the next while browsing through a thesaurus. The ease of use makes World Wide Web a favorite means of window-shopping for neat resources on the Internet.

▶ 1 The World Wide Web (WWW) provides an integrated view of the Internet using clients and servers. Remember, clients are programs that help you seek out information, and servers are the programs that dish up information to the clients. Scattered all over the Internet are World Wide Web servers. Using your WWW client you can easily access these servers and the information they contain.

7 When you are done exploring type **quit** ↵ to quit the public WWW client and close the Telnet connection to CERN.

TIP SHEET

> ▶ Remember, when you use Telnet to access CERN's public WWW client, you are connecting to a remote machine in Switzerland. Sometimes this overseas connection doesn't function as quickly as connections within the United States. In the next section we'll telnet to a fancier public WWW client located in the United States.
>
> ▶ It is difficult to determine whether or not you have a WWW client installed on your Internet host. Check with your system administrator. If you don't have one, the home page of CERN's public WWW client can tell your system administrator where to find a WWW client to install on your Internet host.

There are 64 links to choose from on this page.

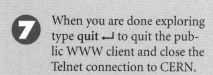

```
                              The World-Wide Web Virtual Library: Subject Catalogue
                                          THE WWW VIRTUAL LIBRARY

            This is a distributed subject catalogue. See also arrangement  by  service
            type[1] ., and other subject catalogues of network information[2] .

            Mail to maintainers of the specified subject or www-request@info.cern.ch to
            add pointers to this list, or if you would like to contribute to
            administration of a subject area.

            See also how to put your data on the web[3]

            Aeronautics              Mailing list archive index[4] . See also NASA LaRC[5]

            Agriculture              See Agricultural info[6] ,  Almanac mail servers[7] ;
                                     the Agricultural Genome[8] (National Agricultural
                                     Library, part of the U.S. Department of Agriculture)

            Archaeology[9]           Separate list
            Astronomy and Astrophysics[10]
                                     Separate list.

            1-64, Back, Up, <RETURN> for more, Quit, or Help:
```

6 You are looking at the subject catalog of the World Wide Web. Press ↵ to scroll to the next page and type u ↵ to scroll to the previous page. To go back to the page you jumped from, type b ↵. If at any point you feel lost, you can press Home ↵ to return to your home page.

2 Rather than menus, the World Wide Web (WWW) uses text. Each page of straight text displayed on your screen contains specially marked phrases, which are actually pointers that lead you directly to the resource being discussed. As with Gopher, these resources may be on the same WWW server or on a WWW server somewhere else in the world. The combination of straight text and jumping make WWW a valuable browsing program on the Internet.

```
> telnet info.cern.ch
Trying 128.141.201.214...
Connected to www0.cern.ch.

UNIX(r) System V Release 4.0 (www0)
```

3 The World Wide Web (WWW) was developed by CERN, a European center for research in high-energy physics that is located in Switzerland. In this section we'll use Telnet to access their public WWW client. One advantage of this client is that it doesn't require a vt100 terminal; you can use it with line-oriented terminal emulation. Type

```
telnet info.cern.ch ↵
```

to connect to this public WWW client.

```
                                          Overview of the Web
                 GENERAL OVERVIEW OF THE WEB
   There is no "top" to the World-Wide Web. You can look at it from many points
   of view. Here are some places to start.

by Subject[1]          The Virtual Library organises information by subject
                       matter.

list of servers[2]     All registered HTTP servers by country

by Service Type[3]     The Web includes data accessible by many other
                       protocols. The lists by access protocol may help if
                       you know what kind of service you are looking for.

   If you find a useful starting point for you personally, you can configure
   your WWW browser to start there by default.

   See also: About the W3 project[4] .
     [End]

1-4, Back, Up, Quit, or Help:
```

```
                                          Welcome to the World-Wide Web
              THE WORLD-WIDE WEB

  This is just one of many access points to the web, the universe of
  information available over networks. To follow references, just type the
  number then hit the return (enter) key.

  The features you have by connecting to this telnet server are very primitive
  compared to the features you have when you run a W3 "client" program on your
  own computer. If you possibly can, please pick up a client for your platform
  to reduce the load on this service and  experience the web in its full
  splendor.

  For more information, select by number:

A list of available W3 client programs[1]
Everything about the W3 project[2]
Places to start exploring[3]
The First International WWW Conference[4]

  This telnet service is provided by the WWW team at the European Particle
  Physics Laboratory known as CERN[5]
    [End]
1-5, Up, Quit, or Help:
```

Type 3 to jump to this page.

4 When you connect to this WWW server, you will see the *home page*. You will always start here when you use this public WWW client at CERN. Rather than menus, WWW pages provide straight text. Notice that the text includes numbers in square brackets—as in [1] or [9]. These are pointers to other documents, which you can jump to by typing the bracketed number. The pointers are like Gopher's menu items and their hidden addresses.

5 Let's jump to *Places to start exploring*. Type **3** ↵. You are now at the general overview of the World Wide Web with a choice of three different perspectives. Type **1** ↵ to continue exploring by subject.

Browsing the World Wide Web

CERN's line-oriented WWW client is pretty plain. If you can emulate a vt100 terminal as described in Chapter 2, you can take advantage of a much nicer WWW client located at the University of Kansas. In addition to fancier screen displays, this WWW client provides a home page with listings of some interesting Internet resources in the United States. It's easy to get overwhelmed by all the choices and information, but in a short time you'll feel very comfortable with browsing both the World Wide Web and Gopherspace.

TIP SHEET

▶ More and more people are using the Internet, and WWW is a very popular service. For these reasons, you may have to wait a long time to receive a document, or, in some cases, you may not even be able to make a connection.

▶ To see if you have Lynx on your Internet host, type lynx ↵ at your UNIX prompt. If UNIX responds with "command not found," you need to speak with your system administrator about having the software installed. Lynx's home page provides some information about obtaining a copy of the program.

▶ When using Lynx you can jump directly to a resource if you know its hidden address. You'll recognize these addresses because they begin with the characters http://. To jump to one of these addresses, type g. Lynx will prompt you with *URL to open:*. Type the address, beginning with http://, and press ↵. This direct access method saves you from trying to find your way through a series of links.

```
> telnet ukanaix.cc.ukans.edu
Trying 129.237.33.1...
Connected to ukanaix.cc.ukans.edu.
```

▶ **1** The name of the client we'll be using is Lynx. To access it, type

telnet ukanaix.cc.ukans.edu ↵

and, at the *login* prompt, type www ↵.

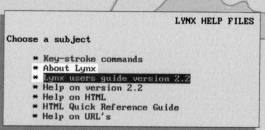

7 Lynx also provides a nice help facility. Type **?** to access help, and Lynx will allow you to read its User Guide on your terminal. The other sections on HTML and URLs are technical descriptions of how the addresses of WWW work. These are more appropriate for an advanced user. When you are done using Lynx you can quit by typing q and then y when asked if you really want to quit.

You can mail yourself files that you like.

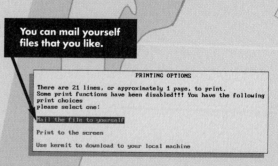

6 How can you get your own copy of a document that interests you? When you are viewing the document, type p to access Lynx's printing options. Since you're using a public version of Lynx at the University of Kansas, you can't have Lynx automatically print a paper copy for you. However, one of your choices is to mail the file to yourself. When you select this option, Lynx asks for your e-mail address and then sends you a copy of the file.

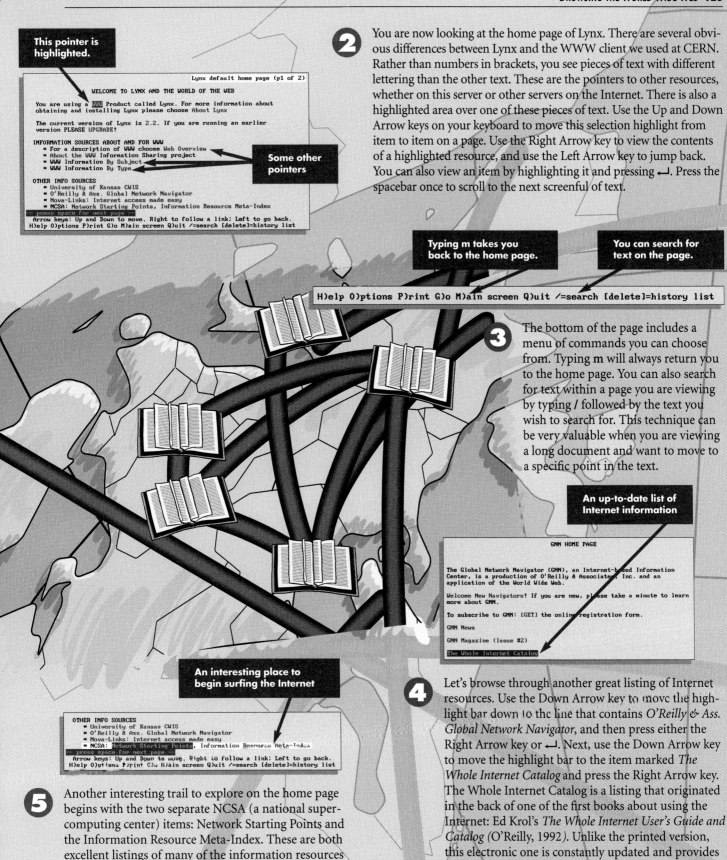

This pointer is highlighted.

```
                              Lynx default home page (p1 of 2)
      WELCOME TO LYNX AND THE WORLD OF THE WEB

You are using a WWW Product called Lynx. For more information about
obtaining and installing Lynx please choose About Lynx

The current version of Lynx is 2.2. If you are running an earlier
version PLEASE UPGRADE!

INFORMATION SOURCES ABOUT AND FOR WWW
     * For a description of WWW choose Web Overview
     * About the WWW Information Sharing project
     * WWW Information By Subject
     * WWW Information By Type

OTHER INFO SOURCES
     * University of Kansas CWIS
     * O'Reilly & Ass. Global Network Navigator
     * Nova-Links: Internet access made easy
     * NCSA: Network Starting Points, Information Resource Meta-Index
-- press space for next page --
Arrow keys: Up and Down to move. Right to follow a link; Left to go back.
H)elp O)ptions P)rint G)o M)ain screen Q)uit /=search [delete]=history list
```

Some other pointers

2 You are now looking at the home page of Lynx. There are several obvious differences between Lynx and the WWW client we used at CERN. Rather than numbers in brackets, you see pieces of text with different lettering than the other text. These are the pointers to other resources, whether on this server or other servers on the Internet. There is also a highlighted area over one of these pieces of text. Use the Up and Down Arrow keys on your keyboard to move this selection highlight from item to item on a page. Use the Right Arrow key to view the contents of a highlighted resource, and use the Left Arrow key to jump back. You can also view an item by highlighting it and pressing ↵. Press the spacebar once to scroll to the next screenful of text.

Typing m takes you back to the home page.

You can search for text on the page.

```
H)elp O)ptions P)rint G)o M)ain screen Q)uit /=search [delete]=history list
```

3 The bottom of the page includes a menu of commands you can choose from. Typing **m** will always return you to the home page. You can also search for text within a page you are viewing by typing **/** followed by the text you wish to search for. This technique can be very valuable when you are viewing a long document and want to move to a specific point in the text.

An up-to-date list of Internet information

```
                    GNN HOME PAGE

The Global Network Navigator (GNN), an Internet-based Information
Center, is a production of O'Reilly & Associates, Inc. and an
application of the World Wide Web.

Welcome New Navigators! If you are new, please take a minute to learn
more about GNN.

To subscribe to GNN: [GET] the online registration form.

GNN News

GNN Magazine (Issue #2)

The Whole Internet Catalog
```

An interesting place to begin surfing the Internet

```
OTHER INFO SOURCES
     * University of Kansas CWIS
     * O'Reilly & Ass. Global Network Navigator
     * Nova-Links: Internet access made easy
     * NCSA: Network Starting Points, Information Resource Meta-Index
-- press space for next page --
Arrow keys: Up and Down to move, Right to follow a link; Left to go back.
H)elp O)ptions P)rint G)o M)ain screen Q)uit /=search [delete]=history list
```

4 Let's browse through another great listing of Internet resources. Use the Down Arrow key to move the highlight bar down to the line that contains *O'Reilly & Ass. Global Network Navigator*, and then press either the Right Arrow key or ↵. Next, use the Down Arrow key to move the highlight bar to the item marked *The Whole Internet Catalog* and press the Right Arrow key. The Whole Internet Catalog is a listing that originated in the back of one of the first books about using the Internet: Ed Krol's *The Whole Internet User's Guide and Catalog* (O'Reilly, 1992). Unlike the printed version, this electronic one is constantly updated and provides an excellent resource. When you are done looking around, type **m** to return to the home page.

5 Another interesting trail to explore on the home page begins with the two separate NCSA (a national supercomputing center) items: Network Starting Points and the Information Resource Meta-Index. These are both excellent listings of many of the information resources available via the Internet. The best part is that you can browse their contents using Lynx.

CHAPTER 14

Searching for Specific Resources on the Internet

 A key reason for using the Internet is to tap into the vast amount of information it makes available. Unfortunately, you need to know exactly where information is located to gain access to it. What do you do if you know what you're looking for but have no idea where to find it in the global network? This chapter discusses three programs offering solutions: Archie, Veronica, and WAIS.

Archie locates files in public ftp archives. You give it a file's name or partial name, and Archie searches its database and tells you about all the files that match that name or partial name. You can use anonymous ftp to retrieve your own copies of the files Archie tells you about.

Veronica appears as a menu item when you use Gopher. It helps you find Gopher servers containing specific information such as introductions to the Internet. You provide Veronica with a word or words that describe your interest and it builds a special Gopher menu consisting of all the menu items in its database that match the words you provide. You then browse the contents of this menu as you would any other Gopher menu.

WAIS (Wide Area Information Server, pronounced "ways") maintains separate indexes of the contents of selected documents, like the indexes you find in the back of a book. You choose an index and provide WAIS with the word or words you're looking for, and it provides a list of the documents in that index that contain those words. WAIS also allows you to read those documents. Even better solutions to resource location are emerging. These include Mosaic, Netscape, OS/2 Warp, and Windows 95.

Finding Things on the Internet

Finding the information you need on the Internet can be a time-consuming task. Even if your exhaustive searching comes up with nothing, you can never be sure that you didn't miss something. This section discusses some ways of improving your likelihood of finding what you are seeking on the Internet.

▶ **1** FAQs, the lists of frequently asked questions and their answers from Usenet newsgroups, are a great resource for locating information. They often provide a list of Internet sites with information pertaining to the interests of the newsgroup. There are also an increasing number of resources—such as Scott Yanoff's list that you retrieved in Chapter 10 —that supply the addresses of other interesting resources on the Internet. You'll find addresses for several of these resource lists in the Appendix at the back of this book.

7 Finally, human language usually provides more than one way to say the same thing. When searching with a computer, think of the different words that express the concept you're interested in—for example "beginner" and "novice." You may need to perform several searches, each using a different word, to find the information you want.

TIP SHEET

▶ **Computers are essentially dumb machines that follow your instructions literally. When selecting words to search for, think about plural and other forms of the word. If you ask the computer to look for the word "dummy," it will ignore all the documents about "dummies" because you have not requested them. You may want to search several times using variations of the word or words of interest. You might also want to search for "dumm" or "dumm*" which will yield both. Wildcards help to overcome the problem.**

▶ **If a particular search yields a null result set, check carefully for typing errors in your search text. The computer will not correct your spelling, and transposed letters can be difficult to spot.**

6 When searching with a computer, be sure to use words that are appropriately descriptive and don't have multiple meanings. If you're choosing between "locomotives" and "trains," for instance, keep in mind that "trains" also refers to teaching someone how to perform a task. If you search for documents using the word "trains," the computer will trace documents based upon both meanings of this word.

2 The greatest information-finding source on the Internet is not a program. It's the users who are constantly out there exploring. People on the Internet are usually glad to help you find information you're looking for. Usenet newsgroups are a great way of contacting people who might know the location of the information you want. Chapters 8 and 9 discuss Usenet. And remember, netiquette says check the group's FAQ for your answer before asking people in the group.

3 There are already several books—such as *The Internet Directory* by Eric Braun—that provide lists of information resources on the Internet. You'll find several of these books listed in the Appendix, and you can expect their number to grow within the next year.

4 The three programs discussed in this chapter—Archie, Veronica, and WAIS— are also excellent ways of tracking down the information you need. None of them covers the entire Internet. You may need to use all three to find the information you're searching for.

5 When searching for information using a computer program, you are likely to encounter two phenomena: information overload and the null result set. Information overload occurs when you search for words—such as "internet"—that are so widely used that the searching program finds hundreds or thousands of possible documents for you. To solve this problem, try searching for more specific words. The null result set is the opposite: Your search text is so specific that nothing matches it. For example, this might happen if you search for "neophyte" rather than "beginner." The resolution to this problem is to search for something a little more general.

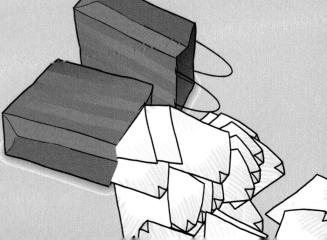

How to Use Archie

Archie is a service that helps you find files in archives that are scattered across the Internet and accessible by ftp. During the night, Archie servers connect with all the ftp sites they know about and make a list of all the files available via anonymous ftp. This information is stored in a database that you can query. All Archie servers have identical databases. If you know the name (or even partial name) of a file, you can ask Archie and it will give you the location of the file—both the address and the path. You can then grab a copy of the file for yourself using anonymous ftp, as described in Chapter 10.

TIP SHEET

▶ **Archie is widely used during the day. If you use Archie at night, you won't have to wait nearly as long for it to perform your search.**

▶ **As you look over your search results and decide where to ftp a file from, try to limit yourself to the United States. Even though it seems really cool to ftp files from other countries and continents, you shouldn't do so if you can get the file from a closer location. Transferring files over unnecessarily long distances is considered bad netiquette.**

▶ **Type archie ↵ at your UNIX prompt to see if you have a program on your Internet host that will automatically talk to the nearest Archie server. If you do not, use Telnet to connect as shown in step 2. If the Archie program on your Internet host doesn't look like the one you used via Telnet, it's probably an old version. Ask your system administrator to update the program.**

▶ **If you want to prevent the results of your Archie search from scrolling by on your screen, type set pager ↵ at the Archie prompt. Then you can use the spacebar to see the next screenful of search results. When you are done paging through them, you can still mail yourself a set as you did in step 5.**

1 Archie is a very popular service and is used around the world. If there were just one Archie server it would collapse from overuse, so there are several. Netiquette dictates that you attempt to use the one nearest to you. The figure shows the addresses of four Archie servers in the eastern United States and a fifth in Nebraska. Please use the one nearest to you.

Archie tells you which host the file is in and the path to it.

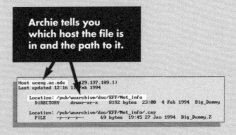

6 Wait about 10 minutes and then check your electronic mailbox for mail from the Archie server. The results give you a machine to connect with using anonymous ftp, followed by the information about the files at that address. The results of my search show that one option is to ftp to uceng.uc.edu, log in as anonymous, and go to the directory /pub/wuarchive/doc/EFF/Net_info, where I will find a directory named Big_Dummy. I will probably find a copy of the electronic book there. If that doesn't work out, I can try some of the other places listed in the search results.

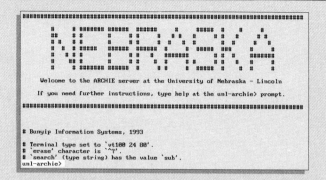

```
# Bunyip Information Systems, 1993

# Terminal type set to `vt100 24 80'.
# `erase' character is `^?'.
# `search' (type string) has the value `sub'.
unl-archie>
```

2 You can connect to Archie via Telnet. Type **telnet** followed by the address of the Archie server you'll be using and ↵. Since I'm on the West Coast, I type

telnet archie.unl.edu ↵

Next, at the *login* prompt, type **archie** ↵. If you are asked for a password, just press ↵. Once you are logged in, Archie will display its opening screen and then its prompt. This is where you will type commands to the Archie server.

```
unl-archie> set search sub
unl-archie> set mailto markhb@shell.portal.com
unl-archie>
```

3 You need to configure Archie to perform the way you want it to. At the prompt, type

set search sub ↵

so you can search for partial words rather than whole words only. At the next prompt, type **set mailto** followed by your Internet address and ↵. This tells Archie where to e-mail the results of your search. These settings will be in effect for the rest of this session. Each time you Telnet to Archie you'll need to re-enter these commands.

The waits are shorter when you search at night.

```
# Search type: sub.
# Your queue position: 1
# Estimated time for completion: 00:07
working... /
```

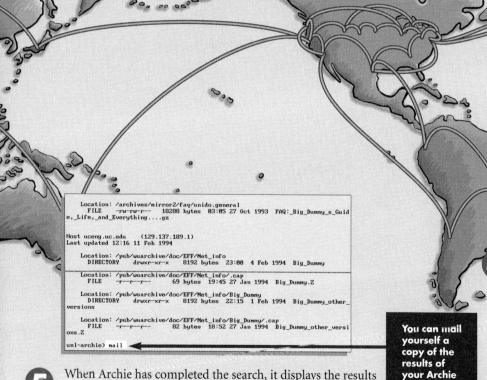

You can mail yourself a copy of the results of your Archie search.

4 Now search for a place where you can grab a copy of The Electronic Frontier Foundation's *Big Dummy's Guide to the Internet* using anonymous ftp. Type **prog big_dummy** ↵. The prog command tells Archie to search its database of filenames. Since you configured Archie to match partial words, searching for big_dummy is effectively searching for big_dummy* where * represents any character or string of characters. Note too that Archie doesn't care if your search word(s) are upper- or lowercase; it matches both. Archie tells you your position in the line of people asking questions, and estimates the time it will take to complete your search.

5 When Archie has completed the search, it displays the results on your screen—a list of files and their addresses. The results of an Archie search usually occupy more than one screen, so you'll see lots of text scrolling by. Immediately after Archie has shown you the results, type **mail** ↵ at the first prompt, and a copy of all these results will be sent to the address you entered in step 3. Now that you've completed the search, type **quit** ↵ to close your connection to Archie.

How to Use Veronica

Like Archie, Veronica allows you to find specific items, but its database consists only of menu items that it finds in Gopherspace. Veronica servers search through Gopherspace at night, keeping a list of all the menu items they find. Using a Gopher client, you ask Veronica to search through its database for your search text. Veronica then creates a custom, one-time Gopher menu for you based on your search. Veronica helps transform Gopher from a means of browsing to a means of finding specific items within Gopherspace.

TIP SHEET

▶ **If you have a local Gopher client, you can connect directly to the University of Minnesota's main menu when you start up by typing**

`gopher consultant.micro.umn.edu ↵`

This can save time if you don't want to have to traverse your local menus. It can also be helpful if your local Gopher menus do not provide access to the University of Minnesota.

▶ **Why search only directory titles in Veronica?** Directory titles provide a convenient way to maximize the results of your search. Directories are containers for files about a specific topic. If you searched using the word "humor" you would get a menu of directories with that word in their labels. But you also get access to all the files in those directories, many of which will *not* have the word "humor" in their name even though they are about "humor." Unfortunately there is no way to find files with a humorous contents that are not in a directory labeled "humor" or that don't have a filename including the word "humor."

▶ **1** To use Veronica you must begin with Gopher. If you haven't already read the sections on Gopher in Chapter 13, please do so before continuing. We'll use the public Gopher client at the University of Minnesota, but you can access Veronica through your local Gopher client as well. Type

`telnet consultant.micro.umn.edu ↵`

and at the *login* prompt, type **gopher** ↵ to run the public client. Remember, you'll need to emulate a vt100 terminal.

6 You can mail yourself copies of any items you find interesting by following the instructions given in Chapter 13. When you are done looking at this menu, type **u** to return to the menu of Veronica servers. Once you've left your special custom menu, you can only return by initiating another search. To exit the Gopher client and close your Telnet connection, type **q**.

```
                Search gopherspace at SUNET: internet beginner
-->  1.  Review of The Internet Companion: A Beginner's Guide to Global Netw..
     2.  Beginner's On-line Internet Training
     3.  Zen and the Art of the Internet -- A Beginner's Guide to the Inter../
     4.  fyi-internet-beginner-FAQ.txt [14Jul92, 90kb]
     5.  Beginner's Guide to The Internet Available
     6.  Zen and the art of the Internet: a beginner's guide to the
     7.  Zen and the Art of the Internet-A Beginner's Guide to the Internet/
     8.  Zen and the Art of the Internet-A Beginner's Guide to the Internet/
     9.  The Internet Companion: A Beginner's Guide to Global Networking/
    10.  The Internet Companion: A Beginner's Guide To Global Networking
    11.  U1206 - The Beginner's Guide to the Internet Program
    12.  "The Beginner's Guide to the Internet"
    13.  Reply to "The Beginner's Guide to the Internet"
    14.  Re: Reply to "The Beginner's Guide to the Internet"
    15.  Re: "The Beginner's Guide to the Internet"
    16.  REVIEW: A Beginner's Guide to the Internet
    17.  The Q&A for Internet beginner
    18.  Internet Beginner's Guide
```

5 Take a look at the menu Veronica creates for you. Sometimes "internet" comes before "beginner" in a menu item, and other times not. Notice also that some of the items are directories and others are files. You can explore the contents of this menu as you would any other Gopher menu.

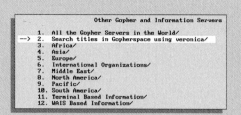

```
        Other Gopher and Information Servers
    1.  All the Gopher Servers in the World/
--> 2.  Search titles in Gopherspace using veronica/
    3.  Africa/
    4.  Asia/
    5.  Europe/
    6.  International Organizations/
    7.  Middle East/
    8.  North America/
    9.  Pacific/
   10.  South America/
   11.  Terminal Based Information/
   12.  WAIS Based Information/
```

2 In the main menu, select the item *Other Gopher and Information Servers*, pressing ↵ when the arrow on the left of your screen points at the item. (Remember, you move this arrow with your arrow keys.) At the next menu select *Search titles in Gopherspace using veronica* and press ↵.

```
            Search titles in Gopherspace using veronica
    1.
    2.  FAQ:  Frequently-Asked Questions about veronica  (1993/08/23)
    3.  How to compose  veronica queries (NEW June 24) READ ME!!
    4.  Search Gopher Directory Titles at PSINet <?>
    5.  Search Gopher Directory Titles at SUNET <?>
    6.  Search Gopher Directory Titles at U. of Manitoba <?>
    7.  Search Gopher Directory Titles at University of Cologne <?>
    8.  Search gopherspace at PSINet <?>
--> 9.  Search gopherspace at SUNET <?>
   10.  Search gopherspace at U. of Manitoba <?>
   11.  Search gopherspace at University of Cologne <?>
```

3 The menu for Veronica lets you choose from several servers and gives you the option of searching only directory titles or all of Gopherspace (that is, directory and file titles). In this case we'll select all of Gopherspace at SUNET since we don't want to limit ourselves to just directories and the other three servers are outside of the United States. Select the item *Search gopherspace at SUNET*. Sometimes the Veronica servers aren't accepting connections—either because of maintenance or because there are already too many users. If your connection is refused you have no choice but to try again at another time.

Internet Restaurant

Today's Special

Veronica's custom menu *created for search of* 'internet beginner'

```
                  Search gopherspace at SUNET
 Words to search for

 internet beginner

            [Cancel: ^G] [Erase: ^U] [Accept: Enter]
```

4 You are now prompted for a word or words to search for. Type **internet beginner** ↵. Veronica will now create a special menu consisting of all the menu items in the database that contain the words "internet" and "beginner," regardless of their order in the item label. You'll notice that searching for "beginner" also yields "beginner's," since Veronica automatically assumes you have a wildcard—which represents any character of set of characters—at the end of each word you're searching for. Veronica doesn't care about uppercase and lowercase; it will match both.

How to Use WAIS

Archie and Veronica deal with filenames, directory names, and menu items. They don't really give you direct access to what's inside the documents. WAIS (Wide Area Information Server) indexes the contents of documents rather than document titles. Using WAIS is more like thumbing through the indexes in the back of books than like using a card catalog that lists book titles only. WAIS currently indexes much less information than either Archie or Veronica. Each WAIS server has its own unique set of indexes that you can search. If you are looking for some specific information that's likely to be contained within a file, WAIS is the search tool for you. There are currently WAIS indexes for everything from the Bible and the Koran to White House press briefings.

TIP SHEET

► If you have a local Gopher client, you can connect directly to the *WAIS Based Information* menu when you start up by typing

  `gopher gopher-gw.micro.umn.edu ↵`

► The World Wide Web is beginning to provide access to WAIS indexes. Check a WWW resources listing to use WAIS through WWW.

► To gain access to a public WAIS client that runs under vt100 terminal emulation, telnet to quake.think.com and type wais ↵ at the *login* prompt. The first time you do so, search for information about swais—the name of this client. Although the public WAIS client is very powerful, it is more complicated to use because of its intricate cycle of selecting databases and searching them to find more databases.

1 There are two ways of accessing WAIS servers: through a WAIS client or through Gopher. In this section we'll use Gopher because it makes WAIS much simpler to use. If you like WAIS, you are encouraged to try the public client listed in the Tip Sheet. To access WAIS through Gopher, type

  `telnet consultant.micro.umn.edu ↵`

and at the *login* prompt type **gopher** ↵ to run the public Gopher client.

7 When you are done looking at the documents in your search result, you can type **u** to return to the menu of indexes and select a new index to search. You can also type **q** at any time to quit Gopher and close your Telnet connection.

These four files in the internet_info WAIS database contain the word "beginner" (even though their titles don't).

6 The result of the search is displayed as a new Gopher menu where each item is a document that was selected because it contains the word "beginner." The order of the documents in the menu is important. The document in the top (number 1) spot contains the word "beginner" more often than the others. It's important to remember this when you get a menu with lots of items as a result of your search. The further you get from the top, the less frequently your word or words will be in the document. Since your WAIS search results are displayed as a Gopher menu, you just select an item to read its contents.

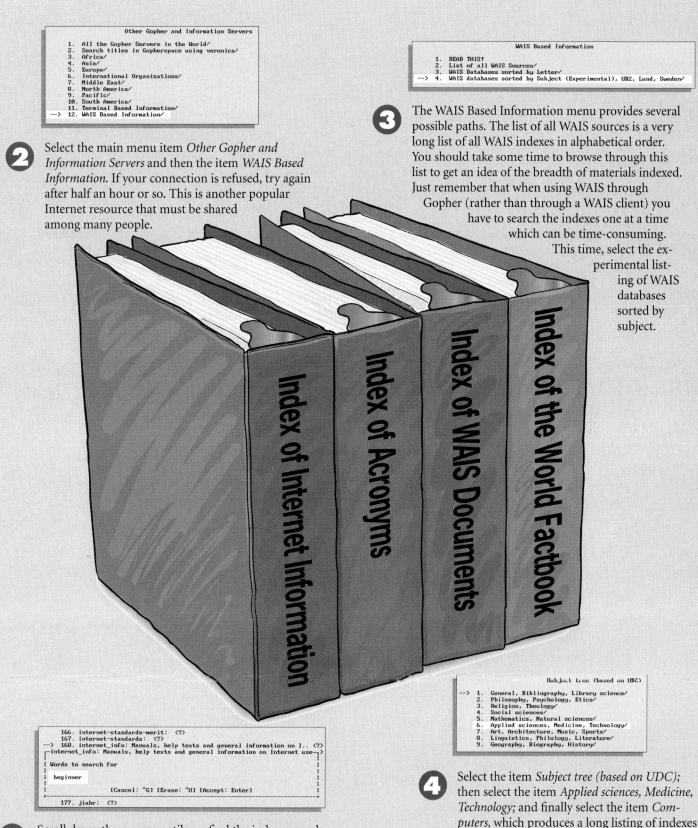

```
                 Other Gopher and Information Servers
       1.   All the Gopher Servers in the World/
       2.   Search titles in Gopherspace using veronica/
       3.   Africa/
       4.   Asia/
       5.   Europe/
       6.   International Organizations/
       7.   Middle East/
       8.   North America/
       9.   Pacific/
      10.   South America/
      11.   Terminal Based Information/
 -->  12.   WAIS Based Information/
```

2 Select the main menu item *Other Gopher and Information Servers* and then the item *WAIS Based Information*. If your connection is refused, try again after half an hour or so. This is another popular Internet resource that must be shared among many people.

```
                        WAIS Based Information
       1.   READ THIS!
       2.   List of all WAIS Sources/
       3.   WAIS Databases sorted by Letter/
 -->   4.   WAIS databases sorted by Subject (Experimental), UB2, Lund, Sweden/
```

3 The WAIS Based Information menu provides several possible paths. The list of all WAIS sources is a very long list of all WAIS indexes in alphabetical order. You should take some time to browse through this list to get an idea of the breadth of materials indexed. Just remember that when using WAIS through Gopher (rather than through a WAIS client) you have to search the indexes one at a time which can be time-consuming. This time, select the experimental listing of WAIS databases sorted by subject.

Index of Internet Information

Index of Acronyms

Index of WAIS Documents

Index of the World Factbook

```
                          Subject tree (based on UDC)
 -->   1.   General, Bibliography, Library science/
       2.   Philosophy, Psychology, Etics/
       3.   Religion, Theology/
       4.   Social sciences/
       5.   Mathematics, Natural sciences/
       6.   Applied sciences, Medicine, Technology/
       7.   Art, Architecture, Music, Sports/
       8.   Linguistics, Philology, Literature/
       9.   Geography, Biography, History/
```

```
      166.  internet-standards-merit:  <?>
      167.  internet-standards:  <?>
 -->  168.  internet_info: Manuals, help texts and general information on I.. <?>
  ┌─internet_info: Manuals, help texts and general information on Internet use─┐
  │                                                                           │
  │ Words to search for                                                       │
  │                                                                           │
  │ beginner                                                                  │
  │                                                                           │
  │               [Cancel: ^G] [Erase: ^U] [Accept: Enter]                    │
  │                                                                           │
      177.  jiahr:  <?>
```

4 Select the item *Subject tree (based on UDC)*; then select the item *Applied sciences, Medicine, Technology*; and finally select the item *Computers*, which produces a long listing of indexes to materials related to computers.

5 Scroll down the menus until you find the index named *internet_info* and select it. Gopher will prompt you for the word or words you want to search for. Type **beginner** ↵.

CHAPTER 15

Painless File Transfer with Winsock FTP

 The previous chapters have shown you the bare essentials of using the Internet with command line text. Beginning with this chapter you will start using the new generation of internet tools. With these tools you will find that you no longer need to know or remember specific commands. In fact, with the Windows interface, about all you need to know is how to point and click the mouse.

The first of these tools is the Winsock FTP. It is a *freeware* program available from several sources. Freeware means that it's free if you use it only for your own personal computing. With this tool you can then download all of the other software that makes cruising the Internet Super Highway as easy as taking a Sunday drive in the country. The Winsock FTP, and all of the other tools discussed in the remainder of this book, eliminate the need to know UNIX commands. The one requirement for using these new super-easy tools is an Internet provider that supports the Windows interface. Several of these are listed in the Appendix. You will also need to have a computer that runs windows and a working knowledge of how to use windows.

How to Access an Ftp Site

The official documentation for Winsock FTP, labeled WS_FTP, says that usage is obvious! Even so, a few examples can't hurt. WS_FTP is used to retrieve files from or send files to the Internet. Most usage will be in retrieving files. All you need to know from a command perspective is how to click the mouse. The rest of the work is done by the software.

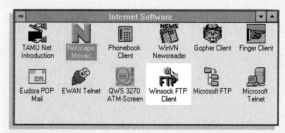

1 When the ftp window software is installed on your computer, just double click the mouse on the Winsock FTP icon. The *Session Profile* window will appear and you will be ready to transfer files after you supply the address of the ftp site.

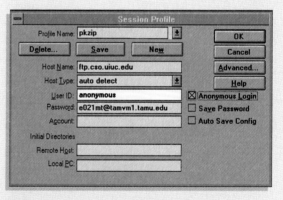

4 Since you will most likely be logging into ftp sites as anonymous, click the mouse on the box next to Anonymous Login. The software will then fill in the User ID box with anonymous, and if it knows your account ID it will put it in the Password box. This is not really a password but just a way for the ftp site to identify the various users. Leave the Host Type box on auto detect unless you know a good reason to change it.

2 The Winsock FTP software usually comes with several commonly accessed ftp site addresses already set up in the Session Profile window. The Oakland site shown is one of these preset sites. When you need to go to a site not already in the profile you click the mouse once on the New button. This clears the various address fields or text boxes.

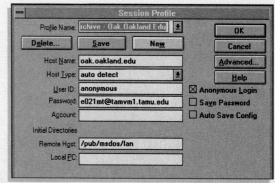

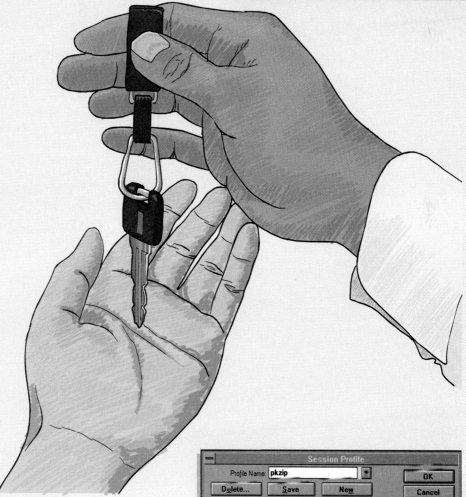

3 You will need to have software to decompress most files that you get through ftp. To get some information on a common one, *PKZIP*, use the mouse to move the cursor to the Profile Name box and type PKZIP. Then move the cursor to the Host Name box and type the ftp address exactly as given.

How to Access an Ftp Site (Continued)

O nce you have transferred to the ftp site, then you need to locate the file that you want to transfer.

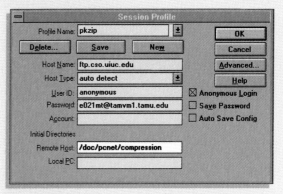

 5 Now you can go down (move the cursor) to the Remote Host box under Initial Directories and type in the directory that you want to go to. The profile is then set up to go to ftp site: ftp.cso.uiuc.edu and directory: /doc/pcnet/compression, which contains information on file compression programs. Now click the OK button and you are on your way to the site.

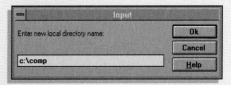

8 Now you are ready to create a directory on your computer to receive the transferred files (if you already have a directory, you will just need to switch to it with the ChDir button under Local System). Click the MkDir button under Local System and you will be asked to type in the new local directory name in the illustrated dialogue box. Click OK and then click ChDir to change to this new directory.

6 When the connection is successful you will see this screen. Notice that the window is split into two file systems. The one on the left is your computer, *Local System*, and the one on the right is for the system you went to by ftp, *Remote System*. Occasionally the system does not go to the directory specified in Remote Host; that is what happened here. In that case, you will need to scroll (use the scroll bar on the right side of the directory window) through the top window of the Remote System to change to the directory that you want.

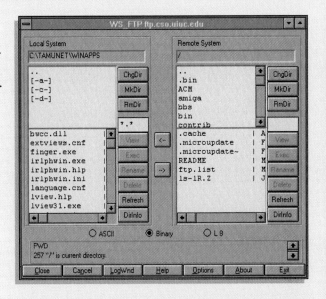

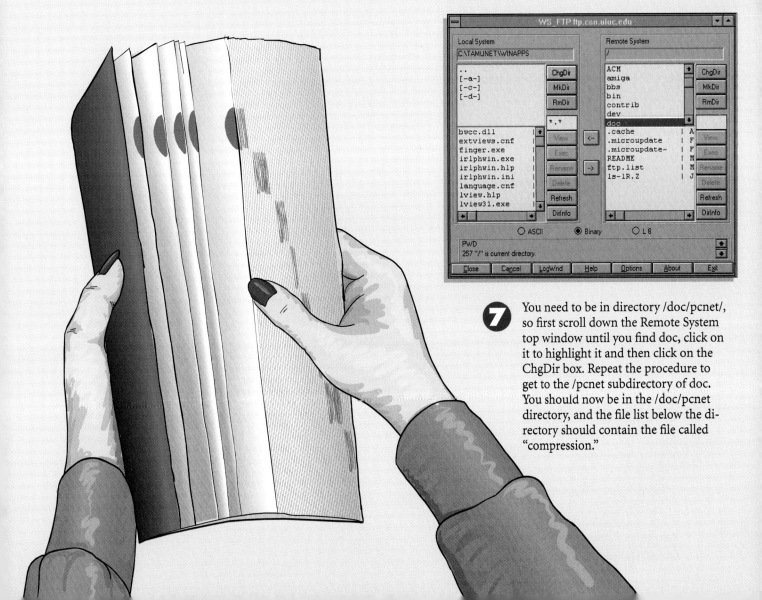

7 You need to be in directory /doc/pcnet/, so first scroll down the Remote System top window until you find doc, click on it to highlight it and then click on the ChgDir box. Repeat the procedure to get to the /pcnet subdirectory of doc. You should now be in the /doc/pcnet directory, and the file list below the directory should contain the file called "compression."

How to Access an Ftp Site (Continued)

O nce you have selected the file you want to transfer and changed to the directory on your system to where it will go, you are ready to do the transfer.

 Before you transfer the file, make sure that you have the correct directory specified for your computer under Local System. Highlight (click on) the name of the file you want to transfer under Remote System.

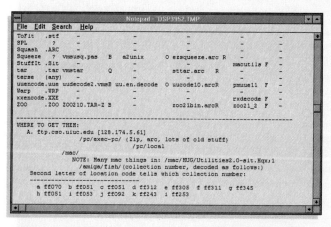

 The file compression that was transferred is a text file, which can be read on your system with a text editor. You could also look at this file before it is transferred by clicking the View button. This gives you information on compression programs and where they may be obtained.

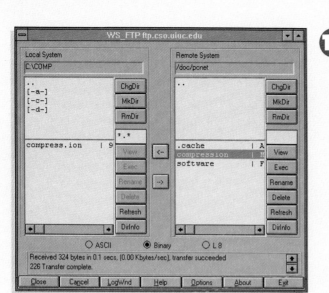

10 There is one more detail before doing the transfer. Notice the three circles marked ASCII, Binary, L8. Unless you know for certain what this should be set for, you should use Binary. This will transfer text and binary files correctly in most cases. If your file is corrupted after the transfer, you can always go back and try another setting.

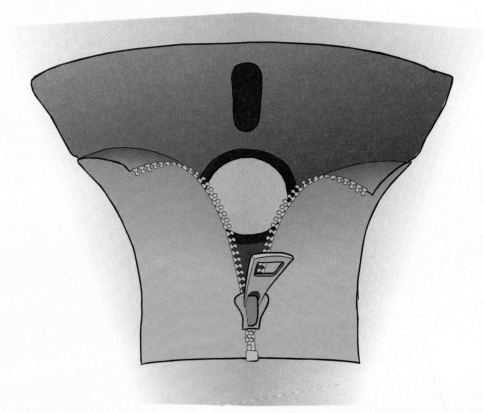

11 To complete the file transfer just click the ← box which shows the file going from the Remote System to your computer, the Local System.

How to Get and Install the Winsock FTP Software

Before you have the Winsock FTP software you will need to resort to the command line style of ftp, discussed in chapters 10 and 11, to obtain it. An alternative would be to ask your Internet service provider for it or to obtain it as part of one of the many Internet starter kits on the market.

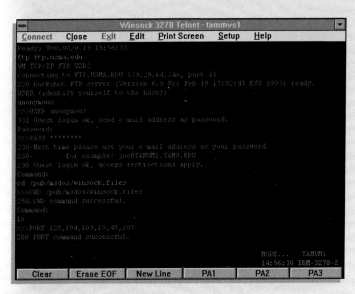

 1 Log onto you favorite command line ftp provider and type **ftp ftp.usma.edu,** press Enter, log in as "anonymous" and change to directory/pub/msdos/winsock.files.

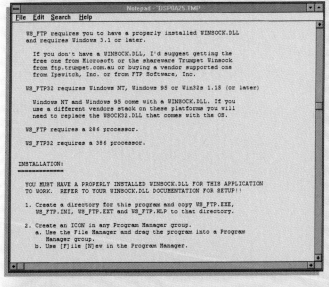 **4** The directions for installing the software are in the .txt file. Installation is straightforward but does require familiarity with the Windows environment.

TIP SHEET

▶ Even though you have a 386 processor or better you are most likely going to install ws_ftp rather than ws_ftp32. The installation is simpler and there is not a perceptible performance gain in ws_ftp32.

▶ The Winsock.dll that you need can be found in several places, one of these is ftp.microsoft.com directory /bussys.

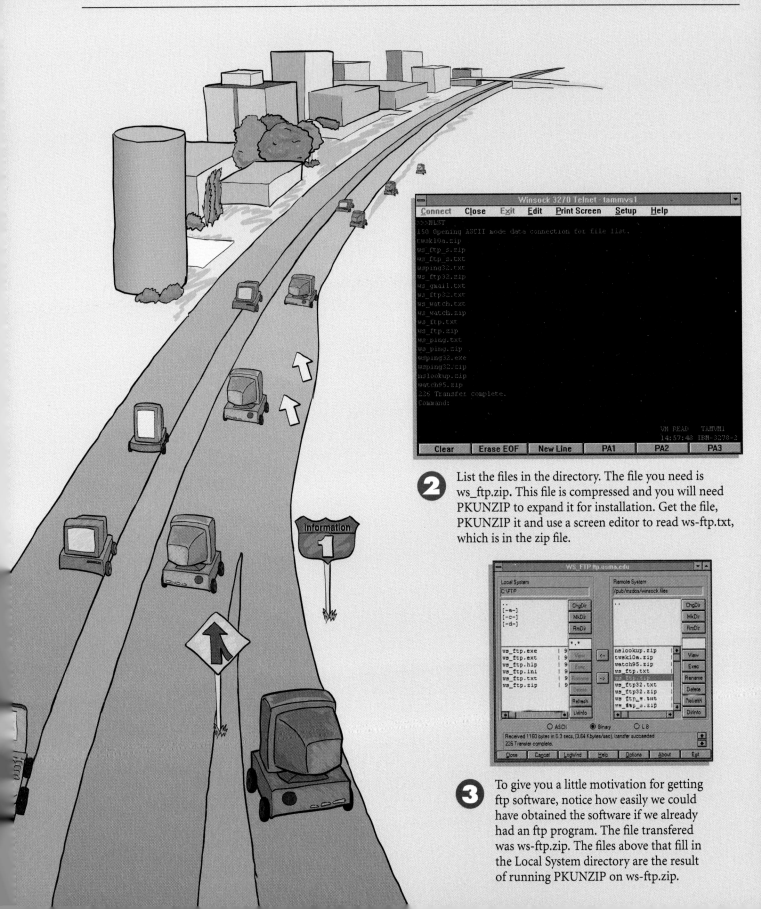

2 List the files in the directory. The file you need is ws_ftp.zip. This file is compressed and you will need PKUNZIP to expand it for installation. Get the file, PKUNZIP it and use a screen editor to read ws-ftp.txt, which is in the zip file.

3 To give you a little motivation for getting ftp software, notice how easily we could have obtained the software if we already had an ftp program. The file transferred was ws-ftp.zip. The files above that fill in the Local System directory are the result of running PKUNZIP on ws-ftp.zip.

CHAPTER 16

Easy Windows Mail Using Eudora

 Eudora is an e-mail program that allows you to send and receive e-mail in the windows environment. It is available as freeware and also as a more advanced commercial product. The program was named Eudora by Steve Dorner. He chose that name from the short story "Why I Live at the P.O." by Eudora Welty.

In order to use Eudora you will need to have an Internet provider that supports *POP* (Post Office Protocol) and provides you with an e-mail address. Eudora logs onto your Internet server account to send and receive mail. The major advantage is that you minimize the time you are logged onto your provider. You can read and compose the mail on your PC without being logged onto the Internet provider's server. Eudora provides a graphical editor for composing and browsing through your e-mail on your own computer. The mail files are also stored on your personal computer.

The only disadvantage to using Eudora arises if you check your e-mail from separate office and home computers. In that case the mail would reside on the computer you accessed it from. Unless your home and office computer were connected, this could prove to be inconvenient. There are some switches that can be set to accommodate two computers.

How to Configure Eudora

To use Eudora you will need an Internet service provider that has POP mail. You will also need an account number and password from this provider. Once you have this you are ready to set up your Eudora Mail software.

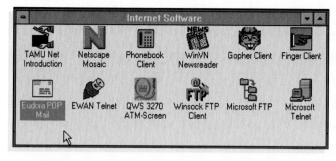

▶ **1** As with all of the window Internet tools, you start Eudora by double-clicking the Eudora Mail Icon.

4 At this point you should leave the other fields blank unless given specific direction by your provider. Now click OK and you are ready to test the software.

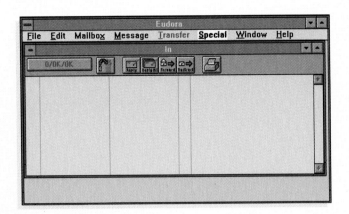

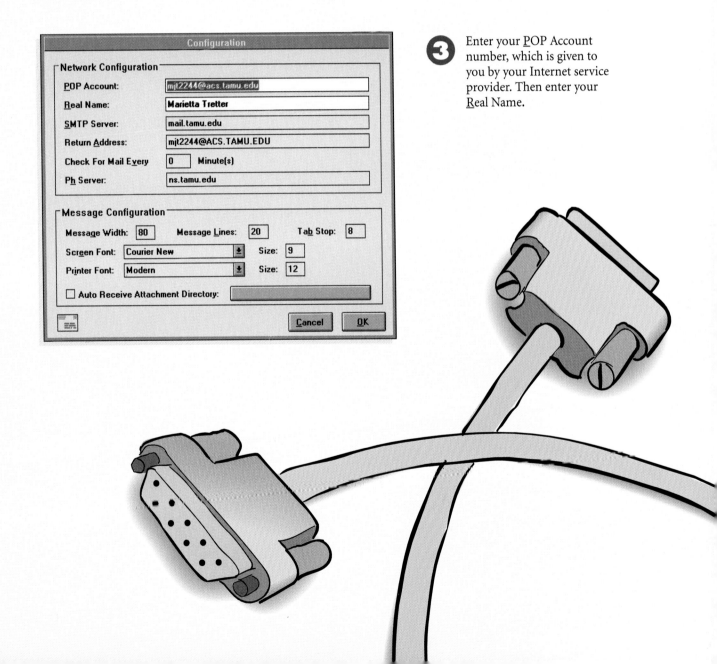

2 Before you can use Eudora you will need to configure it. Note the menu bar at the top of the screen. Pull down the Special menu bar and double-click (select) Configuration.

3 Enter your POP Account number, which is given to you by your Internet service provider. Then enter your Real Name.

How to Send Mail with Eudora

Once Eudora is configured, it is time to test the software. The easiest way to do this is to send a message to yourself. Once this works you can then explore the many features of Eudora, including sending documents.

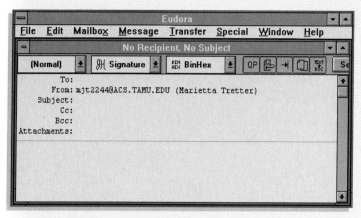

▶ **1** From the Message menu select New Menu. You should see a screen with your POP mail address and real name filled in.

4 Depending on how fast your modem and service provider are, you will see several different small dialogue boxes flash by on your screen. If all the boxes disappear, then the message has probably been forwarded correctly. If any remain, you may need to contact your service provider to correct any problems. Write down any information before contacting the provider.

TIP SHEET

▶ If you would like to end all of your messages with some expression like "May the bird of paradise fly up your nose," select **Signature** from the **Window** menu. Once you have created your message you can have it added to what you send by selecting it in the **Signature** combo box above your message. You won't see it, but the recipient will.

▶ The **Normal** combo box above your message is used to select the priority of your mail. Priority can be higher or lower than normal.

2 To begin with, keep the message simple. In the To field enter your address (the address you see looks different because it is an alias—it is really another way of writing the From address). Next move or Tab to the Subject field and enter a subject. For now, skip the other fields and go to the message field below the line. Enter your message.

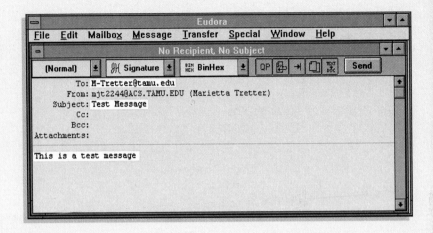

3 To send your message, click on the Send button.

How to Receive Mail Using Eudora

Once you have sent your test mail to yourself check to see if it arrived correctly. Remember that Eudora logs onto the service provider and automatically retrieves mail files and stores them on your computer's hard disk.

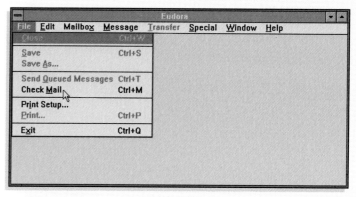

▶ ❶ To check your mail select Check Mail under the File Menu.

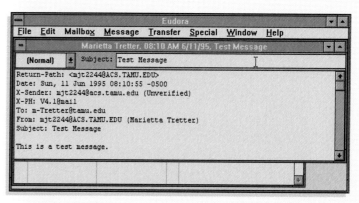

❺ The test message all fits on this small screen. However, to view longer messages you will need to use the scroll bar at the right of the screen.

TIP SHEET

▸ **Eudora usually transfers mail files to your PC and then deletes them from the server. If you check your mail from two different computers, you should select Switches from the Special menu and select Leave Mail on Server option. You can then read the mail a second time from another computer.**

▸ **If you have a slow modem you may also want to select Skip Big Messages under the Switches menu. This will prevent 40K or larger messages from being automatically transferred.**

2 Eudora will ask you for the password that goes with your Internet account or the account you have on the computer that has the POP mail server. Click OK after you have typed in your password. If you make a mistake, simply backspace and correct the password before clicking OK.

3 If you have mail and everything is working correctly you will hear a friendly tone and a mail message will appear. Click OK to see incoming mail.

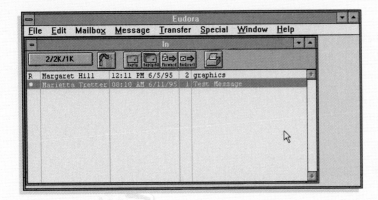

4 To view a specific message just double-click on the message; it will be highlighted and the message screen will appear. If you just want to select a message without viewing it, then click on it once.

How to Reply to a Message

Eudora's graphical editing capability makes it easy to reply to selected parts of a message without retyping the original message.

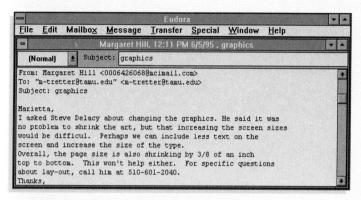

1 Suppose you want to reply to selected parts of a message. Close the message box by double-clicking the box just below the File menu bar.

4 If you want to respond to a particular line or sentence of the original message, move the cursor to that line and then insert a blank line(s) by hitting Enter. If a particular part of the old message is not relevant you can just delete it by Backspacing or highlight and Delete. When you are finished responding, click on Send and your reply will be forwarded.

2 Highlight the message you just closed and click the Reply button. You could also select Reply from the Message menu.

3 Notice that the message now has a > by each line of the original message. This marks the lines from the original message.

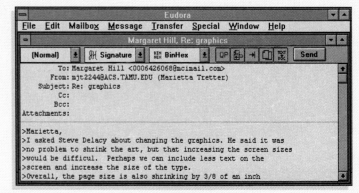

How to Create a Separate Mailbox

You can neatly organize your mail from different sources by creating separate mailboxes. Once you no longer need these mailboxes they are easily removed.

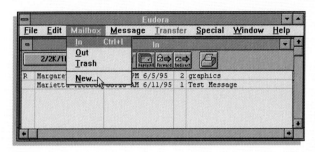

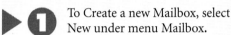

▶ **1** To Create a new Mailbox, select New under menu Mailbox.

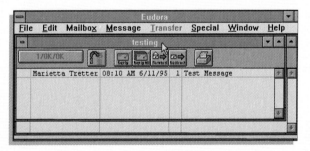

4 Select Testing under menu Mailbox and you should see the message that you transferred into this new mailbox.

TIP SHEET

▶ Note the Size box just above the message names. This gives you information on the number of messages and the approximate size of each.

▶ To remove an empty mailbox, select Mailboxes from the Window Menu and then select Remove. It is best to transfer the messages to the trash before doing this.

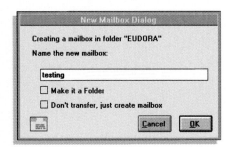

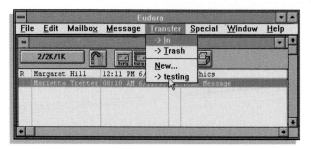

2 Type in the name that you want for the mailbox, in this case it is **testing.** Click OK.

3 Highlight or click on the message you want to transfer to the testing mailbox. Under the Transfer menu select ->testing.

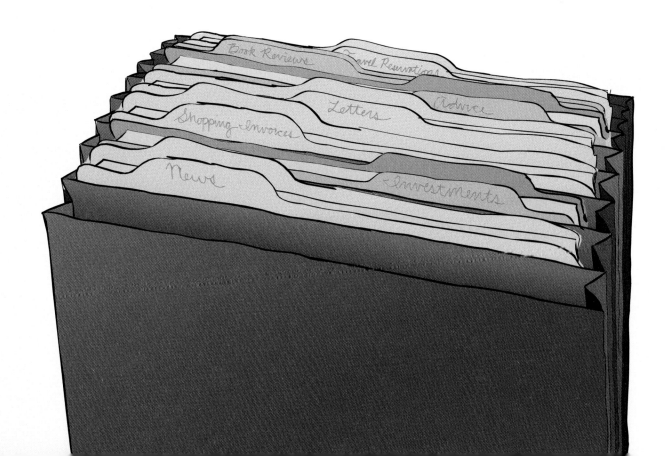

How to Attach a Document to a Message

I t is often necessary to send a document prepared with your word processor or other software. Eudora makes this task almost painless.

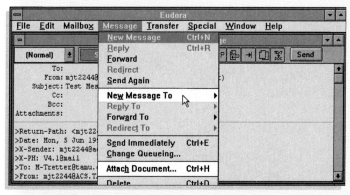

▶ **1** From the Message menu you will
first select New Message. Once you
have set up your message and are
ready to attach a document you will
select Attach Document from the
same menu.

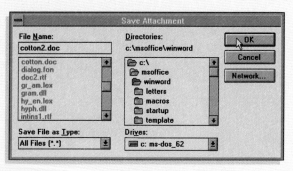

4 In order to check this procedure, try sending
a document to yourself. When you check your
mail Eudora will give you this screen and ask
you how you want to save the incoming document. It is saved here as cotton2.doc, a name
typed in when you receive the document.

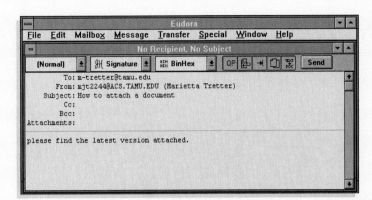

2 Set up your message as you would for sending an ordinary message. Then select Attach Document from the Message menu.

3 Scroll through the Directories until you find the directory containing the document you wish to attach. In this case it is in directory winword. Next, select the file and click OK.

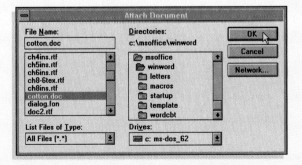

How to Keep Your Mailboxes Neat

If you send and receive a lot of mail, you can quickly create a large collection of unwanted files. In order to keep your disk space clean it is a good idea to frequently send unwanted mail and mailboxes to the trash.

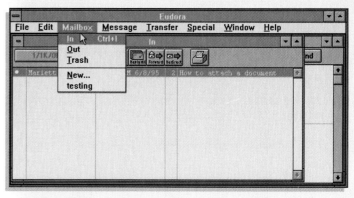

▶ **1** Select the Mailbox you wish to clean up. This includes In, Out, and any you have named, such as Testing.

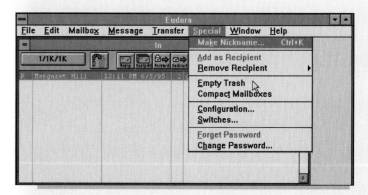

4 Empty the Trash by selecting Empty Trash in Special Menu. For those of you that use a Macintosh, this should look very familiar.

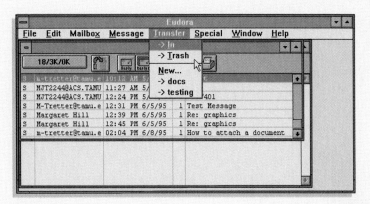

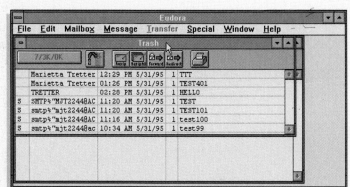

2 Click on the message you wish to remove (it will be highlighted). Then select Trash in the Transfer Menu.

3 Check to see if everything you wish to discard is in the Trash. Do this by selecting Trash in the Mailbox Menu.

How to Get and Install Eudora Software

Eudora is a very useful Mail Handler, and one of its best features is that you can obtain a working version of it for free. There is also a very well written and detailed manual that you can download with the software. Commercial versions are also available.

▶ **1** To obtain a freeware version of Eudora, ftp to ftp.qualcomm.com in directory /quest/eudora/windows/1.4. The commercial version is also available at this site as version 2.0. Be sure to check any downloaded software for viruses before executing.

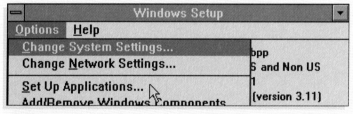

4 Once you have copied the Eudora .exe files to a directory such as C:\Eudora, go to Windows Setup and run Set Up Applications. That's about all there is to installing Eudora. If you need further information, check the manual, which you should have also downloaded.

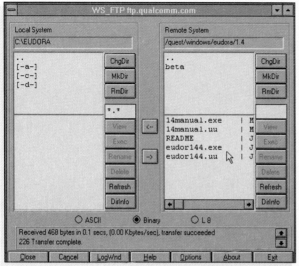

2 You can use Winsock FTP discussed in Chapter 15 to easily transfer the .exe files to your computer.

3 The Readme file indicates that you will need a copy of Winsock.dll. See Chapter 15 for a source for this file. If you have Winsock FTP you then already have one.

CHAPTER 17

WinVN,

a Freeware Newsreader
to Blow Your Trumpet About

 In Chapters 8 and 9 you learned how to work with News groups using command line software. This chapter will introduce you to the window interface newsreader, WinVN. This is a very simple-to-use newsreader that allows you to join groups, read articles, post new articles, and reply to existing articles. The software is free and is constantly being updated and improved by volunteer programmers.

Since WinVN functions in many ways like a mail system, you will need to have an e-mail address from your Internet provider. WinVN is comparable to another window's news reader called Trumpet. The main difference is that WinVN is freeware and Trumpet is shareware (you pay for it if you decide to use it). WinVN offers many options that would take many pages to explain. You should use the WinVN Help menu to explore the many features that are not discussed here.

How to Use WinVN

Since this newsreader has a windows interface you do not need to remember any commands to use it. Simply browse the menus until you find the command you need. It is that easy.

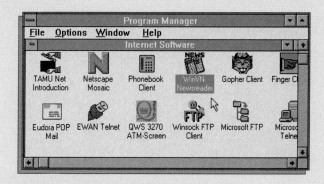

▶ **1** To begin WinVN simply double-click the icon and carefully read the screens as they appear. Your initial use will require some information from your Internet Provider. If you do not have the information, simply cancel and return when you do.

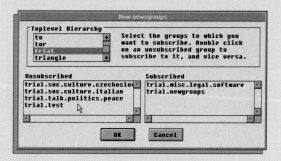

4 Once the list is complete you will be able to subscribe to any of the newsgroups. Select groups by simply double-clicking items of interest in the Unsubscribed column. If you don't know what you want, browse the Toplevel Hierarchy and then the corresponding Unsubscribed list. You can unsubscribe by double-clicking items in the Subscribe column.

2 The first time you use WinVN you will need to enter your e-mail address and your name and organization as you wish it to appear on any of your articles or responses to articles.

3 Whenever you start up WinVN it will put together a list of news groups. If you have a slow modem or a busy Internet provider this could take some time. Click Yes to set up the list.

How to View News Articles with WinVN

O ne has to know how to click the mouse to view articles; it's even easier than reading a newspaper.

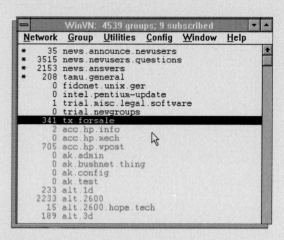

1 The list of groups is compiled in a window format. Double-click the group that you want to look at. A zero means the group is empty. Scroll the window to see all of the groups.

▶ If the format of an article is scrambled and unreadable try clicking ROT13 under the View menu. This is often done to hide potentially offensive material. The reader decides if they want to view it.

▶ When you are viewing an article with responses (a conversation) you can simply press F3 to view the next response in the conversation.

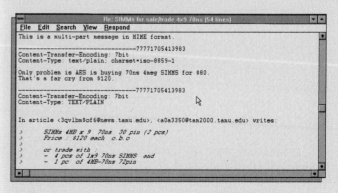

5 This is a reply to the reply to SIMMS for sale.

2 The highlighted article is the main article in the group tx.forsale. The bar on the article underneath it is a reply, and the bar on the article under it is a reply to the reply. This is how WinVN indicates articles and responses. Select and double-click to see the article.

3 This is the article SIMMS for sale.

4 This is a reply to the article SIMMS for sale.

How to Create a New Article and Respond to an Old Article

To get involved in a news group you need the basic tools for creating articles and responding to existing ones. WinVN has some very sophisticated tools that allow you to also share documents and even pictures. Only the basics will be discussed here. You should explore the other possibilities.

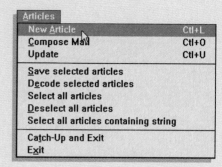

▶ **1** To create a New Article in a group open the Main Window of the group you want to post to (double-click the group name). In the Articles menu select New Article. The main group shown is tx.forsale. A dialogue box will appear and you can type in the name of your new article.

7 Go back and update the group window (under Articles menu) and you should see your response marked by the indented vertical bar.

6 Net etiquette dictates that you eliminate as many lines of the original message as possible before sending your response. Keep only those relevant to your response. Just highlight and delete the unneeded lines. Don't delete the initial address lines. Once you have the original message pared down, just type your response by moving the cursor to an appropriate place on the window. Then select Post Article.

TIP SHEET

▶ **As soon as you send your new article or response it is posted. So make sure it is what you want to do before clicking the Post Article selection.**

▶ **Notice that there is an Attach File option under the Posting menu. This allows you to include pictures, documents, and so forth. You may have to experiment some to find the best options for using this feature.**

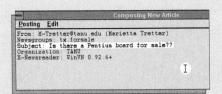

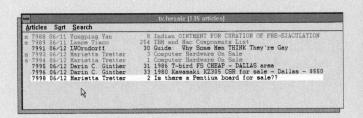

2 A box appears for your new article. Do not change any of the first lines in this box. Note the Subject box has the new article name typed in the dialogue box. Move the cursor below the typed lines and type your article. When you are finished go to the Posting menu and select Post Article. That's all there is to it.

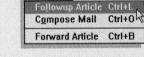

4 If you want to respond to an existing article, select the article by double-clicking on it. In the Article Respond menu bar select Follow-up Article bar. A dialog box appears with the title already entered. Click OK and you will see the original article message with > preceding each line.

3 Go back to the group main menu and under the Articles menu select Update. You should then see your new article with the subject name that you gave it.

5 A Posting screen appears with the information for the article you are responding to already filled in, so just click OK.

How to Get and Install WinVN

WinVN is free for the asking. You will need to have Winsock 1.1 or higher to use it. It is available from several sources. One source is to ftp to sunsite.unc.edu in directory /pub/micro/pc-stuff/ms-windows/winsock. With WinVN you definitely get more than you pay for.

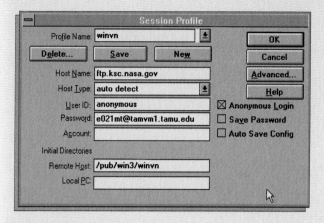

 WinVN is available on many sites. Some sites have older versions, so beware. The best site is ftp.ksc.nasa.gov because it is up to date and has a fast server.

TIP SHEET

▸ Some of the ftp sites for WinVN have source code and documentation available. These files will be denoted by SRC or DOC in their name.

▸ An older site that you might try is titan.ksc.nasa.gov. directory /pub/win3/winvn.

2 Note the files in directory /pub/winvn/win3 are in Unix format. It is best to transfer one file at a time and rename it to avoid PC file problems. Transfer files to an appropriate WinVN directory on your computer.

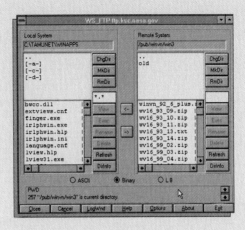

3 To install WinVN, first unzip the files. Read the Readme files and then use Set Up Applications under Windows Setup to install WinVN.exe in your Internet program group.

4 The very first time you run WinVN this dialog box will appear. You will need to get NNTP and SMTP information from your Internet provider. You can try to leave TCP port set at nntp, which will work in most cases.

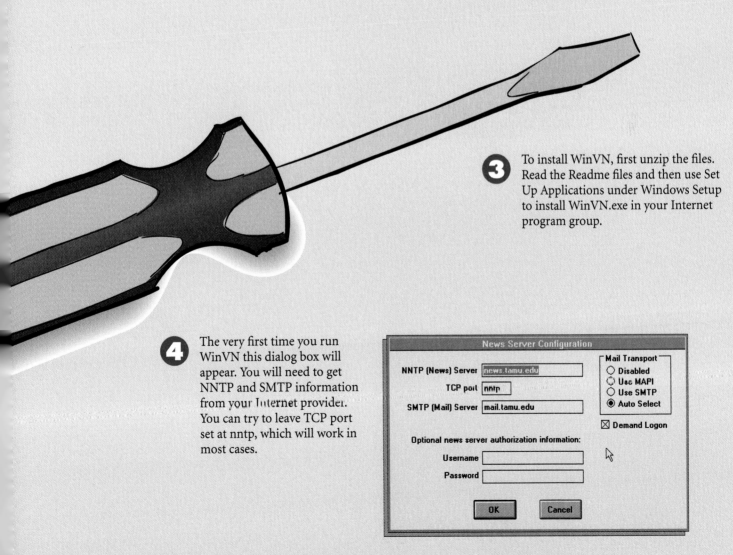

CHAPTER 18

Cello and the World Wide Web

To most people, cruising the Internet means using a friendly World Wide Web (WWW) browser. Cello is one of the simplest forms of these browsers. Cello was created by an attorney for the Legal Information Institute at Cornell. It is an alternative to the popular Mosaic browser. Its simple format makes it look more like a predecessor to Mosaic than a successor. In addition to HTTP (Hypertext Transport Protocol—all WWW documents are in hypertext format), it can be configured to support ftp, gopher, CSO phonebook databases, and Usenet. One drawback to Cello is that it does not support interactive forms for such things as user feedback. Cello allows you to view graphics as well as text. To use Cello you will need an Internet service provider who may also supply the Winsock TCP/IP stack necessary to run it.

How to Start Up Cello

A s with all the window Internet software, your basic skill requirement will be the ability to click the left mouse button. You do not need to remember any commands since all of the commands appear in the menu bar and Cello also offers an extensive Help menu.

The Cello page has a very simple format and is ideal for those who find the display of many buttons confusing. It offers an alternative to Mosaic or Netscape for browsing the World Wide Web.

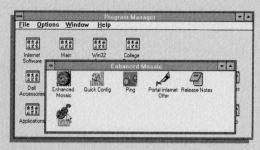

▶ **1** To start up Cello simply double-click its icon after getting onto the Internet.

7 The up-arrow button is used to go back to the previous screen. Cello keeps this information locally in your computer so it doesn't have to download it each time you page back through the current document.

6 The Stop button is used to stop the downloading of information. If you have a slow modem or connection you may decide not to wait for some information to be downloaded, so just click the Stop button to stop the process.

TIP SHEET

▸ **If your Cello access to the Web seems slow, check some of the configuration options available in the Help menu.**

▸ **If you use the Internet during prime daytime hours it may be very slow. Try non-peak hours if you are having trouble getting into a site or page. Some Internet providers offer free or reduced-cost access at non-peak times.**

2 The Menu bar contains all of the Cello commands available. The Help menu is extensive and very readable. Use the Help menu to explore all the capabilities of Cello.

3 The button with the little house on it is where you click to get back to the beginning of the Home Page, which is shown here. Click this at any time.

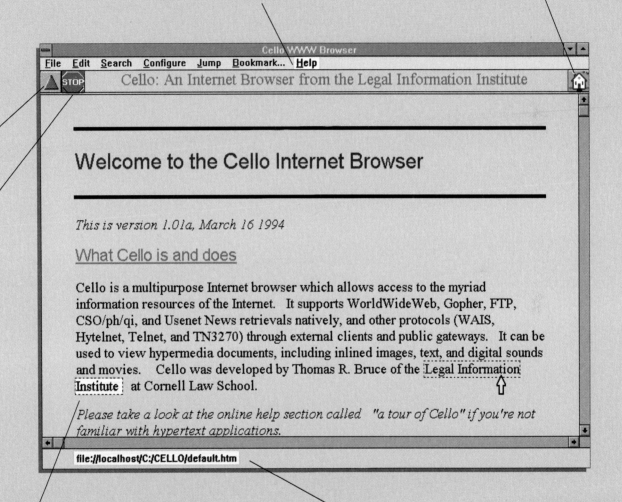

5 The text shown in outline boxes represents hypertext. This is the beauty of Web browsing. This text contains links to the site or document so all you have to do to get it (or go there) is to double-click on the hypertext. You will find these boxes scattered throughout all Web pages. Click some and see what happens.

4 The message at the bottom of the screen shows you where you are currently. Watch how it changes as you visit sites on the Web.

How to Navigate the Web with Hypertext

It is not difficult to spend hours viewing hypertext documents on the WWW. You can literally travel the world and outer space without getting out of your chair.

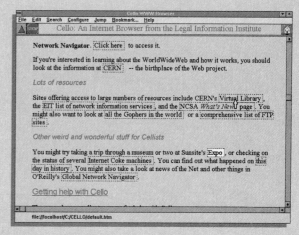

▶ **1** Use the vertical scroll bar on the right-hand side of the window to move down through Cello's opening document (home page). Double-click on the word Expo in the outlined text. That will take you to Sunsite.

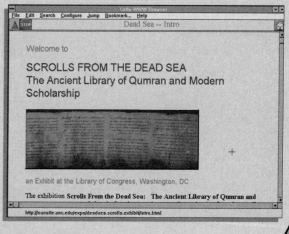

4 This has taken you to an actual display of a Dead Sea Scroll. Pretty amazing, isn't it? You can continue viewing whatever is of interest in this manner.

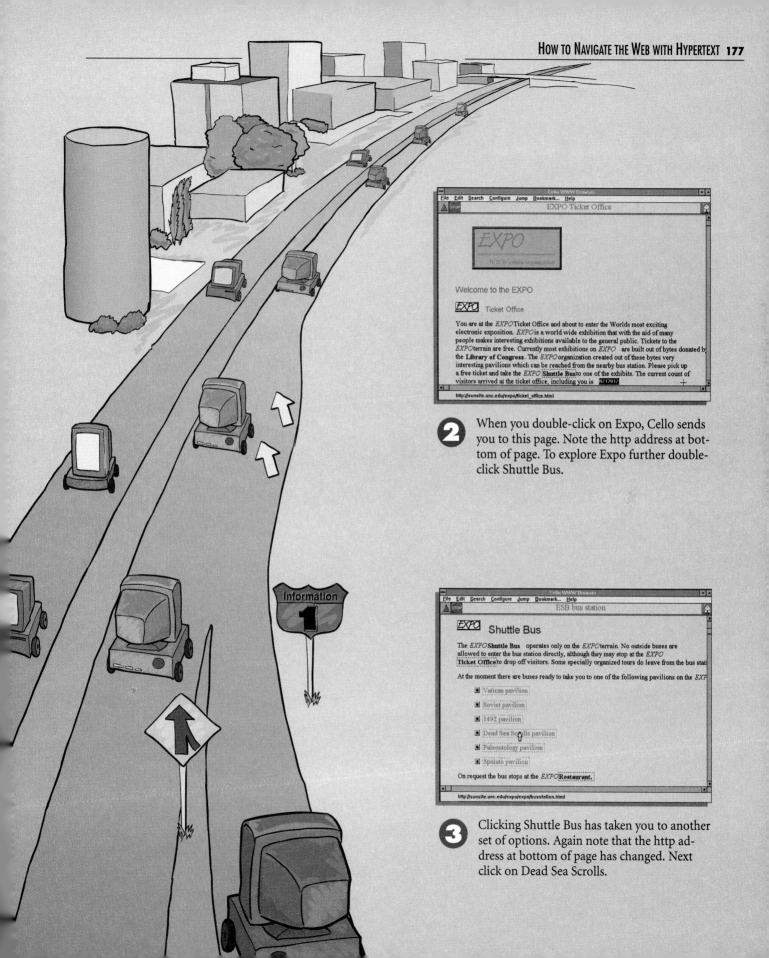

2 When you double-click on Expo, Cello sends you to this page. Note the http address at bottom of page. To explore Expo further double-click Shuttle Bus.

3 Clicking Shuttle Bus has taken you to another set of options. Again note that the http address at bottom of page has changed. Next click on Dead Sea Scrolls.

How to Keep Track of Where You Have Been

When you cruise the Internet it is often easy to get distracted and forget exactly how you got to some really interesting new "stuff." Cello has Bookmarks that let you keep track of things you want to go back to.

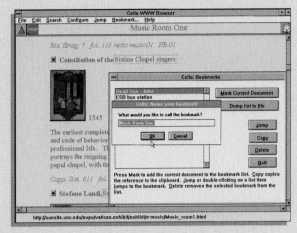

1 When you find yourself in an interesting place that you don't want to lose track of, click Bookmark in the Menu bar. This brings up the Cello:Bookmarks window.

TIP SHEET

▶ If you get an error message say-ing the bookmark could not be saved, you probably have a copy of Cello that is in read only for-mat. Go to your Cello directory, remove the cello.bmk file and cre-ate a new file called cello.bmk.

▶ Whenever you get an error mes-sage in Cello you can get more in-formation from the Help menu under Problems: Error Messages.

2 In the Cello:Bookmarks window click Mark Current Document. This will bring up the Cello:Name your Bookmark dialogue box. The box has the name of the document which you can use. If you prefer a more reasonable name move the cursor to the box and type what you want. Click OK.

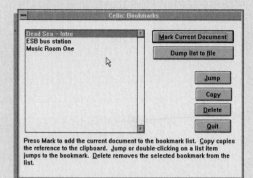

3 You should then see the new bookmark in the list. Note directions for use at the bottom of the window.

4 Creating the bookmark puts it in a permanent file. You can then go back to this location anytime you use Cello by selecting Jump in the Bookmark menu. The bookmark will remain in the file until you delete it.

How to Do Some Other Interesting Things

Cello has multiple uses and functions, including sending mail and working with gopher or WAIS. All of these cannot be covered here. However, usage is so intuitive that typical users can figure out many new uses by exploring the Help and Menu bars.

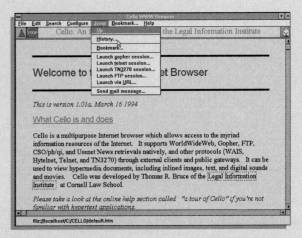

1 The Jump menu has a gold mine of options. If you want to get back to a document before you close your Cello session, you can do so by going to History.

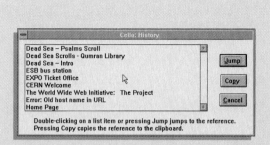

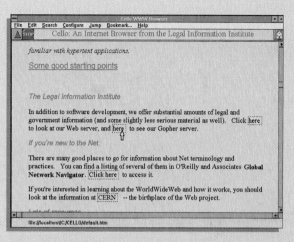

2 Under the History window you will see all of the documents you have seen in the current session. To return to one of these, highlight it and then click the Jump button. Notice the directions at the bottom of the History window.

3 You can get to gopher by clicking the Here box in the Cello home page or by clicking the Launch gopher session. You need to set up the address of this in the Configuration menu if it has not been done by your Internet provider. See Chapter 13 for more information on Gopher.

4 If you know the address of a hypertext document—many magazines and newspapers publish these on a regular basis—you can go to it directly by entering it as a URL (Universal Resource Locator). To get to the URL dialogue box, click Launch via URL under the Jump menu.

How to Get and Install Cello

C ello is a freeware program that can be obtained from many sources. Many books supply it with the text. Many Internet service providers include it in your startup package. It's available from Cornell via ftp. Installation is simple; however, if your Provider does not supply Cello you may have to spend some time configuring it.

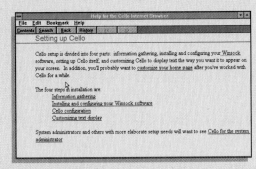

► **1** Cello Help files offer information on configuration and setup. It is important to note that you will need the Winsock software. Of course you need to install Cello before you can read the help file.

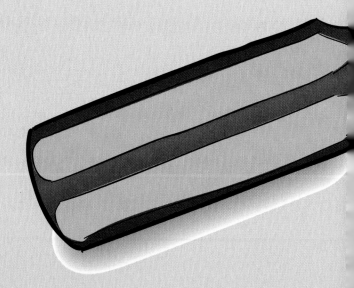

TIP SHEET

► Check to see if your Internet provider will supply the Winsock TCP/IP or recommend a supplier. It will make installation easier.

► Always run a virus check on any software that you get by ftp before you run any executable (.exe) files. Failure to do this could damage your files or even your computer.

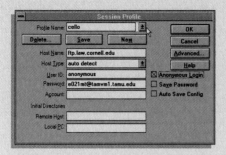

2 Cello is available from the source by ftp to ftp.law.cornell.edu in the directory /pub/Lii/Cello. See Chapter 15 for Winsock FTP.

3 The file you need to download or transfer to your computer is cello.zip. You will need a copy of PKUNZIP to decompress it—see Chapter 15 for a source for this.

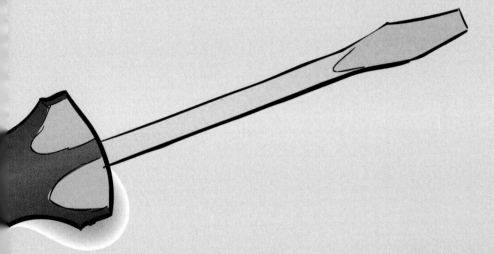

4 To get Cello installed:(a) Install Winsock TCP/IP stack; (b) Unzip Cello.zip into a directory such as c:\cello; (c) Move cello.ini into your c:\windows directory; (d) Click the windows setup icon and then click on set up applications.

CHAPTER 19

How to Conquer the World with Mosaic

 Mosaic is a program that makes cruising the Internet a simple pleasure. It was written by the National Center for Supercomputer Applications (NCSA) at the University of Illinois. It is constantly undergoing changes and improvements. This chapter will display screens from two versions of Mosaic. One is an enhanced version which simplifies the window interface by creating useful hypertext links that automatically perform some of the menu bar and button functions. The other is the true NCSA Mosaic in its latest form.

Mosaic can almost eliminate the need for many of the separate Internet programs discussed in previous chapters. It can serve as a news reader, WAIS search, telnet, and ftp resource, as well as take you on a visual tour of an art gallery, display the text of a book, or even show a movie. The really amazing part of this program, though, is that it can do all of this without the user having to know any specific commands or operating systems such as UNIX. Mosaic truly is one of the Internet programs that makes the Internet available to everyone.

Because of Mosaic's popularity and ease of use there are now similar programs appearing that attempt to do more with a somewhat simplified interface, including Cello and Netscape. However, no matter what version of Mosaic you have, you will most likely find the variations offer few hurdles in usage. The programs are so easy to use that one can adapt quickly to the many variations.

How to Start Up Mosaic

Since this program has a window interface, all you need to do is get on your Internet server and then double-click the Mosaic icon. To use Mosaic in its simplest form you just click on the hypertext—text highlighted by color and underlining. This text has links to the documents and sites that make up the World Wide Web.

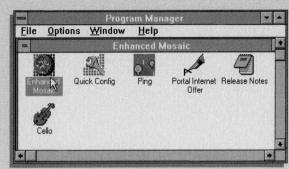

▶ **1** Double-click the Mosaic icon to get the program started. This icon may vary slightly depending on the version of Mosaic you have. In this case it is a modified or enhanced version distributed in some Internet tradebooks or by a service provider.

TIP SHEET

▶ Since the menu and button bars change with the many changing flavors of Mosaic, you need to explore the menus (especially Help) and all of the various buttons. There has never been a fatality associated with this type of exploration.

▶ The address in the URL box starting with http (for web document) indicates the computer it is on (ncsa.uiuc.edu) and the directory it is in (/SDG/Software/etc). You can find these addresses almost anywhere on the Web, in newspapers, magazines, and so forth.

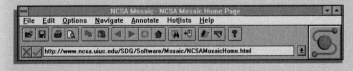

5 The boxes with the X and check next to the http address are used to go to those addresses when they are clicked. Otherwise the window box indicates your current URL address.

2 This particular version, or flavor, of Mosaic has simplified the Menu bar and Button bar at the top of the window. It has replaced many of the button and menu functions with hypertext links within the initial Home Page document. Note the Help Hypertext window and the Help Menu bar.

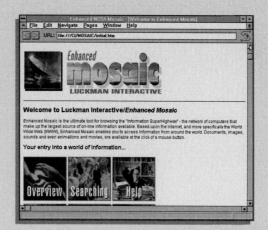

3 The < and > buttons at the left top of the window are used to page forward and backward through all Mosaic screens or documents. In the case illustrated it is the Enhanced Mosaic Home Page. The URL box next to these paging buttons indicates the current location on the Web. *URL* stands for Universal Resource Locator and it lets you go directly to Web or Internet sites.

4 The Window shown here is from the latest version of the original NCSA Mosaic. Note that there are many more buttons and a more complex menu bar. The function of the < and > buttons is the same as the enhanced version. The little House button is used to return to the Home page—as in Cello.

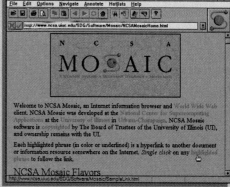

How to Tour an Art Gallery

One of the most novel aspects of Web browsers, such as Mosaic, is the ability to display color pictures almost instantaneously on your computer screen. This will be demonstrated by a quick tour of two art galleries, the Louvre and the Krannert Art Gallery.

▶ **1** To start the tour of the art gallery you must first know where it is. Enhanced Mosaic makes this easy by clicking the Recreation graphic. If this is not available you can search the Web for the information or get the address from a multitude of publications.

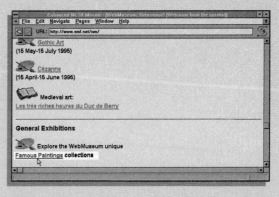

4 You are now given some exhibit options. In this case Famous Paintings will be chosen.

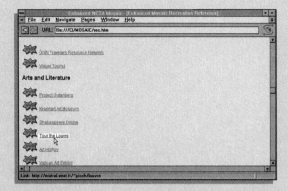

2 Using the Scroll bar on the right side of the Mosaic window, find the hypertext associated with the museum you wish to tour—in this case, click Tour the Louvre.

3 The WebMuseum Network asks you to go through the closest site. Some judicious clicking resulted in using the emf site which happened to be the only active site at the moment.

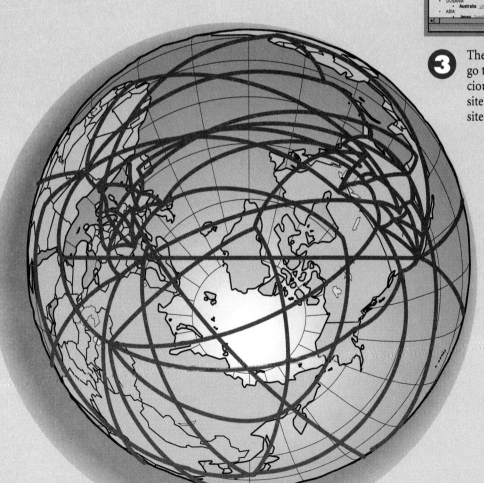

How to Tour an Art Gallery (Continued)

Most art galleries initially give you a small image of the artwork. Usually you can click on the image and it will display a full screen version of the artwork.

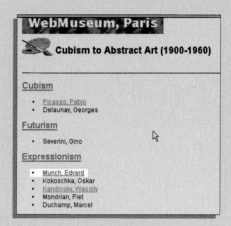

▶ **5** The screen now displays options for various types of art. In this case select Edvard Munch, an expressionist.

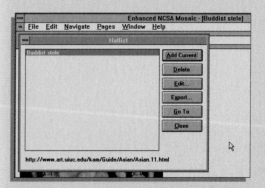

10 If you would like to return to this image at a future Internet session, you can create a Hotlist item from the menu bar. Pull down the items in the menu bar until you find Hotlist as a submenu—location of this submenu may vary depending on the version of Mosaic. The next time you start up Mosaic you can again select Hotlist and go directly to any item listed there.

6 When the small image attempted to appear, there was an error in loading. When the error box (where the image snapshot should have appeared) was clicked, Mosaic was then able to display the large image. This is a good lesson to remember when using the Internet: Although your first attempt may fail, an alternative may likely succeed.

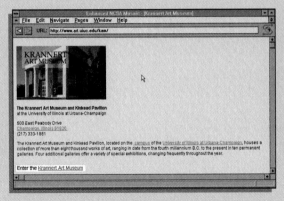

7 Returning to the U.S., the next museum will be the Krannert Art Museum at the University of Illinois. Click on Enter the Museum to begin the tour.

8 After scrolling through the museum exhibits, Asian Art is chosen. This time the small images load successfully.

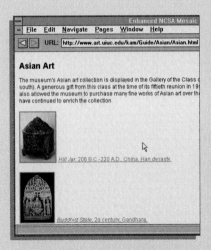

9 Again, by clicking on the small image, the large image appears.

How to Use URL— Universal Resource Locator

You can get to many Web resources by simply clicking on the highlighted hypertext. However, there are many locations on the Web that you may want to access directly. This is when you use the Open URL option in the File menu. This can also be used for ftp, gopher, and Telnet, and to join news groups.

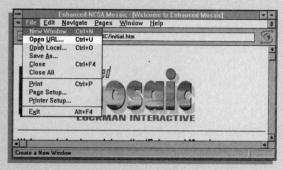

► **1** To type in a Web address first click Open URL in the File menu.

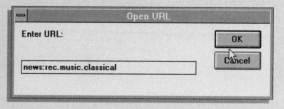

6 News groups can be joined and read as with WinVN, described in Chapter 17.

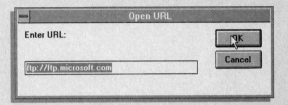

2 The most typical use of Open URL is to access a Web document directly. You must have the exact address which indicates the computer and file directories. These addresses always begin with http.

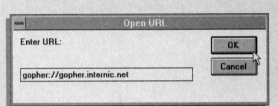

3 You can transfer files with Mosaic using ftp in the Enter URL box. This works in basically the same way as the Winsock ftp discussed in Chapter 15.

4 You can also use Mosaic to do gopher browsing, as explained in Chapter 13.

5 Use Telnet to connect to a remote computer site. This is a function described in detail in Chapter 12.

How to Ftp with Mosaic

osaic allows you to go to a remote site, search through directories, and transfer selected files to your computer. The directories you search are hypertext, so all you have to do to look in a directory is click on the highlighted text. It works like Winsock FTP described in Chapter 15.

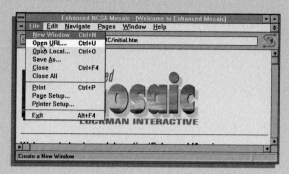

1 To search for a file and transfer it to your computer, begin by selecting Open URL under the File menu.

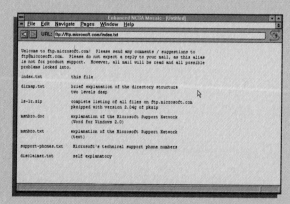

6 When you click on a text file, it will be displayed on your screen rather than being set up to transfer.

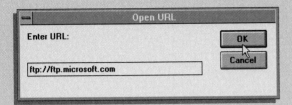

2 In the text box type **ftp://** followed by the address of the ftp site you wish to access.

3 The initial access to Microsoft.com shows the directories and some files in hypertext. To access the Softlib directory click the highlighted text.

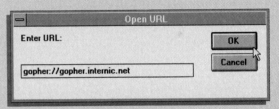

4 In the directory Softlib are several .exe files. Scroll through the list to select the file you want to transfer to your system. In this case click on the file Animate.exe.

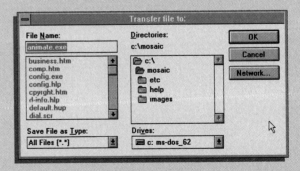

5 When you click on the binary file you want to transfer, a Transfer window appears. Select the directory you want to transfer the file to on your computer and click OK. This will produce a binary file transfer.

How to Access Gopher Space with Mosaic

With Mosaic you can access gopher space as described in Chapter 13. The nice thing is that you practically eliminate the need for extra gopher client software.

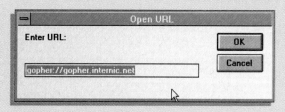

▶ **1** Select Open URL under the File menu and type **gopher://** followed by the address of the gopher site.

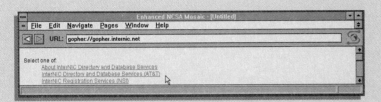

2 The Gopher menu is displayed in highlighted hypertext. Just click on the text to go to your selection.

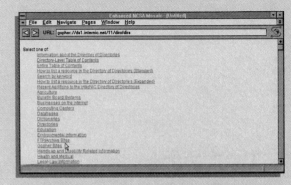

3 At each level of the gopher menu you scroll through the selections in highlighted hypertext and click on the one you want to see.

4 When cruising the Web, if you come across a highlighted hyperlink to a gopher site, just click it and you will be linked to the gopher menu.

How to Do Searches with Mosaic

The variety of searches that you can perform with Web browsers seems to be constantly increasing. This is in fact one of the distinguishing features of many of the variations of Mosaic and its offshoots. This section explores some of these search options.

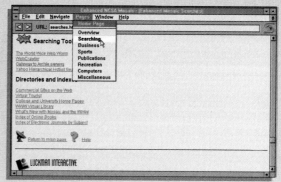

1 In Enhanced Mosaic, Netscape, and the like, Search engines (software) are built into home pages or button bars. To access several search techniques you simply click on the menu option or button bar for searching. This brings up hyperlinks to old and newer search engines, including WebCrawler and Yahoo.

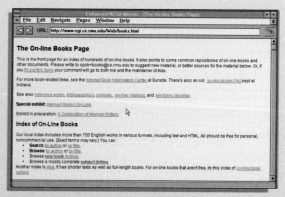

5 Under Directories and Indexes, clicking Index of Online Books produces this option page. A surprising number of books are available on the Internet. Much of the credit for this goes to the Gutenberg project (try a search for this topic).

2 Yahoo is a new search method that has a lot of easy-to-use features, including a limitation on the number of matches. In this case the search is for the occurrence of the string *cather*.

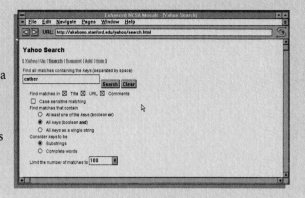

3 The result of the Yahoo search for cather produced three matches.

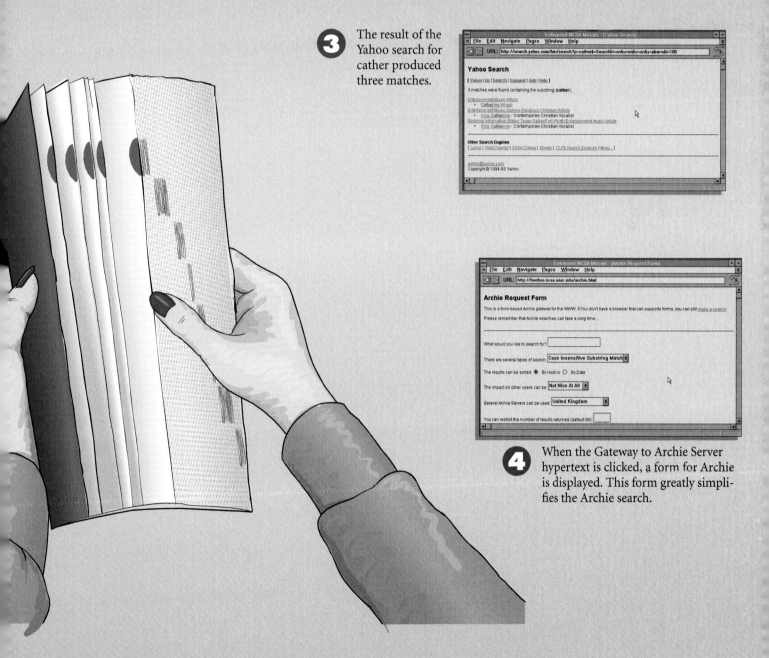

4 When the Gateway to Archie Server hypertext is clicked, a form for Archie is displayed. This form greatly simplifies the Archie search.

How to Telnet Using Mosaic

When you need to log onto a remote computer as a user you can use Telnet as described in Chapter 12. Mosaic allows you to Telnet without having to run separate Telnet software. Unfortunately, once you Telnet to a site you lose the user-friendly capability of the Mosaic interface. You will be on your own once you log into the remote computer.

1 From the File menu select Open URL and type **Telnet://** followed by the computer address, which in this case is **acs.tamu.edu**. Click OK.

5 Some sites allow guest login by giving you information on the login screen. If you have not previously accessed a site, be sure to carefully read the login screen to see if there is a guest login user name and password. Some guest accommodating systems also send a sequence to determine if your computer is correctly receiving text. Again, be careful to read all of the information on the login or startup screen for a Telnet site.

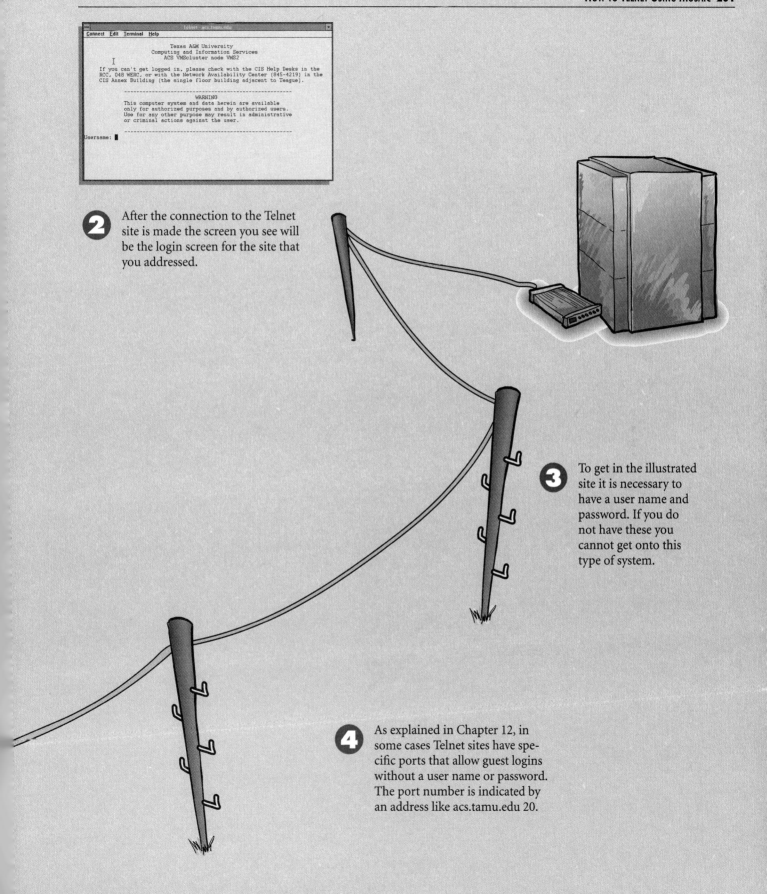

```
                    telnet - acs.tamu.edu
 Connect  Edit  Terminal  Help

                    Texas A&M University
                Computing and Information Services
                   ACS VMScluster node VMS2
        I
    If you can't get logged in, please check with the CIS Help Desks in the
    RCC, 048 WERC, or with the Network Availability Center (845-4219) in the
    CIS Annex Building (the single floor building adjacent to Teague).

    --------------------------------------------------------
                           WARNING
        This computer system and data herein are available
        only for authorized purposes and by authorized users.
        Use for any other purpose may result in administrative
        or criminal actions against the user.

    --------------------------------------------------------
 Username: █
```

2 After the connection to the Telnet site is made the screen you see will be the login screen for the site that you addressed.

3 To get in the illustrated site it is necessary to have a user name and password. If you do not have these you cannot get onto this type of system.

4 As explained in Chapter 12, in some cases Telnet sites have specific ports that allow guest logins without a user name or password. The port number is indicated by an address like acs.tamu.edu 20.

How to Do a WAIS Search with Mosaic

Recall from Chapter 14 that a WAIS search indexes the contents of documents rather than the title. Mosaic can use a hypertext link to do this search.

▶ **1** From the File menu select Open URL and type **http://** followed by **server.wais.com/directory-of-servers.html**. This is the hyperlink to the WAIS home page.

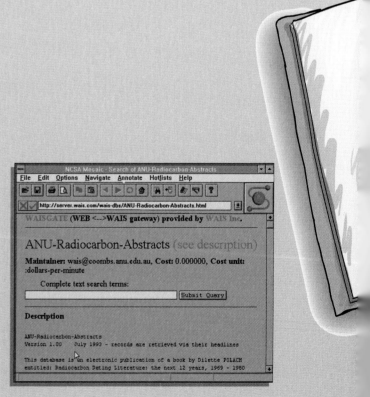

4 ANU-Radiocarbon-Abstracts was selected with this result.

2 The first page of the WAIS home page is displayed. Note it is under restoration— a typical situation for the dynamic World Wide Web!

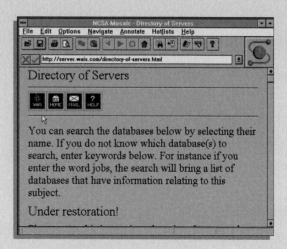

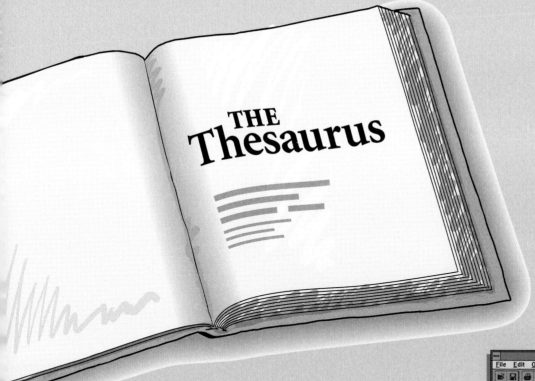

3 The WAIS button was clicked on the home page. The next step is to type in a search string in the Find box or to scroll through the index and select one.

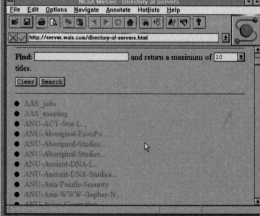

How to Get the News with Mosaic

Mosaic can also serve as a handy news reader. You can go directly to a news group or subscribe to various news groups.

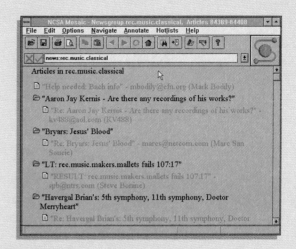

1 If you know the name of the news group then simply type **news:** followed by the news group name—**rec.music.classical** in this case—in the File menu option, open URL, text box. In this version of Mosaic you simply click the check box to go to the typed in item.

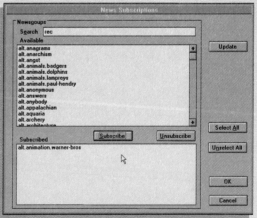

4 To subscribe to a news group, simply highlight the group by clicking on it and then clicking on Subscribe. You may also remove your subscription by clicking Unsubscribe.

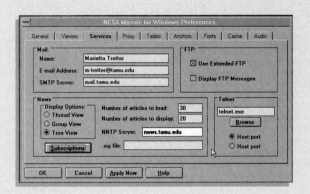

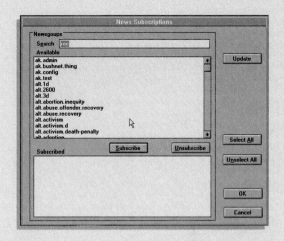

2 To find out what news groups are available and to subscribe to them, you will first need to complete a preference form. To do this, find Preferences in the pulldown menu—it can be under different menu bar options depending on the version of Mosaic you have. Go to the Services folder and fill in the name of your NNTP server (this should be available from your Internet service provider). Then click the Subscriptions button.

3 After you click the Subscriptions button you will be asked if you want a list of news groups. If you click yes you will get a list similar to the one displayed.

How to Get and Install Mosaic Software

There are many flavors of Mosaic. Fortunately, the most up-to-date version is free. Some enhanced versions are free in the sense that they are enticements to subscribe to a service. This section shows you how to get and install Mosaic 20b4.

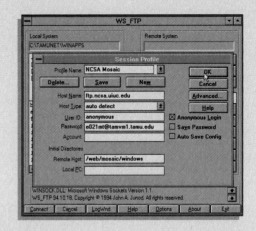

1 The latest version of the original Mosaic is available free by ftp to ftp.ncsa.uiuc.edu.

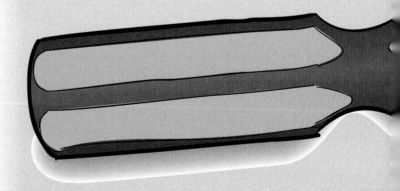

TIP SHEET

- ▶ You will need to have a SLIP or PPP setup (or ethernet connection), usually obtained from your Internet provider, before you can run Mosaic on the Internet.

- ▶ Run is an option under the File menu in Windows. Type Setup.exe (include the path on the setup file) in the Run window text box.

- ▶ When the version of Mosaic changes you see something like mos20c2.exe (a previous version to mos20b4, for example, was mos20a7).

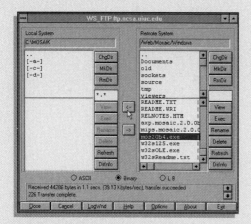

2 The files you need to transfer are mos20b4.exe and w32s125.exe. You need Win32 software to run Mosaic. It's a good idea to view the Readme file to see if you might already have Win32.

3 Once you have transferred the files and checked them for viruses, you can go to DOS and type **w32s125**. This will inflate the Win32 files (w32s125 is called a self-extracting file). Then go back to Windows and run Setup.exe from the directory in which you have the extracted Win32 files.

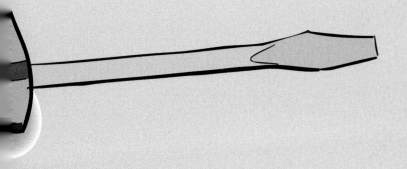

4 In DOS type **mos20b4** to run the self-extracting Mosaic file. This will put the Mosaic files in C:\Mosaic. Go back to Windows and run Setup.exe. (If setup isn't there look for a file install.exe) This will install Mosaic and set up the Mosaic icon if all goes well. Then dial up your Internet provider and double-click the Mosaic icon—it should work.

CHAPTER 20

Advanced Mosaic

Mosaic by itself has many strong features. There are also some free add-ons that can make it even more powerful. One of these is Adobe Acrobat. This program allows you to create publication-quality documents with text and graphics that can be viewed and printed by anyone with a computer. This is accomplished by including a free copy of Adobe Acrobat with the document.

A program similar in nature to Acrobat is Ghostview, which allows the user to read and print documents in Postscript format without a Postscript printer. This program is more complicated to install than Acrobat and not as portable.

Another program which is fun and useful for preparing multimedia film clips is the movie viewer for QuickTime format movies. The movies are short clips which can easily take up over a megabyte of disk space. It's not quite like seeing a movie with your VCR, but it's pretty impressive given the current state of computer movies.

The World Wide Web is based on the home page format. With little more additional software than a text-only word processor you can build your own home page that could be made available on the Internet.

How to Get and Use Adobe Acrobat

The Adobe Acrobat home page calls the software the fastest and most inexpensive way to move beyond paper. You do this by "printing" files to the *PDF* (Portable Document Format). This gives you documents with color, graphics, fonts, easy navigation and printing, plus the convenience of electronic access. When you send a free copy of Acrobat Reader to a Windows or Macintosh user, they can print or view a PDF document with their existing hardware and software.

1 The first step in using the software is to get it. To do this get to the Adobe home page address: http://www.adobe.com.

7 Acrobat allows you to read and print very professional looking documents like the one you see here. It is well worth the investment in installation.

2 Next, select Free Adobe Software and you will see the hyperlink to download Acrobat.

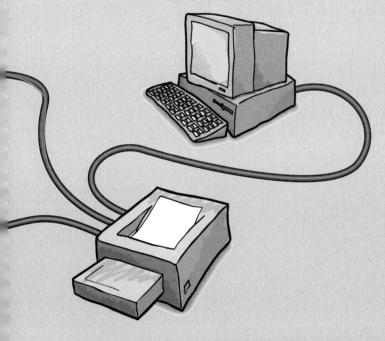

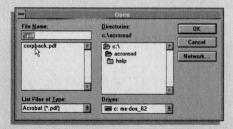

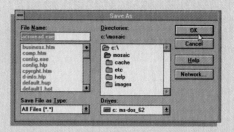

3 A dialogue box appears with acroread.exe. You must select the directory on your computer that it will be stored on. Select the directory and click OK.

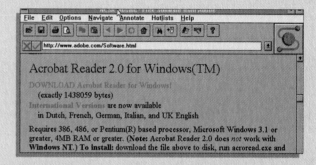

4 It's always a good idea to read any online installation instructions, as freeware programs tend to change with the weather.

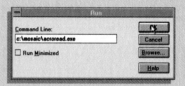

5 To install acroread.exe, simply select Run under the window's File menu, type in **acroread.exe** with its path, click OK and it is installed. This is one of the easiest Mosaic add-ons to install.

6 When you encounter a file with the .pdf extension you simply open it under Acrobat to view or print it.

How to Go to the Movies with Mosaic

There are an abundance of movie clips on the Internet. In order to view them you need an appropriate viewer. There are several different formats for this, including Mpeg and QuickTime. QuickTime will be set up in this section.

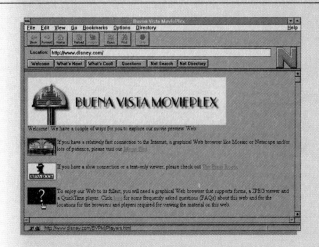

1 One of many sources for the QuickTime viewer software is at http://www.disney.com.

5 Next use PKUN-ZIP to unzip qtw11.zip and put the files in your windows\system directory. If you have a Preferences viewer in your version of Mosaic, just add a viewer preference with Associate Mime Type of: video/quicktime; with extensions .mov; to application c:\windows\mplayer.exe. QuickTime uses the existing windows control panel from mplayer.

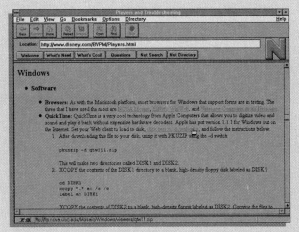

2 Selecting the ? gives information and a hypertext link to the software.

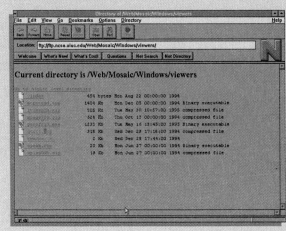

3 Selecting Click Here to Download brings up a hyperlink menu of choices. Note from the previous screen that the QuickTime viewer is qtw11.zip.

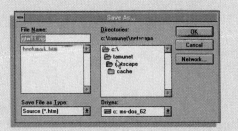

4 Click on qtw11.zip and this dialogue box asks you to set up the directory to receive QuickTime. Select the directory and click OK.

How to Go to the Movies with Mosaic (Continued)

Once QuickTime is installed you can then proceed to enjoying the show.

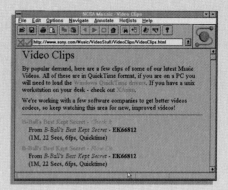

▶ **6** When you get video clips, they need to be in the correct QuickTime format. In this case they need the .mov file extension rather than .qt. The address http://www.sony.com offers many musical video clips in QuickTime format.

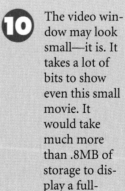

10 The video window may look small—it is. It takes a lot of bits to show even this small movie. It would take much more than .8MB of storage to display a full-screen high resolution movie. You can enlarge the movie and decrease the resolution by clicking the ^ box or dragging the lower righthand corner.

Note that each video indicates the amount of storage space required and its running time. For instance, Cleopatra's Cat takes .8MB of storage and runs for 22 seconds.

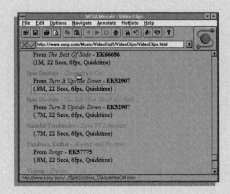

The media player has controls much like a CD player or tape recorder. Click the > arrow to start.

 Downloading Cleopatra's Cat takes a couple of minutes, which may seem like hours. When it is loaded, the Media player and screen appear.

How to Get and Use Ghostview to View and Print Postscript Files

P ostscript is a page setup printer language that usually needs special software and printers. Ghostview lets you view and print Postscript files without this special hardware. Many professional publications are in Postscript format. Ghostview is probably the most complicated freeware program to install.

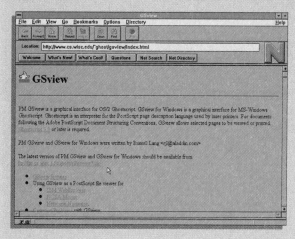

1 Versions of Ghostview are listed in the GSView home page at http://www.cs.wisc.edu/ghost/gsview/index.html.

4 If your version of Mosaic has the Preferences/Viewers window, then set it up as Associate MIME, Type of Application/postscript; with extensions .eps,.ai,.ps; To this Application c:\name and path of your version of Ghostscript and Ghostview.

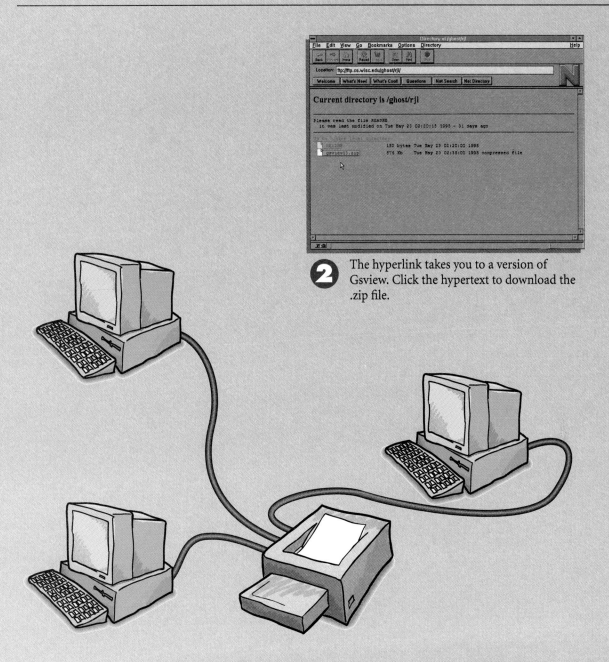

2 The hyperlink takes you to a version of Gsview. Click the hypertext to download the .zip file.

3 The path to the location of your Ghostview and Ghostscript software is the crucial information that needs to be supplied to your mosaic.ini file if that is used by your version of Mosaic. Read the included readme files for specific directions for the version of Ghostview that you have downloaded.

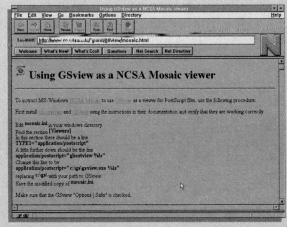

How to Get and Use Ghostview to View and Print Postscript Files (Continued)

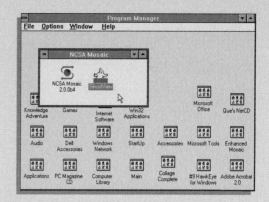

Once Ghostview is installed you still need to set up Ghostview in order for it to work correctly.

▶ **5** Unlike most other add-ons to Mosaic, Ghostview has an icon, which means that it can be run independently of Mosaic. When you first install it you need to run it outside of Mosaic to complete the installation.

6 Start Ghostview by clicking the icon, select Ghostscript

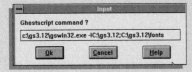

Command under the Options menu. Type in the path for the version of Ghostscript that you have installed. Note that the path lists all the related files and directories that were created when the files were unzipped.

7 If you get errors when trying to view a .ps file you have probably entered the path information incorrectly in the previous step. Check the documentation and Help menu that came with your version of Ghostview.

8 Once you can open a .ps file without an error message, you should see an impressive picture or text.

How to Build Your Own Home Page

Home pages, which are the main document and display of the WWW, are very easy to build in *HTML* (hypertext markup language). Keep in mind that once you build your page, the only way you can make it available to the WWW is to store it on an Internet Service provider. This can be very expensive, but not necessarily.

▶ **1** To get started building your home page, all you need is a word processor that can store documents in text only—this means no control characters or other formating features. There are also many specialized editors which you can locate by doing a search on the web. Many of these editors are free. All that has been used for these examples is Word 6.0 in text only mode.

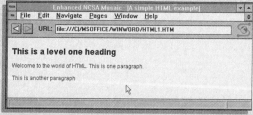
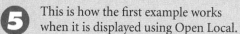

5 This is how the first example works when it is displayed using Open Local.

▶ **The best source of information on HTML is the Internet itself. Search for information on HTML or home page.**

▶ **Before you build the home page to beat all home pages, occasionally check the output to make sure you are doing what you think you are.**

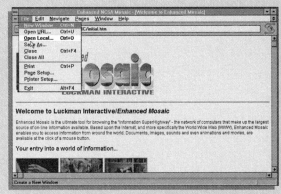

2 Once you have your home page, or as you are building it, you can view the actual page by using Open Local under the Mosaic file menu.

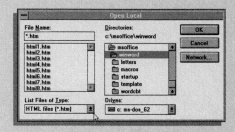

3 The file extension that your version of Mosaic wants may differ from the .htm that is shown. Some, for example, use .url to indicate a home page. It is easy to change the file extension if you guessed the wrong one. The List Files of Type will give you a hint to the file extension.

4 Here is the first HTML example:

```
<Title>A simple HTML example</Title>
<H1>This is a level one heading</H1>
Welcome to the world of HTML.
This is one paragraph.<P>
This is another paragraph<p>
```

All text *tags* have a beginning and end such as <Title> and </Title>. <p> is the only exception. <p> indicates a paragraph. Note the difference between beginning and ending tags. Tags are not case sensitive, which means that whether you type in upper- or lowercase makes no difference.

How to Build Your Own Home Page (Continued)

The best way to get an understanding of the various tags is by example.

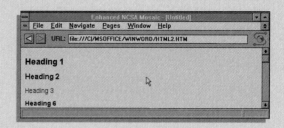

▶ **6** The text showing effect of different headings 1–6, and the result:

```
<h1> Heading 1</h1>
<h2> Heading 2</h2>
<h3> Heading 3</h3>
<h6> Heading 6</h6>
```

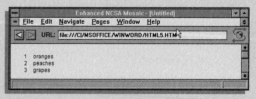

9 A numbered list, note that case is unimportant in tags:

```
<ol>
<LI> oranges
<LI> peaches
<li> grapes
</ol>
```

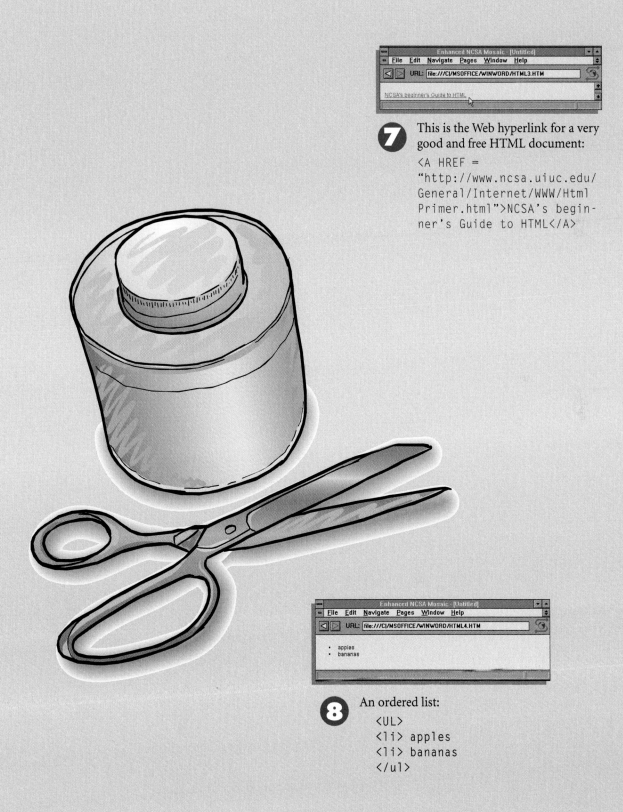

7 This is the Web hyperlink for a very good and free HTML document:

```
<A HREF =
"http://www.ncsa.uiuc.edu/
General/Internet/WWW/Html
Primer.html">NCSA's begin-
ner's Guide to HTML</A>
```

8 An ordered list:

```
<UL>
<li> apples
<li> bananas
</ul>
```

How to Build Your Own Home Page (Continued)

There are many tags to work with—this gives you only some of the basic ones. You can also insert graphics and sounds and just about anything else you can think of. Check the Internet for more details.

13 This is the text for the big example:

```
<Head>
<TITLE> A Longer Example</Title>
</Head>
<BODY>
<H1>A Long Example</h1>
This is a simple HTML document. This is the
first paragraph.<p>
```

This is the second paragraph, which shows special effects. This is a word in <i>italics</I>. This is a word in <B>bold</B>. This is a block quote.

```
<Blockquote>
How now Brown Cow
</BLOCKQUOTE>
```

Here is an in-lined GIF image: <IMG SRG = "myimage.gif">.

```
<P>
<H2> A Second Level Header</H2>
```

Here is a section of text that should display as a fixed-width font: <P>

```
<PRE>
IF Y = 1 THEN J = 2
K = Y*J
</PRE>
This is a forced break:<BR>
WRA Computing<BR>
999 SOMEWHERE<BR>
COWTOWN TX 671234-2233<BR>
<P>This is the end of the sample document.
<p>
<ADDRESS>Me
(me@mycomputer.univ.edu)</ADDRESS>
</BODY>
```

TIP SHEET

- An HTML handbook is available at http://www.leeds.ac.uk/ucs/www/handbook. This has a list of many editors. Look for directory handbook-4_HTML.html.

- Check http://microsoft.com for a free add-on Word HTML editor. It modifies Word on your system, so make sure you want to do this or back up your existing copy.

▶ **10** An example showing indentation:

```
<DL>
<DT> WHITE HOUSE
<DD> Where the President lives
with his family.
<DT> PENTAGON
<DD> Where the military lives
with its top brass.
</DL>
```

11 Indentation and bullets:

```
<UL>
<LI> A few New England states:
        <UL>
        <li> Vermont
        <LI> New Hampshire
        </UL>
<LI> One Midwestern state:
        <UL>
        <LI> Wisconsin
         </UL>
</UL>
```

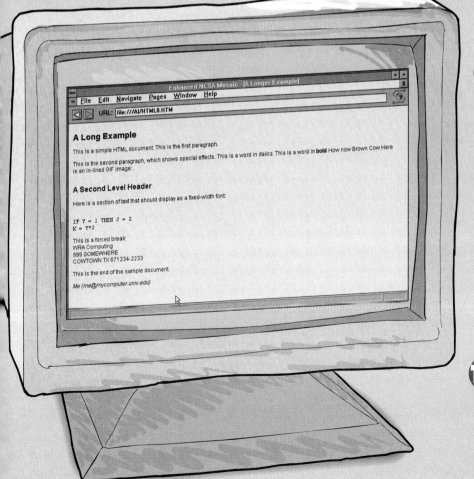

12 This is an example showing bold text, fixed spacing, and e-mail address.

CHAPTER 21

New Internet Tools

 All aspects of the Internet are dynamic. Everything is constantly changing, and in most cases, improving. A popular Web browser can suddenly be eclipsed in a matter of weeks by a new product. The current trend is to include Internet software with the operating system that comes with your computer. OS/2 Warp is building an Internet presence, and Microsoft is launching its own network with access tools incorporated into Windows 95. Mosaic's dominance of the Web browser software is being seriously challenged by Netscape, which is strictly shareware (you are asked to pay a fee if you use it) as opposed to freeware (you are never asked to pay a fee).

Although the user may sometimes be overwhelmed by the choices, it is good to be able to have so much competition working to make things easier and more appealing to use. The Internet itself is again the best source of information on the new products that are constantly appearing.

OS/2 Warp and Windows 95 Approach the Internet

Microsoft and IBM both have big plans for the future of the Internet. IBM has somewhat of a head start with OS/2 Warp, which was available about a year before Microsoft's much publicized (and criticized) Windows 95. However, Windows 95 promises much more than OS/2 with its Microsoft Network. The question remains: Will it deliver what it promises, and when?

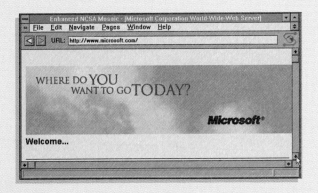

1 The best source of information on Microsoft is at http://www.microsoft.com. This is also a source of some interesting free software.

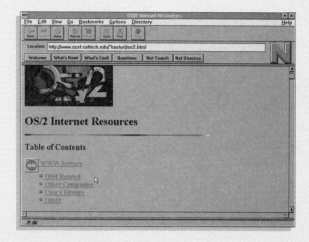

2 Windows 95 beta testers were offered built-in access to MSN, the Microsoft Network. This promises interactive TV, online banking and shopping, and many other consumer services. Although the network is open to beta testers, none of these new and innovative resources have actually materialized before the official release of Windows 95. Some of these innovations require major changes in Internet resources and management and will not appear spontaneously.

3 IBM's OS/2 Warp Internet interface is more conservative than Microsoft's, and because of this has actually delivered a product. There are established OS/2 Warp Internet resources available.

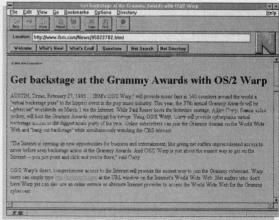

4 Check http://www.ibm.com for some interesting OS/2 Warp Internet applications on the Internet.

Netscape, a Strong Competitor to Mosaic

Netscape has been almost an overnight success. It functions the same as Mosaic, and if you can use Mosaic you will have little trouble adapting to it. It offers functions similarly to those of some of the enhanced versions of Mosaic. Unlike Mosaic, which is free, it is shareware, and if you decide to use the software after a trial period you are expected to pay for it.

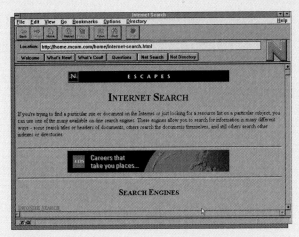

1 One of the more useful features of Netscape is that several very useful Internet search engines are just a button click away with the Net Search button below the menu bar.

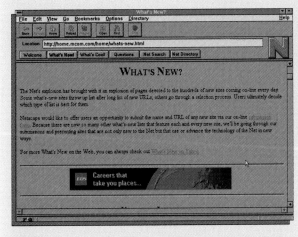

4 At a loss as to what the latest new item is on the Internet? Just click the What's New button.

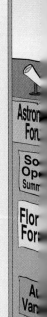

TIP SHEET

▶ **The version of Netscape changes constantly. Check or search the Internet for the latest version.**

▶ **Try http://home.mcom.com/ comprod/mirror/index.html for version 1.2.**

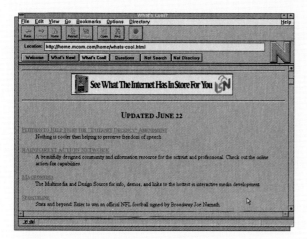

2 The What's Cool button brings up a wide range of topics.

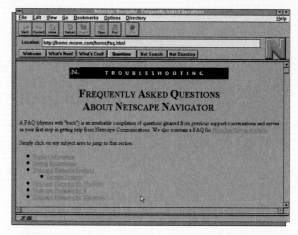

3 Having trouble with Netscape or need more information? Then click the Questions button.

CHAPTER 22

Some Internet Resources

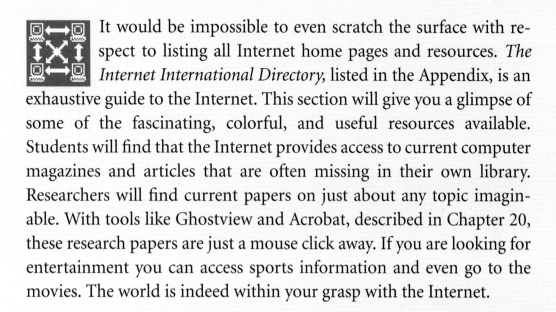 It would be impossible to even scratch the surface with respect to listing all Internet home pages and resources. *The Internet International Directory,* listed in the Appendix, is an exhaustive guide to the Internet. This section will give you a glimpse of some of the fascinating, colorful, and useful resources available. Students will find that the Internet provides access to current computer magazines and articles that are often missing in their own library. Researchers will find current papers on just about any topic imaginable. With tools like Ghostview and Acrobat, described in Chapter 20, these research papers are just a mouse click away. If you are looking for entertainment you can access sports information and even go to the movies. The world is indeed within your grasp with the Internet.

Business Resources

Many business resources, such as stock quotes, data bases, and law information, are free with Internet access. The number of resources increases daily.

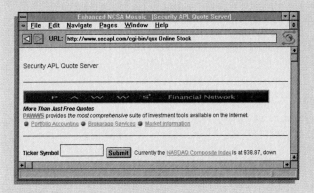

▶ **1** For stock quotes type:
```
http://www.secapl.com/cgi-bin/
qsx Online Stock
```

▶ **Try typing in the top level directory and leaving off the exact file name in your URL. In most cases this will give you a broad selection of topics. For example, try typing**

```
http://www.atm.ch.cam.ac.uk/Movies
```

without the moviequery.html (a file name).

▶ **If you find a favorite site and you get a message saying it is no longer at that site, read the message carefully, as they usually include a hyperlink to the new location.**

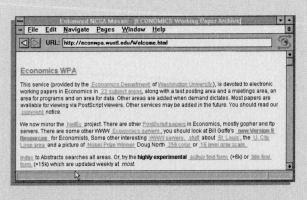

6 Need some economic references? Go to:
```
http://econwpa.wustl.edu/
Welcome.html
```

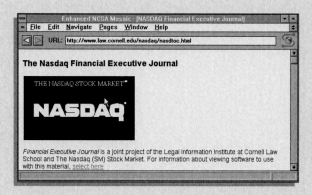

2 For the NASDAQ Journal type:

http://www.law.cornell.edu/nasdaq/
nasdtoc.html

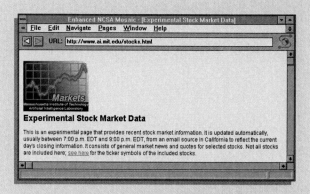

3 For stock market information type:

http://www.ai.mit.edu/stocks.html

4 The Security and Exchange Commission database is at:

http://town.hall.org/edgar/
edgar.html

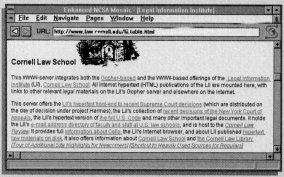

5 Cornell Law School information is yours at:

http://www.law.cornell.edu/
lii.table.html

Entertainment Resources

R ead a book or a magazine, watch a movie, check a movie review, check on your favorite sport, brew some beer. You can do it all and more on the Internet.

▶ **1** Get *Wired*, the magazine, at:
`http://www.wired.com`

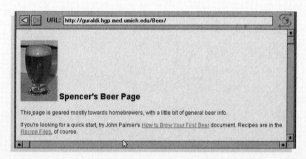

8 Can't find a beer to suit you? Try brewing your own with help from:
`http://guraldi.hgp.med.umich.edu/Beer`

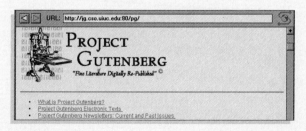

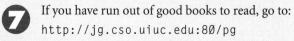

7 If you have run out of good books to read, go to:
`http://jg.cso.uiuc.edu:80/pg`

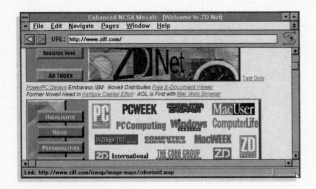

2 Ziff-Davis publishes a lot of magazines that have a huge amount of Internet information. Preview these publications at:

`http://www.ziff.com`

3 If you want to know what is going on in the art world, check out:

`http://www.msstate.edu/`
`Fineart_Online/home.html`

4 No, it's not about Superman, but you might find some useful information at:

`http://www.atmos.uiuc.edu`

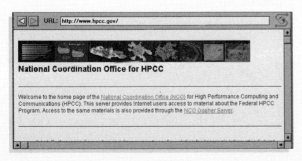

5 Want to tour the Virtual World? Go to:

`http://wings.buffalo.edu/world`

6 Do you like high performance computing better than high performance cars? Go to:

`http://www.hpcc.gov`

Entertainment Resources (Continued)

I f you don't like to read for entertainment, then try some of these resources.

▶ **1** If you're planning a trip, don't leave home without checking:

```
http://nearnet.gnn.com/gnn/metal/
travel/index.html
```

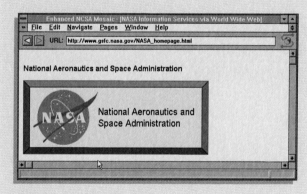

8 Rumors say that they sometimes show current shuttle pictures at this site:

```
http://www.gsfc.nasa.gov/
NASA_homepage.html
```

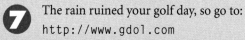

7 The rain ruined your golf day, so go to:

```
http://www.gdol.com
```

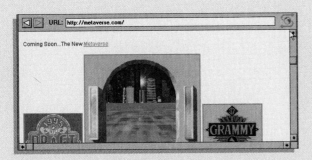

2 Hall of Fame, here you come:

`http://metaverse.com`

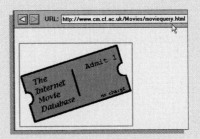

3 Check out that movie before you spend your money:

`http://www.cm.cf.ac.uk/`
`Movies/moviequery.html`

4 Check how many home runs Babe Ruth made, or almost any other sports topic at:

`http://www.atm.ch.cam.ac.uk/`
`sports/sports.html`

6 Want to see the Late Show early, check:

`http://bingen.cs.csbsju.`
`edu.letterman.html`

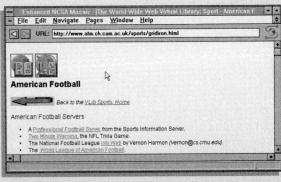

5 Can't get enough football on TV? Check this site:

`http:-//www.atm.ch.cam.ac.uk/`
`sports/gridiron.html`

APPENDIX

Selected Internet Resources

 This Appendix provides the next level of information you need to explore the Internet. The books mentioned here cover many topics in greater depth than is possible in this book. The lists of various resources give some sense of the breadth of information available on the Internet and tell you where to go to find it. Equipped with this information, you'll be ready to explore the vast, global Internet.

Sometimes you may have difficulty connecting to some of the resources listed in this Appendix. Do not be discouraged and do not stop trying to retrieve the files listed. The astounding growth of the Internet means that occasionally you have to wait your turn in line. Also, because of the volume of changes some ftp files incur, the site will sometimes change directory names or file names. If you don't find the exact reference, be sure to explore the directories and files for similar names.

Getting Connected

There are a large number of Internet service providers—companies that will provide you with an account on an Internet host. You can use your home or office computer and a modem to connect to the host over the telephone. Some providers charge a uniform fee while others offer discounts or free service for people in a limited geographical area. For example, Prairienet is free to residents of Illinois. Generally speaking, you must pay for the telephone call between your personal computer and the host computer, which makes it important to find a nearby service provider. In some cases, providers allow you to access them through special low-cost long distance phone lines. Here is a list of four service providers, located in California, that provide access through low-cost long distance. If you do not already have access to the Internet you should check your local resources through newspaper ads, yellow pages, and so forth. New Internet providers appear every day and many are in small communities. You can, of course, check the well known providers such as America Online, CompuServe, or Delphi. Readily available magazines such as *Computer Shopper* and *PC Magazine* have ads and information on many Internet providers.

One Internet address:

```
http://www.frontiertech.com/isp.html
```

claims to offer software and information on connecting to almost every provider in existence.

Paper Books about the Internet

There are already dozens of books about the Internet, and more appearing every month. Here are just a few that will be useful to you after you've begun to explore the Internet.

Braun, Eric. *The Internet Directory: The Most Complete Guide to Resources on the Internet.* New York: Fawcett Colombine, 1994.

This book brings together a large number of lists available on the Internet, with the added insurance of verified addresses. The drawback to this kind of book is that, because the Internet changes so rapidly, the book is outdated almost as soon as it's published. However, if you don't want to track down all the component lists on your own, you'll appreciate the one-stop shopping provided by this book.

Dern, Daniel. *The Internet Guide for New Users.* New York: McGraw-Hill, 1994.

The book provides comprehensive coverage of the Internet, along with a chapter on UNIX. It's a great book to buy when you're ready to move beyond the information presented in this one.

Estrada, Susan. *Connecting to the Internet: An O'Reilly Buyer's Guide.* Sebastopol, CA: O'Reilly & Associates, 1993.

This book provides a comprehensive listing of many services that give you access to the Internet, along with an explanation of some alternative means of connecting.

Hahn, Harley, and Stout, Rick. *The Internet Complete Reference.* Berkeley, CA: Osborne/McGraw-Hill, 1994.

The title says it all.

Krol, Ed. *The Whole Internet User's Guide & Catalog.* Sebastopol, CA: O'Reilly & Associates, 1992.

This is a good, comprehensive book about the Internet; it offers a mixture of technical and social information.

Angell, David and Heslop, Brent. *Mosaic for Dummies Windows Edition.* Foster City, CA: IDG Books Worldwide, Inc. 1995.

This is a very comprehensive book that will take you will past the "dummy" stage.

Hahn, Harley and Stout, Rick. *The Internet Yellow Pages.* 2nd Edition. Berkeley, CA: Osborne McGraw Hill. 1995.

A very complete directory of most of what is available on the Internet.

Pike, Mary Ann. *Special Edition Using the Internet.* 2nd Edition. Indianapolis, IN: Que Corporation.

Just about everything you need to know about installing and using much of the Internet software tools. It includes a software CD-ROM to get you started on the Internet.

Paper Books about UNIX

If you would like to learn more about UNIX than the elementary treatment provided in this book, consider buying a book devoted solely to UNIX. UNIX actually comes in several different versions. There are many books that cover one particular variety. One example is

Pew, John. *Guide to Solaris.* Emeryville, CA: Ziff-Davis Press, 1993.

Rather than trying to figure out which version of UNIX your Internet host uses, you could buy a book that attempts to cover all versions of UNIX. Here are two that might be especially useful to beginners.

Todino, Grace; Strang, John; and Peek, Jerry. *Learning the UNIX Operating System.* 3rd Edition. Sebastopol, CA: O'Reilly & Associates, 1993.

This is a very brief overview of UNIX that provides only the most basic information you need.

Waite, Mitchell; Prata, Stephen; and Martin, Donald. *The Waite Group's UNIX Primer Plus.* 2nd Edition. Carmel, Indiana: SAMS Publishing, 1990.

This book offers a more comprehensive approach to UNIX than the above book; it also includes a chapter on the text editor vi.

Hahn, Harley. *A Student's Guide to UNIX*, New York, NY: McGraw Hill, Inc. 1993.

This is a well written guide to UNIX and the Internet.

A Book about vi

If you're going to be using the vi text editor, you may want to bone up on some of its intricacies and idiosyncrasies. This book provides a comprehensive look at this text editor.

Lamb, Linda. *Learning the vi Editor.* 5th Edition. Sebastopol, CA: O'Reilly & Associates, 1990.

Electronic Books and Documents about the Internet

Several books about the Internet are available in electronic form over the Internet. These frequently have the advantage of being more up to date than paper books about the Internet.

The most up-to-date sources of information on the Internet are often available in documents on the Internet. The best way to find these ever-changing documents is to use a key word search. For example, a search for HTML—hypertext markup language—leads you to a handbook on HTML, which you can view and print on your own computer system (see Chapter 20).

LaQuey, Tracy and Ryer, Jeanne C. *The Internet Companion: A Beginner's Guide to Global Networking.*

This book is being made available online so that potential buyers can see if they like it. To get a copy, anonymous ftp to ftp.std.com, and in the directory /OBS/The.Internet.Companion, get the file named internet.companion. You'll find an order form in the same directory as the book. Use the order form to order a paper copy of the book using electronic mail if you decide you want a paper copy.

Electronic Lists of Resources on the Internet

As you'll discover in this book, the Internet is full of electronic resources listing the types of services and information it offers. Here are a few key resource listings that will help you explore.

Comprehensive Lists of Internet Resources

Anonymous ftp to ftp.rpi.edu. In the directory /pub/communications get the file internet-cmc.txt. You can also access this file using the World Wide Web, as described in Chapter 13. After starting Lynx, type **g** and then, at the *URL:* prompt, type

```
http://www.rpi.edu/Internet/Guides
```

The World Wide Web version provides immediate access to the resources in the document.

This document is John December's *Internet and Computer Mediated Communication List,* a comprehensive and frequently updated guide by subject to the many resources the Internet has to offer. This guide provides an excellent starting point for Internet exploration.

O'Reilly's *Whole Internet Catalog* and Global Network Navigator service is accessible via the World Wide Web. After starting Lynx, type **g** and then, at the *URL:* prompt, type

```
http://nearnet.gnn.com/wic/newrescat.toc.html ↵
```

The *Whole Internet Catalog* classifies Internet resources by subject. The weekly updates make it very timely.

You will find a number of files covering specific topics and the resources available on the Internet.

This set of listings is also available over the World Wide Web using Cello, Mosaic, or Lynx at:

```
hhtp://http2.sils.umich.edu
```

This is a growing set of documents assembled by graduate students in the Library School at the University of Michigan. Each guide provides a comprehensive listing of Internet resources for a specific topic. This resource is well worth a visit.

Anonymous ftp to rtfm.mit.edu, and in the directory

```
/pub/usenet-by-group/alt.internet.services
```

get the file named

```
/Internet_Services_FAQ
```

This is a regularly updated FAQ that answers most beginner questions.

Anonymous ftp to rtfm.mit.edu, and in the directory

```
/pub/usenet-by-group/alt.internet.services
```

get the file

```
Updated_Internet_Services_List
```

This is a list prepared by Scott Yanoff of interesting services and databases available over the Internet. Check it monthly to make sure you have the most up-to-date information.

A List of Mailing Lists

Anonymous ftp to rtfm.mit.edu, and in the directory

```
/pub/usenet-by-group/news.announce.newusers
```

get the files

```
Mailing_Lists
```

This is an updated list of the currently active mailing lists. There is a brief description of each group along with information about how to subscribe.

A List of Newsgroups

Anonymous ftp to rtfm.mit.edu, and in the directory

```
/pub/usenet-by-group/news.announce.newsgroups
```

get the files

```
List_of_Active_Newsgroups,_Part_I
```

and

```
List_of_Active_Newsgroups,_Part_II
```

This is an updated list of the currently active newsgroups. Remember that a site administrator may choose which groups to carry. Your site may not make some of the groups on this list available.

A List of Ftp Sites

Anonymous ftp to rtfm.mit.edu. In the directory

```
/pub/usenet-by-group/news.answers/ftp-list
```

get the file named faq.

This is a FAQ about anonymous ftp and archives on the Internet. Among other things, it provides some valuable netiquette lessons about anonymous ftp.

Anonymous ftp to rtfm.mit.edu, and in the directory

```
/pub/usenet-by-group/news.answer/ftp-list/sitelist
```

get the files part1 through part20.

This is a list in 20 parts of most of the anonymous ftp sites on the Internet along with addresses and the types of information they carry. This file is updated regularly. It is also very large. You can find a copy of this list in the news.newusers.questions directory on rtfm.mit.edu.

Usenet Documents

Anonymous ftp to rtfm.mit.edu, and in the directory

```
/pub/usenet-by-group/news.announce.newusers
```

get the file

```
Welcome_to_news.newusers.questions!_(weekly_posting)
```

If the file isn't there, try again after a day or two.

The file answers some very basic Usenet questions and discusses how to use Usenet.

A List of FAQs

Anonymous ftp to rtfm.mit.edu, and in the directory

```
/pub/usenet-by-group/news.announce.newusers
```

get the files List_of_Periodic_Informational_Postings,_Part_1_7 through _7_7.

This is a list (currently in seven parts) of FAQs, the Usenet newsgroups that post them, and how often they're updated. Many FAQs are available for anonymous ftp from rtfm.mit.edu in their newsgroup's respective subdirectory within the directory /pub/usenet.

Project Gutenberg

Project Gutenberg converts literary classics into electronic form. These electronic books are available via ftp (discussed in Chapters 10, 15, 19, and 22). The ftp archive is located at mrcnext.cso.uiuc.edu in the directory etext. Anonymous ftp is allowed. Look at the file called NEWUSER.GUT for an explanation of the project's goals and check the file INDEX100.GUT for a listing of the books that are currently available.

INDEX

SYMBOLS

& (ampersand), 27

A

absolute pathname, 35
addresses. *See also* electronic mail
  for Web sites, 192
  http, 186
  in Mosaic URL box, 186
  overview, 14–15
  simplifying with aliases, 56–57
administrators, mailing list, 63. *See also* mailing lists
Adobe Acrobat, 209, 210–211
aliases, simplifying addresses with, 56–57, 60
America Online, 8, 9
antivirus software, 98
Archie, 109, 128–129
  request form, 199
art galleries, on the World Wide Web, 188–191
articles. *See also* newsgroups
  posting in WinVN, 169
ascii files, transfer considerations, 98, 99

B

beer brewing, 236
Big Dummy's Guide to the Internet, 118, 139
binary files, transfer considerations, 98–99
Bin Hex option box, Eudora, 156
BITNET network, 68
BMUG (Berkeley Macintosh Users Group), 9
books. *See also* Project Gutenberg
  about the Internet, 114, 118, 241, 242–243
  electronic, 3, 118, 245–246
browsers. *See* Gopher; World Wide Web; Mosaic; Netscape

bulletin board systems (BBSs), 9
bundling files, 104–105
business resources, 234–235

C

cables, 4
case
  in addresses, 14
  in commands, 48
  in flags, 38
  in searches, 52
cc: prompt, electronic mail, 24, 28–29
Cello browser, 173
  Bookmarks, 178–179
  getting and installing, 182–183
  Jump button, 181
  navigating the Web with, 176–177
  sending messages with, 180–181
  starting, 174–175
change directory (cd) command, UNIX, 37
character strings, 52
CIS. *See* CompuServe
client/server concept, 116
commands
  ftp. *See* ftp (file transfer protocol) program
  UNIX. *See* UNIX
compressing and decompressing files, 101, 102–103, 137, 140
CompuServe (CIS), 8
computer networks. *See* networks
connecting to Internet, 20–21, 242
copying files, 40, 122. *See also* ftp (file transfer protocol) program
Cornell Law School information, 235

D

deleting
  electronic mail text, 24
  files and directories, 40
  items from mailbox, 30–31, 58, 60
DIALOG, 109
digests, electronic mail, 68
directories. *See also* files
  deleting, 40
  listing contents of, 38–39
  managing files in, 40–41, 96–97
  managing and navigating, 36–37, 94–95
  structures, 34, 36–37
directory structures, creating and navigating, 34, 36–37
directory titles, using for searches in Veronica, 130
domains, 15
dumb terminals, 16–17

E

editing, letters with vi, 50–51
editors. *See* text editors
electronic bulletin board systems (BBSs), 9
electronic frontier, 8–9
electronic mail (e-mail) 4. *See also* mailing lists; newsgroups
  addresses, 12–13, 14–15, 56–57
  canceling messages, 24
  confidentiality of, 24
  deleting material in, 24, 30–31
  distinguishing old from new, 26
  Elm program, 60–61
  emphasis and expressions in messages, 86–87
  etiquette. *See* etiquette online; netiquette
  Eudora program for, 145

FAQs (frequently asked
    questions), 88–89, 126,
    143
Mail program. *See* Mail
    program
multiple recipients, 24, 28
Pine program, 58–59
POP (Post Office Protocol)
    for, 145
replying to, 28–29
scrambling/unscrambling
    messages, 84
undeleting, 31
using, 23
electronic malls, 8
Elm mail program, 60–61
e-mail. *See* electronic mail; Mail
    program
emoticons, 86
emulators, terminal, 18–19, 105
Enhanced Mosaic home page,
    187
entertainment resources,
    236–239
error messages, in Cello, 178
etiquette, online
    FAQs (frequently asked
        questions), 85
    in file transfer, 128
    guidelines, 86–87
    helping new users, 72
    insults, 72, 87
    offensive material, 87
    unnecessary politeness, 68
Eudora, 145
    attaching documents to
        messages, 156–157
    configuring, 146–147
    creating a separate mailbox,
        154–155
    deleting messages from
        mailbox, 158–159
    getting and installing,
        160–161
    priority of mail, 148
    receiving mail with, 150–151
    replying to messages,
        152–153
    sending mail with, 148–149
Expo, in Cello, 177

F

FAQs, 88–89
    finding information via, 126
    getting lists of, 249
    saving for future reference,
        80–81
files. *See also* directories
    bundling, 104–105
    compressing and
        uncompressing, 101,
        102–103, 137, 140
    deleting, 40
    in electronic mail. *See*
        electronic mail
    managing, 40–41, 96–97
    naming, 36, 100, 103
    removing. *See* deleting
    renaming, 40
    transferring. *See* ftp (file
        transfer protocol)
        program
    transferring with Mosaic,
        194–195
file transfer protocol. *See* ftp
finding information. *See*
    searching the Internet
flags, 38
flamers, 72, 85
freenet, 108
freeware, 227
freeware news reader, 164
ftp (file transfer protocol)
    program, 93
    Archie program in, 128–129
    bundling files, 104–105
    compressing files, 101,
        102–103
    copying files with, 138–139
    Local System, 139
    navigating within directories,
        96–97
    public-domain news readers
        on, 82–83
    Remote System, 139
    retrieving files, 98–99
    transferring files to Local
        System, 140–141
    via Winsock FTP, 136–137

ftp commands, list of, 94
ftp sites
    connecting to, 94–95
    list of, 248

G

gateways, 12
Ghostview, 209, 216–219
global wide area networks, 5
Gopher, 113, 116–117
    accessing and navigating,
        116–117, 118–119
    accessing WAIS via, 132–133
    browsing Internet with, 115
    browsing with Mosaic, 193,
        196–197
    exploring, 118–119
    Veronica program in,
        130–131
graphical programs, modem
    speed needed for, 21
graphical Windows interface,
    accessing newsgroups
    with, 82–83
gzip and gunzip file compression
    programs, 102–103

H

hardware
    Internet requirements, 11
    terminals. *See* terminals
help
    with newsgroups, 76
    with UNIX, 42–43
home directory
    building your own, 220–225
    on host computer, 35–36
    HTML tags for, 222–225
    returning to in Cello, 175
home page, 9
hosts, 14, 15, 33
HTML (hypertext markup
    language)
    building home page with,
        220–225
    editor, 224
    example of tags, 222–225